The People of the Apocalypse

Find out what is next on the Bible prophecy calendar of events by studying the people God will use during the end times

By: Evangelist Larry E. Wolfe
http://www.btmi.org

"The People of the Apocalypse"
By: Evangelist Larry E. Wolfe

ISBN: 978-0-6151-7103-6

Unless otherwise specified, all Scripture quotations are based on the Authorized King James Version
Copyright 2007 by: www.btmi.org

For more information visit: www.btmi.org
Printed in the United States of America
First Edition, July 2007

INTRODUCTION

The study of the prophetic Scriptures in recent years has escalated as recorded by Daniel the prophet:

"Seal the book even to the time of the end: many shall run to and fro and knowledge shall be increased...And he said, Go thy way Daniel: for the words are closed up and sealed till the time of the end." *(Daniel 12:4, 9)*

Daniel's prophecy of the heightened activity of those who *"shall run to and fro"* refers to this increased study of his writings and the other prophetic Scriptures that are tied to his book. The result is *"knowledge shall be increased"* when God opens up those truths that were formerly *"closed up and sealed till the time of the end"*.

"The People of the Apocalypse" is an examination of these Scriptures focusing upon the people who are found in the prophetic Word and their impact upon *"the time of the end"*.

The first seven chapters of this study serve as an introduction to the lives of these people as they lay the groundwork for understanding the time and circumstances in which "The People of the Apocalypse" will appear.

This study lays emphasis upon the literal method of interpreting the Scripture for the plain common sense interpretation provides the most accurate rendering as the following quote underlines:

"Many of the interpretations placed upon the Bible's revelation of the future presuppose that it just cannot mean what the words plainly seem to say, therefore, another explanation is required. That is the common source of the alternative prophetic views. Men come to the Bible and look at prophecy. Ideas have come to them from various quarters, and they admit that, at the first reading, they would understand these words simply to mean one thing, yet they maintain that the words do not mean what they plainly appear to say. That is unbelief. That is, we need someone to interpret for us what God has said, and that makes the interpreter the authority, not God. If someone speaks to me in a foreign language and I have another to interpret, I utterly depend on what the interpreter tells me. Thus, when prophetic teachers say what God means when He has said something different,

3

we would have to trust in them, and not in what the Bible says if we accept such adjusting of the plain language of God. That is the problem source. That is the common pattern in all of the alternative prophetic views that are to be found amongst God's people, an alternative to the simple understanding that what God says is precisely what He means."

("A Correct Understanding of Pre-Millennial Truth-An Aid to Faith" pp.19 "Watching and Waiting" by: Ivan Foster)

By utilizing the literal method of interpretation, certain Scriptures will take on new meaning in passages that have controlled the prophetic thinking of many of those who are Bible believers.

The Lord's answer to His disciples found in Matthew 24:3-31 is one of these passages that have been scrambled by many Bible teachers in order to make it fit a certain theory. However, it must be interpreted literally, in chronological order, without any exceptions in order to gain the proper sense of the timing of the end times, for this key passage, the Lord's masterpiece, forms the foundation for understanding all other prophetic Scripture.

With this discourse (Matthew 24:3-31) as the cornerstone of end times prophecy, "The People of the Apocalypse" unfolds the events of the End of the Age, the 70th Week of Daniel, the Great Tribulation, the Second Coming of Christ and the Day of the Lord. All of these events are indicated chronologically in the Lord Jesus Christ's Matthew 24 Olivet Discourse.

Each of the chapters in "The People of the Apocalypse" is a stand-alone Bible prophecy message within itself. Therefore, repetition of key information and documentation concerning certain people is necessary in order for each individual message to be clearly set forth.

TABLE OF CONTENTS

1

The Coming Events

God's purposes for the 70th Week of Daniel are stated clearly: *"Seventy weeks are determined upon thy people and upon thy holy city to finish the transgression, and to make an end of sins, and to make reconciliation for iniquity, and to bring in everlasting righteousness and to seal up the vision and prophecy, and to anoint the most Holy." (Daniel 9:24)*

This information given to Daniel the prophet by the angel Gabriel, the messenger of God, distinctly spells out God's plan during this heralded end times period. This one verse records:

I. The Prophesied Time Period:
   A. 70 Weeks
   B. 490 Years
II. The Points of Focus:
   A. Daniel's People: The Jews
   B. Daniel's Holy City: Jerusalem
III. The Purposes of God:
   A. To finish the transgression
   B. To make an end of sin
   C. To make reconciliation for iniquity
   D. To bring in everlasting righteousness
   E. To seal up the vision and prophecy
   F. To anoint the most holy

The remaining 70th Week of Daniel (Daniel 9:27) will be focused upon Daniel's people the Jews, and upon Jerusalem, Daniel's holy city, just like the first 69 weeks/483 years which are now recorded history (Daniel 9:25, 26).

This unfolding of the Jew's future was God's prophetic answer to Daniel's mighty prayer of Daniel 9:4-19 as he was praying for the present situation concerning his people and their sinful condition, past and present, and their 70 year captivity. In his prayer he specifically mentions his people and his holy city Jerusalem repeatedly during this lengthy and spiritually powerful prayer.

In response, he was given an immediate and precise answer concerning a much larger, more important revelation outlining 70 weeks of years [490 years]. During this answer the program of the ages for the Jews and their holy city Jerusalem is unveiled, showing the beginning: *"from the going forth of the commandment to restore and to build Jerusalem" (Daniel 9:25)* to the end *"even until the consummation" (Daniel 9:27).*

First of all, in order for the remaining 70th Week to begin, there must be a Jewish people (Daniel 9:24), or nation who, of necessity, must be in their Promised Land (Deuteronomy 30:5) and in possession of their holy city Jerusalem (Daniel 9:24).

While the *"times of the Gentiles" (Luke 21:24)* continue *"until the fullness of the Gentiles be come in" (Romans 11:25)*, the present-day Jews:
1. Are once again a recognized people/nation,
2. Are dwelling in the Promised Land of Israel,
3. Are occupying their holy city Jerusalem.

Thus, the Lord has already put in place the first three pre-requisites for the 70th Week of Daniel. He is now setting the stage for the start of the last week, or seven years, to take place. But, there are more events and conditions necessary, as described in Scripture, in order for these final seven years to begin as the following words of the Lord Jesus Christ indicate:
*"And Jesus answered and said unto them, Elijah truly shall **first** come, and restore all things. But I say unto you, That Elijah is come already, and they knew him not but have done unto him whatsoever they listed. Likewise shall also the Son of man suffer of them. Then the disciples understood that he spoke unto them of John the Baptist."* (Matthew 17:11-13)

The event He is referring to when He said, *"Elijah truly shall **first** come, and restore all things"* is also recorded in the last prophecy of the Old Testament:
*"Behold I will send you Elijah the prophet **before** the coming of the*

great and dreadful day of the Lord: And he shall turn the heart of the fathers to the children, and the heart of the children to their fathers, lest I come and smite the earth with a curse." (Malachi 4:5, 6)

One of the major events on God's agenda is the sending of this last Elijah-like prophet. He will be an integral part of the Lord's preparation of the people, both Jew and Gentile. He will be sent before the climactic and unparalleled time of God's judgment of the earth and its population, called the Day of the Lord, which begins during the last half of the 70th Week of Daniel (Matthew 24:15-29).

His ministry will begin prior to the mid-point of the 70th Week when the *"abomination of desolation" (Daniel 9:27; Matthew 24:15)* occurs and stops the regular sacrifice that began earlier through the *"restore all things" (Matthew 17:11; Mark 9:12)* ministry of this last Elijah-like prophet.

The Lord will once again be sending prophets to His people the Jews. These prophets will not just be affecting the land of Israel as in Old Testament days. But, like *"the two prophets"* of Revelation 11:3-14, this last Elijah will most likely have a worldwide ministry during his end times tenure as he ministers to the hearts of God's people thereby restoring a key part of those *"things"* which have been foreordained by God.

It would not have been necessary for the Lord to send this last Elijah if the Jews had received John the Baptist, as the Lord Jesus Christ indicated in Matthew 11:13, 14:
*"For all the prophets and the law prophesied until John [the Baptist]. And **if** ye will receive it, this is Elijah, which was for to come."*

But the Jews did not receive it. If they had, the Lord would have continued with His Day of the Lord program as already spelled out in the Old Testament. Instead their rejection of John the Baptist and the Christ he was heralding has brought Jew and Gentile alike to this very time in the plan of God.

During the close of this age and before the beginning of the Day of the Lord, God will surely send this last Elijah-like prophet to *"restore"* those things that He requires. Peter also spoke of this

9

"restitution [restoration]" in his second sermon:
*"And He shall send Jesus Christ, which before was preached unto you: Whom the heaven must receive **until** the times of restitution of all things, which God hath spoken by the mouth of all His holy prophets since the world began." (Acts 3:20, 21)*

Peter indicates that the return of the Lord Jesus Christ will not occur *"until the times of restitution [restoration] of all things"* thus confirming that the Lord Jesus Christ's Second Coming will occur **after** this last Elijah-like prophet restores all things and is ministering to the hearts of men. In the process, he will be fulfilling his service to the Lord by heralding the soon return of the long awaited Messiah, the Lord Jesus Christ.

This word *"restitution"*, a noun only used this one time in the New Testament, has the same Greek root as the verb *"restore"* that the Lord Jesus used in Matthew 17:11 meaning "to restore to its former state" indicating Elijah's two-fold restoration ministry:
1. The spiritual revival of the hearts of God's people (Malachi 4:5, 6)
2. The physical restoration of the "*holy covenant*" practices
   (Daniel 11:28-32; Matthew 17:11; Mark 9:12)

This same Greek root is also found in the word *"shall turn again"* in Malachi 4:5:
*"And behold I will send to you Elias the Thesbite, before the great and glorious day of the Lord comes; who **shall turn again** the heart of the father to the son, and the heart of a man to his neighbor, lest I come and smite the earth grievously." (Septuagint)*

This verse is found in the Septuagint, the Greek Old Testament, a translation of the Hebrew text that was the people's Bible before and during New Testament times and is still actively used today by certain orthodox Christians in Eastern Europe.

Over 90% of the Old Testament quotations in the New Testament find their source in this translation, which the Lord Jesus utilized when He spoke of Elijah's future ministry of restoration in Matthew 17:11, which will occur **_before_** the Day of the Lord begins.

While the 70th Week of Daniel has as its focus the Jews and

10

Jerusalem, it is merely the prelude to the Day of the Lord which begins during the 70th Week. The Day of the Lord is in reality the world's time of the end climactic ultimatum from the Lord, for it deals with the entire population of planet earth, Jew and Gentile alike, and is the most prophesied event in all of Scripture.

Understanding the necessary conditions and events that must occur before the 70th Week of Daniel begins is vital. But, God's Day of the Lord must be the primary consideration because the 70th Week provides the conditions He requires in order to begin His final time of the end judgment, which the prophet Malachi called: *"the great and dreadful day of the Lord" (Malachi 4:5).*

By utilizing the prophetic timeline given by the Lord Jesus Christ in Matthew 24:3-31, it is clear that the Day of the Lord will begin ***"immediately after*** *the tribulation" (Matthew 24:29a)* indicated by the notable sign of the Day of the Lord/Second Coming of Christ: *"the sun be darkened, and the moon shall not give her light, and the stars shall fall from heaven, and the powers of heaven shall be shaken." (Matthew 24:29b)*

This sign was originally recorded in Joel 2:31: *"The sun shall be turned into darkness, and the moon into blood, **before** the great and the terrible day of the Lord come."*

It is also referred to in Revelation 6:12-17. This significant sign will occur the same day the Lord returns to rapture the saints before His wrathful judgment, the Day of the Lord, begins. The Lord's teaching in Luke 17:22-37 emphasizes *"the same day"* rescue then retribution plan He has used throughout the Biblical record. His vivid account of the rapture in Luke 17:34-36 describes this simultaneous rescuing of believers while unbelievers are left behind to face the coming judgment.

The disciples, not understanding this truth, immediately asked, *"Where, Lord"* wanting to know the specific location. The Lord answered: *"Wherever the body [corpse (Matthew 24:28)] is, thither will the eagles [vultures] be gathered together." (Luke 17:37)*

11

The Lord is indicating not only the certainty of this event but also its worldwide scope for regardless of where a dead body is found on the planet vultures will definitely be present.

He then answered the disciples question as to exactly where these events would take place by indicating the far reaching global effects of His certain, *"same day"* Second Coming and subsequent Day of the Lord judgment.

But, before all this, the Lord will send this last Elijah-like prophet, mentioned above, who will *"restore all things" (Matthew 17:11)*. His ministry will be much like the first Elijah, who in God's wisdom set the stage for the coming of the second Elijah, John the Baptist, who in like manner has accomplished the same for this third and future prophet of God.

He, like the first and second Elijah, will be completely led by the Holy Spirit of God, knowing and announcing God's plan as it unfolds. The first Elijah knew with absolute certainty exactly where, when and what God was planning in order to accomplish His will for His people as he gave the now famous ultimatum to king Ahab concerning the 3-1/2 year drought (I Kings 17:1).

Elijah's preparation for this notable day caused him to have earth shaking faith as he immersed himself in the Word of God thereby receiving the Holy Spirit's understanding that the Lord was about to bring a period of drought upon the earth in response to the idolatrous conduct of His people, the Jews (Deuteronomy 11:16, 17).

He later pronounced another great ultimatum to God's people: *"How long halt ye between two opinions? If the Lord be God, follow Him: but if Baal, then follow him" (I Kings 18:21)*. This was followed by the renowned contest between God and Baal (I Kings 18:22-40).

His mighty prayer is recorded near the end of this contest:
*"Lord God of Abraham, Isaac, and of Israel, let it be known this day that Thou art God in Israel, and that I am Thy servant, and that I have done all these things at Thy word. Hear me, O LORD, hear me, that this people may know that Thou art the LORD God, and that Thou **hast turned their heart back again**." (I Kings 18:36, 37)*

This brought down from heaven the all-consuming fire of God eliciting the submission and worship of the people. This Holy Spirit filled prayer by God's servant was what it took for God to turn their hearts, which in like manner is what it will take at the end of the age when the last Elijah will accomplish his ministry.

The second Elijah, John the Baptist, as the Lord Himself came to him on the banks of Jordan the day He was made known publicly at His baptism, announced, *"Behold the Lamb of God who takes away the sin of the world" (John 1:29).*

In the three days recorded in John 1:19-36, John the Baptist would experience the culmination of his ministry. On the first day the unbelieving Jews asked him *"Art thou Elijah?"* The second day he saw *"Jesus coming unto him, and said, Behold the Lamb of God which takes away the sin of the world"* and the third day *"And looking upon Jesus as He walked, he said, Behold the Lamb of God!"*

John knew who Jesus was, and exactly what He came to do for all of mankind long before the Lord Jesus Christ died on the Cross of Calvary for the sins of mankind. He was completely accurate in his proclamations concerning the Christ, the Jewish Messiah, the blessed Lord Jesus Christ Who came to save His people from their sin. John's *"baptism of repentance"* served to turn the hearts of God's people, preparing them for the Lord's first coming as *"the Lamb of God"* to bring salvation to all people who would receive Him.

With two Elijahs now past, some conclusions can be drawn from the Biblical record concerning the third and last Elijah. This powerful Jewish prophet will come during the end of the age, before the Day of the Lord, to *"restore all things"* in the spirit and power of his two predecessors.

If God continues to be *"the same yesterday, today and forever" (Hebrews 13:8),* this prophet's ministry will increase in a progressive manner. The scope of his ministry will grow from being strictly to the Jews in the land of Israel to include all of the saints in the existing Church worldwide.

This can be predicted with certainty for the central purpose of his

ministry will be similar to the two Elijahs before him:
1. They Called the people of God to repentance
2. They Confronted the political leader
3. They Condemned the false religious leaders

We can look to the Scripture with confidence and great expectation concerning this mighty prophet of God, for he too will call the people of God to repentance and revival. He also will confront the political leader of that day, the Antichrist. It will also be his duty, as God's Holy Spirit filled voice, to condemn the religious leader, the false prophet.

He will be instrumental in the restoration of the *"holy covenant" (Daniel 11:28-32)*. He will be the likely leader of a great company of men who will evangelize the Jews (Daniel 11:33, 12:3) as *"all Israel shall be saved" (Romans 11:26)* when their Deliverer, the Lord Jesus Christ, will *"bring in everlasting righteousness" (Daniel 9:24)* at the end of the 70th Week of Daniel. (Revelation 11:15, 14:1)

This Elijah-like prophet will revive the people of God spiritually, turning their hearts, but, he will also be responsible to physically *"restore all things"* referring to the things of the *"holy covenant"* including temple worship (Revelation 11:1, 2) which is also recorded in the book of Daniel:
*"Then shall he [Antichrist] return into his land with great riches; and his heart shall be against **the holy covenant**: and he shall do exploits, and return to his own land...he shall be grieved and return, and have indignation against **the holy covenant**: so shall he do; he shall even return, and have intelligence with them that forsake **the holy covenant**. And arms [forces] shall stand on his part, and they shall pollute the sanctuary of strength, and shall take away the daily sacrifice, and they shall place the abomination that maketh desolate. And such as do wickedly against **the covenant** shall he corrupt by flatteries; but the people that do know their God shall be strong and do exploits." (Daniel 11:28, 30-32)*

This passage shows that there will be those Jews who fall away and forsake the restored *"holy covenant"* referring to the covenant God originally made with the nation of Israel at Mount Sinai (Exodus 19:3-6).

The Jews renewed obedience to this covenant underlies the restoration of temple worship and the offering of the daily or regular morning and evening sacrifices that are those specifically indicated here in these verses.

The wicked and deceitful activities of the Antichrist focusing upon his personal and progressively-building contempt for the *"holy covenant"* recorded above, along with those Jews who forsake this covenant, which is the *"falling away"* of II Thessalonians 2:3, occur **before** he has his image placed in the temple of God.

This event, the setting up of Antichrist's image *"in the holy place"* *(Matthew 24:15),* marks the mid-point of the 70th Week of Daniel (Daniel 9:27) and the ending of *"the regular/morning and evening sacrifice"* *(Daniel 8:11-14, 9:27, 11:31, 12:11).*

The Antichrist's *"intelligence with them that forsake the holy covenant"* *(Daniel 11:30)* could well be the catalyst that brings this horrific event to pass. The Lord Jesus Christ in His unfolding of the end of the age indicated the importance of this prophecy when He said:
"When ye therefore shall see the abomination of desolation spoken of by Daniel the prophet, stand in the holy place (whoso reads, let him understand") (Matthew 24:15).

This is but one of the two Old Testament prophecies utilized by the Lord Jesus as He chronologically unfolded the end of this age, which culminates with His Second Coming, to the four disciples of His inner circle (Matthew 24:3-31).

The *"abomination of desolation"* *(Matthew 24:15)* marks the mid-point of the 70th Week of Daniel and the end of the restored *"holy covenant"* temple worship of God by the Jews. The second Old Testament prophecy He referred to says:
*"**Immediately after** the tribulation of those days shall the sun be darkened, and the moon shall not give her light, and the stars shall fall from heaven, and the powers of heaven shall be shaken."*
(Matthew 24:29)

This major prophetic sign and its global effects are referred to in at least fourteen different Bible passages: Isaiah 5:30, 13:10, 24:23; Ezekiel 32:7, 8; Joel 2:2, 10, 30-31; Amos 1:18; 8:9; Zephaniah 1:15; Matthew 24:29; Mark 13:24, 25; Luke 21:25; Acts 2:20; Revelation 6:12, 13).

These heavenly wonders are the sign marking three major events:
1. The End of the Great Tribulation (Matthew 24:29),
2. The Second Coming of Christ for the gathering of the elect/rapture of the saints (Matthew 24:30, 31),
3. The Beginning of the Day of the Lord's Wrath (Joel 2:30, 31; Revelation 6:12-17)

Revelation 7:1-8 adds still another significant event in this series which occurs just before the Second Coming of Christ. It is the sealing of the 144 Thousand, which takes place before the gathering of the elect/rapture (Revelation 7:9-17) so that the testimony of the Lord Jesus Christ continues on earth throughout the Day of the Lord.

These two prophecies are the most significant O.T. end times passages in all of Scripture as they vividly provide the believer with the actual timeposts unveiling the Lord's chronological structure which He so simply and precisely communicated to His disciples during His last days on earth.

This step-by-step unfolding of the end times is demonstrated by the Lord's usage of time-indicating words such as:
*"The end is **not yet**....All these are the **beginning** of sorrows...**Then** shall they deliver you up to be afflicted...**And then** shall many be offended...But he that shall endure **unto the end**...**Then** shall the end come...**Then** let them which be in Judea...**For then** shall be great tribulation...**Then** if any man shall say unto you...**Immediately after** the tribulation...**And then** shall appear the sign of the Son of man...**and then** shall all the tribes of the earth mourn..."*
(Matthew 24:6-30)

The simplicity that is in Christ Jesus is unmistakably understandable. Whether it be to the Lord's disciples, the newborn babe in the far reaches of Africa, or the seasoned prophecy professor, the Lord gave Matthew 24:3-31 in His familiar and effective way so that all you need is the Word of God and you can grasp the truth

16

necessary for understanding any doctrine of Scripture including His Second Coming and the time of the end.

Since He is the Author of all Scripture, the information that was given to Daniel describing *"the abomination of desolation"* provides additional insight concerning Elijah's end of the age restoration of the Old Covenant worship of God.

The first reference to *"the abomination of desolation"* occurs in Daniel's vision of chapter eight. The purpose of this vision focuses upon the Antichrirst, his Actions and the Actual Time his actions will have effect, in (Daniel 8:1-8) The Ascertaining of His Country, (Daniel 8:9) The Ascendancy of the Antichrist, (Daniel 8:10-14) The Actual Time/Actions of the Antichrist.

The detail of Daniel 8 is given in order to accurately pinpoint the country from which the Antichrist will rise with the choice coming from one of the *"four notable ones toward the four winds of heaven"* *(Daniel 8:8)*. Then Daniel 8:9: (*"and out of one of them came forth a little horn"*) shows the Antichrist coming from one of these *"four kingdoms...in the latter time [end time] of their kingdoms" (Daniel 8:22, 23)* as clearly interpreted by the angel.

These four countries came from the kingdom of Alexander the Great when upon his death his empire was divided into: Syria (North), Egypt (South), Turkey/Armenia (East), and Greece (West). In chapter eleven the Antichrist is identified as *"the king of the north" (Daniel 11:6, 7, 11, 15, 40)* indicating that he will rise from the country of Syria.

Although this vision includes the rise and fall of certain kingdoms from a long past era, the timeframe and emphasis of this revelation is *"the time of the end...the last end of the indignation" (Daniel 8:17, 19)* indicating exactly when these events will take place. The major event, as indicated by the Lord in Matthew 24:15, is the Antichrist's primary goal of ending the *"holy covenant"* temple worship of the true and living God.

Paul's illuminating record of this horrendous event is the last and most powerful indication of the Antichrist's vile intent:

"Let no man deceive you by any means: for that day [Day of the Lord] shall not come, except there come a falling away first, and that man of sin [Antichrist] be revealed, the son of perdition; who opposeth and exalteth himself above all that is called God, or that is worshipped; so that he as God sitteth in the temple of God, showing himself that he is God." (II Thessalonians 2:3, 4)

This will bring an end to the restored temple worship of God at the mid-point of the 70th Week when the Jews will be worshipping in the temple of God as stated by the Apostle John:

"And there was given me a reed like a rod: and the angel stood, saying, Rise, and measure the temple of God, and the altar, and them [the Jews] that worship therein. But, the court [of the Gentiles] which is without the temple leave out, and measure it not; for it is given unto the Gentiles: and the holy city shall they tread under foot forty and two months." (Revelation 11:1, 2)

The ending of the worship of God stands out as the major event of the Antichrist's tenure as it is recorded in the book of Daniel four times, underscored by the Lord Jesus Christ, and described by the apostle Paul.

The issue is worship! In a word, worship defines the primaary reason for the Antichrist's action. The majority of the world's inhabitants will worship this one man who is Satanically energized and given Satanic authority to rule like none other before him.

But, there are those "obstinate" Jews who will continue to worship Jehovah in the temple of God at Jerusalem...and, those "rebellious" Christians who worship Jehovah who also will not take the mark of the beast. They all must be brought into submission or be eliminated.

The Antichrist's history, culminating with the ending of the regular sacrifice in God's temple, is the primary prophetic focal point of the book of Daniel for the development and progression of the visions in the book of Daniel focus around this one major event:
1. Nebuchadnezzars vision of four kingdoms emphasis is the 4th kingdom (Daniel 2).
2. Daniel's vision of four kingdoms, ten nations, little horn, emphasis is the 4th kingdom (Daniel 7).

3. Daniel's vision of four kingdoms, four divisions, little horn, abomination/daily sacrifice ceasing (Daniel 8)
4. Daniel's vision of the prince that shall come, daily sacrifice ceasing/abomination of desolation (Daniel 9)
5. Daniel's last vision: kingdoms of Persia and Greece (Daniel 10)
6. Daniel's last vision (cont.) four kingdoms, four divisions, king of the north, daily sacrifice ceasing/abomination of desolation (Daniel 11)
7. Daniel's last vision (cont.) daily sacrifice taken away, abomination desolation (Daniel 12)

While numerous facts are repeated in these visions, the major repetitive emphasis shown here is the Antichrist and his implementing of *"the abomination of desolation"* clearly referred to by the Lord Jesus Christ (Matthew 24:15) in His cronological unfolding of the end times.

This is the only reference from the book of Daniel given by the Lord which records the end of the restored temple worship of God. It is immediately followed by the beginning of Antichrist worship in God's temple when his image is set up in the holy place.

The Lord progressively unfolds this series of visions by giving Daniel the interpretation of Nebuchadnezzar's vision bringing to his mind the truth of the four coming kingdoms with the fourth in focus.

Five decades later, in chapter seven, the Lord expands this four-kingdom concept with the fourth emphasized, including the *"ten horns"* with *"the little horn" (Daniel 7:8)* as the end times archenemy of God being the significant character.

In his chapter eight vision, similar ground is covered with *"the little horn" (Daniel 8:9)* coming out of one of the four divisions of Alexander the Great's empire which four divisions are part of the previous ten horns. He, *"the little horn" (Daniel 8:11, 12)* will put a stop to the regular daily sacrifice in the temple of God.

In chapter nine, having now settled in the mind of Daniel the truth of the coming of one who will oppose God and end the regular sacrifice, this *"little horn"* of chapters seven and eight *"confirms the*

19

covenant for one week" eventually causing the daily sacrifice to cease at the mid-point of this last week or seven years, which is the 70th Week of Daniel (Daniel 9:27).

The last vision given in Daniel 10-12 continues to underline what has already been revealed in the previous four visions. Only the remaining two of the previous four kingdoms are named, Persia and Greece, with the focus upon the four divisions of Alexander's empire once again supplying the source region for the Antichrist.

The angel mentions this fourfold division by utilizing the words *"four winds of heaven" (Daniel 11:4)* as in Daniel 8:8, indicating their relative location to the holy land as North, South, East and West. Then he skips over the centuries between and begins dealing with the future generations and end times rise of the last *"king of the north" (Daniel 11: 21-45),* who is the Antichrist.

This is exactly what occurred in Daniel 8:1-8 where the four kingdoms and the four divisions *"toward the four winds of heaven"* were introduced together. This is repeated in Daniel's last vision where *"the four winds of heaven" (Daniel 11:4)* are immediately followed by the introduction and generational rise of the last *"king of the north"* who is the Antichrist.

He, once again, is shown to be the one responsible for stopping the temple worship of God and the setting up of the abomination of desolation when he has his own image set up in the holy place (Daniel 11:31). This interpretation, based on the repetition of a pattern in the Biblical texts of chapters eight and eleven, was developed in the 19th century by noted prophecy scholar Dr. Samuel P. Tregelles. He not only dedicated himself to the study of the prophetic Scripture, but was also a recognized expert in Old Testament languages.

He has been called the greatest Biblical scholar of the nineteenth century as his writings were known worldwide and his concise scholarship was acknowledged both in Europe and America. He authored numerous works including "Heads of Hebrew Grammar" and "Hebrew Reading Lessons" for the student, and was reputed to be the recommended expert on prophecy by his contemporary, Charles Haddon Spurgeon.

His commentary on the book of Daniel "Tregelles on Daniel" is one of the most scholarly and exceedingly helpful volumes in the study of this important book of Old Testament time of the end prophecy.

His interpretation, utilized above, is based on the only mention of the taking away of the *"daily sacrifice...the abomination that makes desolate" (Daniel 11:31)* in the step-by-step end times narrative of Daniel's last vision. Tregelles rightly decided that this must be the same one that occurs at the mid-point of the 70th Week of Daniel (Daniel 9:27) which is clearly referred to by the Lord Jesus Christ in Matthew 24:15.

If the narrative of chapter eleven is reviewed, there is no logical pause, break or time lapse in the text, except between Daniel 11:4 and 11:5 after the *"four winds of heaven"*, representing the four divisions of Alexander's kingdom, appear. Then the *"kings of the south...north"* have a detailed documentation of their generations and respective activities up to and including the time of the end.

His careful analysis of the Biblical text, combined with his excellent knowledge of the Hebrew and Chaldee/Aramaic provide unusual insight as he time and again proves his interpretation based upon the text and the text alone.

His alignment of Daniel 7:21-25 and Daniel 8:9-19 concerning *"the little horn"* compared with Daniel 11:36-41 prove that all three texts are referring to the same person, the coming Antichrist ("Tregelles on Daniel" pp.83). He held to the Biblical teaching that present-day Syria will be the country of origin for the Antichrist showing that the Assyrian of old will continue to be Israel's great enemy at the time of the end.

His timely refutation of the false theory teaching the "at-any-moment rapture and coming of Christ" found in his short volume "The Hope of Christ's Second Coming" is compelling to say the least. In twenty-four precise chapters, this book illuminates his Biblical position as it was written during the rise of this false theory in the mid-nineteenth century.

Even though the majority of the Jews will follow the Antichrist in that day, the implicit obedience of certain Jews to the Lord Jesus Christ will definitely become reality when the Day of the Lord begins for the Lord will open that time with the 144 Thousand (Revelation 14:1; Psalm 110:3).

These young men (the 144 Thousand), being mature saints of God, are called *"the servants of our God...which were sealed" (Revelation 7:3, 4)* and are later described as *"following the Lamb wherever He goes" (Revelation 14:4)* underlining their full and complete obedience to the Lord Jesus Christ.

"The woman" of Revelation 12, who represents the faithful of the nation of Israel, is also made up of Israelites who obediently flee (Matthew 24:16) to a place prepared of God (Revelation 12:6). These will likely be the women, children and older men who will spend the last half of the 70th Week of Daniel in the wilderness where they will be nourished by God (Revelation 12:14).

The 144 Thousand chosen, called and faithful young men do not flee with *"the woman"* for they are seen after the mid-point of the 70th week of Daniel when they are sealed (Revelation 7:1-8) immediately after the sign of the Day of the Lord (Revelation 6:12-17).

This seal, which is the signature of God physically written on their foreheads (Revelation 14:1), will provide them with protection during the Day of the Lord:
"And it was commanded them [locusts] that they should not hurt the grass of the earth, neither any green thing, neither any tree; but only those men which nave not the seal of God in their foreheads." (Revelation 9:4)

They also appear later *"with the Lamb"* at the end of 70th Week of Daniel and during the Day of the Lord (Revelation 14:1, 17:14) respectively as they remain upon earth during the Day of the Lord, after the gathering of the elect/rapture.

In addition, there will be the *"two witnesses"* of Revelation 11:3-17 who also will minister during the last half of the 70th Week of Daniel and the Day of the Lord as prophets of the judgment of God.

22

They too will not be gathered with the elect/raptured for their ministry continues before and after the rapture occurs, according to the Lord's precise timeline in Matthew 24:4-31.

This chronological timeline indicates the following sequence:
1. The Beginning of Sorrows (v.4-8)
2. The Great Tribulation (v.9-14)
3. The Great Tribulation Detailed (v.15-28)
4. The Sign of the 2nd Coming of Christ/Day of the Lord (v.29)
5. The Second Coming of Christ/Gathering of The Elect/Beginning of the Day of the Lord (v.30, 31)

The time called *"the beginning of sorrows" (Matthew 24:8)*, although not strictly defined in years, months or days by the Lord, encompasses a lengthy period. The unparalleled rise of *"false Christs" (Matthew 24:4, 5)* such as the Jehovah's [false] Witnesses, Mormons/Latter Day [false] Saints, Seventh Day Adventists and the Christian Science cults among others have all occurred within the past two centuries.

The 20th century produced the most horrendous display of World War I and World War II (Matthew 24:6). The 21st century now continues with an increasing number of famines, pestilence and earthquakes (Matthew 24:7) revealing that we have been living within *"the beginning of sorrows"* and are presently closing in rapidly on the Lord's return.

As the Lord has already begun preparing the world for His Day of the Lord judgment, He has also begun preparing His earthly people, the Jews, for the time of unparalleled wrath from heaven also known as *"the time of Jacobs trouble" (Jeremiah 30:7)*.

He continues to move forward as the Jews are in their Promised Land (Deuteronomy 30:5, Matthew 24:16) and have miraculously become a nation [Daniel's people] with Jerusalem [Daniel's holy city] (Daniel 9:24) in their possession now [2007] for four decades.

The Lord's sending of the last Elijah-like prophet, spoken of in Malachi 4:5, 6; Mathew 17:11; Mark 9:12, appears to be on the very doorstep of His prophetic plan to *"restore all things"* which must

23

occur during *"the beginning of sorrows"(Matthew 24:8)* and prior to *"the great tribulation" (Matthew 24:21)*. That is the time when the faithful of the nation of Israel will be fleeing (Matthew 24:15-28; Revelation 12:6) during the Antichrist's global war with the Church saints (Daniel 7:21-25; Revelation 13:1-1). During this time, Satan's primary focus will be centered upon the Jews in the land (Daniel 11:21-12:1; Revelation 12:17).

Like the successful evangelists of old and his two predecessors [Elijah and John the Baptist] whom the Lord sent to His people, his emphasis will be upon repentance. This provides the Lord with the ability to turn the hearts of His earthly people the Jews and Gentiles within the Church, which is the Body of the Lord Jesus Christ.

It is likely that the Church will provide the seedbed for the powerful group of evangelists, [144 Thousand]. They will be sealed and remain as *"the servants of our God" (Revelation 7:3)* upon earth (Revelation 9:4, 14:1-5) during the *"great and dreadful day of the Lord" (Revelation 8, 9, 15, 16.)* It will begin "immediately after" the rapture/gathering of the elect out of the shortened great tribulation (Matthew 24:22; Revelation 7:9-17).

The 144 Thousand will be sent to evangelize and instruct, during (Daniel 11:32-35) and after the great tribulation (Daniel 12:3; Revelation 14:1-5), those whom God will save when *"all Israel shall be saved" (Romans 11:26; Isaiah 59:20)* at the end of the 70th Week of Daniel:
"For whosoever shall call upon the name of the Lord shall be saved. How then shall they call on Him in whom they have not believed? And how shall they believe in Him of whom they have not heard? And how shall they hear without a preacher? And how shall they preach, except they be sent?" (Romans 10:13-15)

Therefore, out of *"the saints"* mentioned in Daniel 7:18, 21, 25, 27, who comprise the global end times Church of Jesus Christ, will come the last Elijah-like prophet (Malachi 4:5, 6; Matthew 17:11), the martyrs (Revelation 6:9-11), the *"two witnesses" (Revelation 11:3)*, *"the woman" (Revelation 12:1-17a)*, and *"the rest of her [physical] seed which keep the commandments of God, and have the testimony of Jesus Christ" (Revelation 12:17b)*. It is from this group that God will call and then eventually seal the 144 Thousand *"servants of our God"* *(Revelation 7:1-8)*.

In addition, there will be those Jews who hear and believe the instruction of the 144 Thousand causing the Lord to turn their hearts when *"all Israel shall be saved" (Isaiah 59:20; Romans 11:25, 26).*

These Jews are the one third that remain after the Lord brings them:
"Through the fire, and will refine them as silver is refined, and will try them as gold is tried: they shall call on My name, and I will hear them: I will say, it is My people: and they shall say, The LORD is My God." (Zechariah 13:9)

Unfortunately, as the verses prior reveal, two thirds will die during this *"time of Jacob's [Israel's] trouble" (Jeremiah 30:7)* also known as the seven trumpet plagues which occur during the beginning of the Day of the Lord:
"Awake, O sword, against My shepherd, and against the man that is My fellow, saith the LORD of hosts: smite the shepherd, and the sheep shall be scattered: and I will turn mine hand upon the little ones. And it shall come to pass, that in all the land, saith the LORD, two parts therein shall be cut off and die; but the third part shall be left therein." (Zechariah 13:7, 8)

This unprecedented slaughter will cause the prior holocausts inflicted upon the Jews to pale in comparison to the horrendous and unparalleled judgment, which proceeds from the hand of God.

The sixth trumpet judgment alone will claim one third of the earth's population (Revelation 9:18) which is God's judgment upon the earth and its unrepentant inhabitants (II Peter 3:3-10; Revelation 9:20, 21, 16:9-11). Gods purification of Israel (Isaiah 1:24-28; Ezekiel 7:19, 20; Amos 5:18, 19; Zechariah 13:8, 9; Malachi 3:1-3) will continue to unfold as described in these seven trumpet judgments (Revelation 8, 9, 11).

The primary purpose of the Day of the Lord is the purification of God's earthly people, the Jews, just as the primary purpose of the Great Tribulation is the purification of the Church of Jesus Christ in preparation for His Coming to take them home (Ephesians 5:26; Titus 3:14; I John 3:1-3; Jude 24).

He will utilize the wicked purposes of men to bring many sons unto glory having their hearts revived and purified. During the time called *"the great tribulation"* *(Matthew 24:21; Revelation 7:14)*, also known as Satan's *"great wrath"* *(Revelation 12:12)*, there will be many faithful martyrs (Revelation 6:10, 11, 20:4) as they will *"love not their lives unto the death"* *(Revelation 12:11)*.

It will be this martyrdom of His own brethren, referred to as *"fellow servants also and their brethren"* spoken to the martyrs in Revelation 6:11, that will bring the exact number to His predetermined will. These are those whose names are written in the Lamb's book of life from the foundation of the world, who are called out from the *"remnant [rest] of her [physical] seed"* *(Revelation 12:17b)*.

They are the ones who are the *"called and chosen and faithful"* *(Revelation 17:14b)* going with the Lord to fight the *"ten horns"* at the battle of Armageddon (Revelation 17:12-14a). This exact, predetermined number of 144 Thousand sons of Israel will battle spiritually and physically along with the Lamb, the Lord Jesus Christ, during the *"great and dreadful day of the Lord"* having been sealed and protected from the devastating judgment of God (Revelation 9:4).

Here is the end times Israel of God. It is these prime servants of God who are selected for His spiritual and physical army during the most privileged and crucial days of time that redeemed men will ever walk the face of planet earth.

These will be those young holy priest/warriors in the Lord's army (Psalm 110:3) who have earned the honor of standing on Mount Zion with the Lamb, the Lord Jesus Christ, serving Him, the King of kings and Lord of lords with every ounce of their being.

They are seen taking part in one of the most powerful worship scenes ever recorded in the Word of God as heaven and earth meet, singing in beautiful harmony the *"new song"* which is sung only by those designated participants as they exalt and worship the Father before His heavenly throne (Revelation 14:1-5).

This worship scene occurs at the end of the 70th Week of Daniel, after the first three elements of God's plan for the Jews (Daniel 9:24a) are completed:
1. *The transgression is finished*
2. *Sin is ended*
3. *Reconciliation for iniquity has been made*

These three negative events involving Israel's rebellion against God are over, and the last three positive elements:
1. *To bring in everlasting righteousness*
2. *To seal up the vision and prophecy*
3. *To anoint the most holy*
are soon to be accomplished as God's marvelous plan continues to unfold (Daniel 9:24b).

The 70th Week comes to an end at the sounding of the 7th Trumpet: *"And the seventh angel sounded: and there were great voices in heaven, saying, The kingdoms of this world are become the kingdoms of our Lord, and of His Christ; and He shall reign for ever and ever. And the four and twenty elders, which sat before God on their seats, fell upon their faces, and worshipped God, Saying, We give Thee thanks, O Lord God Almighty, which art, and was, and art to come; because Thou hast taken to Thee Thy great power, and hast reigned. And the nations were angry, and Thy wrath is come, and the time of the dead, that they should be judged, and that Thou should give reward unto Thy servants the prophets, and to the saints, and them that fear Thy name, small and great; and should destroy them which destroy the earth. And the temple of God was opened in heaven, and there was seen in His temple the ark of His testament: and there were voices, and thundering, and an earthquake, and great hail."* *(Revelation 11:15-19)*

This significant proclamation from heaven, followed by the magnificent display of worship, signals the occurrence of a series of major events in the unfolding chronological end times plan of God. First of all, the 3-1/2 year ministry of the *"two witnesses"* comes to its conclusion (Revelation 11:3-14).

The greatest event of all in this series is announced immediately by *"great voices from heaven, saying, The kingdoms of this world are become the kingdoms of our Lord, and of His Christ, and He shall reign for ever and ever." (Revelation 11:15)*

These may well be the actual lyrics of the *"new song"* being sung by the harpers in heaven and the 144 Thousand on earth in Revelation 14:1-3 for both of these events occur simultaneously to the praise and glory of God.

The eternal, earthly rule of Christ over the physical kingdoms of earth has now begun. The end times Israel of God, the 144 Thousand on Mount Zion (Revelation 14:1), will receive their Messiah, the Lord Jesus Christ as King of the nation of Israel. This is not unlike the time when all of the twelve tribes of Israel received David as their king recorded in I Chronicles 12:1-40.

This event of old marks the first time all of the tribes of Israel came together in harmony for the coronation of David, God's first anointed king from the tribe of Judah. This King-making, of the last Anointed King, *"The Lion of the Tribe of Judah" (Revelation 5:5),* will once again be accomplished as the twelve tribes gather to receive the Lord Jesus Christ as their earthly King at the end of the 70th Week of Daniel.

This will occur when the One who has made reconciliation for the sins of Israel will be received as their King by the end times Israel of God. They are the 144 Thousand, those who *"follow the Lamb wherever He goes...and have been redeemed from among men being the first fruits unto God and the Lamb." (Revelation 14:4)*

This major prophetic event has been announced in the Old Testament:
"Yet have I set My King upon My holy hill of Zion;" (Psalm 2:6)

The patriarch Jacob also prophesied of it over 3500 years ago:
"The Scepter shall not depart from Judah, nor a lawgiver from between his feet until Shiloh come, and unto Him shall the gathering of the people be." (Genesis 49:10)

Micah the prophet also refers to this great gathering:

"Therefore will He [Messiah] give them [Israel] up until the time [End of the 70ᵗʰ Week/End of The Time of Jacob's Trouble] that she [Israel] which travails has brought forth [all Israel saved]: then the remnant [remainder/rest] of His brethren [the woman/faithful of Israel] shall return unto the children [sons] of Israel [the 144 Thousand]." *(Micah 5:3)*

End of the Age Conditions in the Land of Israel

Daniel's prophecy provides insight into how conditions will be shaped in the land of Israel prior to and during the first half of the 70ᵗʰ week. It is clear from Daniel 9:27 that the majority of Israelites will agree with the covenant confirmed by the Antichrist for the seven-year duration of this last week:

"And he shall confirm the covenant with [the] many for one week." *(Daniel 9:27)*

This confirming of the covenant by the Antichrist will likely be centered upon guaranteeing Israel peace during this tumultuous time when there will be *"wars and rumors of wars"* *(Matthew 24:6)* throughout the earth.

"The holy covenant" of Daniel 11:28-32 is not referring to the Antichrist's covenant but indicates the restored Old Covenant (Exodus 19:5, 6), which appears to be accepted by the Antichrist and honored initially by the majority of Jews.

Later, the Antichrist's heart *"shall be set against the holy covenant"* and eventually he has *"indignation against the holy covenant, so shall he do, he shall even return and have intelligence with them that forsake the holy covenant"* *(Daniel 11:28, 30)*.

These verses show the progression of the Antichrist's actions:
1. He deceitfully confirms a covenant with the many in Israel at the beginning of the 70th Week (Daniel 9:27)
2. He accepts the restored (Matthew 17:11) *"holy covenant"* (Daniel 11:23)
3. He turns against the restored *"holy covenant"* (Daniel 11:28)

29

which is the precursor to the "*abomination of desolation*" (Daniel 11:31)

The Jews who align with the Antichrist play right into his hand: *"And such as do wickedly against the covenant shall he corrupt by flatteries: But the people that do know their God shall be strong and do exploits" (Daniel 11:32)*

Three different groups of Jews are shown within the land:
1. The first group of Jews mentioned by Daniel in this passage are those who depart from their prior allegiance to *the "holy covenant"* and choose to "*forsake the holy covenant*" which is the "*falling away*" recorded by the Apostle Paul. (II Thessalonians 2:3)
2. The second group is "*the people that do know their God...they that understand among the people shall instruct many*". In simple terms, these are Jews who remain faithful and are active in the land (Revelation 12:17b) after the mid-point of the 70th Week.
3. The third group called the "*many*" (Daniel 11:33) are Jews seeking the truth, being instructed by those "*that do know their God...they that understand among the people.*"

Exactly when the restoration of the *"holy covenant"* takes place is not clearly specified. But, it will be part of the ministry of *"Elijah"* to *"restore all things" (Matthew 17:11)* which will likely take place prior to the 70th Week of Daniel.

The Antichrist's involvement with the *"daily sacrifice"* begins after he confirms a covenant with the Jews, at the beginning of the 70th Week of Daniel, and continues 2300 days or *"evenings and mornings"* (Daniel 8:14).

Just what his involvement will include also is not specified, but it could be that he will preside over, and possibly have a position of authority regarding the Jews temple worship shortly after confirming the 'peace' covenant at the beginning of the 70th Week of Daniel.

Some apply this Daniel chapter eight vision to the history of Antiochus Epiphanes, a type of the Antichrist, who desecrated the temple during his assault upon the Jews and their worship during the

2nd Century B.C.

But Gabriel, who interpreted the vision for Daniel, states exactly when the vision will occur: *"O son of man: for at **the time of the end** shall be the vision.*
*Behold I will make thee know what shall be in **the last end** of the indignation: for at the time appointed **the end** shall be."*
(Daniel 8:17, 19)

In addition to Gabriel's specific interpretation, there are three events which occur in this vision that were not fulfilled in the 2nd Century B.C. by Antiochus Epiphanes:
1. He did not *"cast down some of the host and of the stars to the ground, and stamped upon them"* (Daniel 8:10).
2. He did not *"magnify himself even to Prince of the host/stand up against Prince of princes"* (Daniel 8:25).
3. He was not: *"broken without hand [human agency-NASV]"* (Daniel 8:25).

However, each of those events will occur during the end times:
1. *"And his [great red dragon/Satan] tail drew the third part of the stars of heaven, and did cast them to the earth".*
   (Revelation 12:4).
2. The Antichrist will open *"his mouth in blasphemy against God, to blaspheme His name, and His tabernacle, and them that dwell in heaven". (Revelation 13:6)*
3. The Antichrist will *"be broken without hand".*
   (Daniel 2:34, 35; Revelation 19:20)

This passage recording the 2300 days the Antichrist is involved with the *"daily sacrifice"* implies that he may early on during the 70th Week of Daniel have an integral position of authority regarding the Jews worship and may preside over the *"evening and morning"* or *"regular sacrifice".*

Daniel 8:12 gives the reason the Antichrist is given this access:
*"**And on account of transgression** the host will be given over to the horn along with the regular sacrifice; and it will fling truth to the ground and perform its will and prosper."(NASV)*

This verse not only supplies the likely cause for the Antichrist's intrusive ability to invade these sacred areas, but it also underlines the events that will occur during those days prior to the *"abomination of desolation"* at the mid-point of the 70th Week of Daniel:

1. The host will be given over to the horn
   [During the first half of the 70th Week]
2. *The regular sacrifice"* will also *"be given over to the horn"*
   [During the first half of the 70th Week].

It is because of sin, transgression in particular, a word that emphasizes the settled attitude of open and full rebellion against God, that he is able to accomplish it. This is the same word used in Daniel 9:24:

*"Seventy weeks are determined upon thy people and thy holy city, to finish the **transgression"*** describing the first purpose the Lord has decreed these 70 weeks or 490 years.

The Lord Jesus Christ spoke of this last and most blatant rebellion of the Jews:

"I [the Christ] am come in My Fathers name, and ye receive Me not: if another [the Antichrist] shall come in his own name, him ye will receive." (John 5:43)

The majority of Jews will in fact continue to reject their Messiah, the Lord Jesus Christ, in that day and instead embrace the Antichrist, just as they did their *"Caesar" (John 19:15)* of old.

This last rejection of the Messiah will occur after Elijah has restored all things providing the Jews with all the outward evidence that God sent him, giving them the opportunity to worship the Lord according to the *"holy covenant"*. Instead they will commit the *"transgression"* as they collaborate with and receive the Antichrist worshipping him in open rebellion against God.

This *"transgression"* or rebellion by those who *"forsake the holy covenant"* provides the Antichrist with the ability to intervene as the host will be given over to him along with the regular sacrifice. Eventually he will end the regular sacrifice and set up his image in the holy place at the mid-point of the 70th Week of Daniel.

The climax of these events begins when:
"He [Antichrist] shall be grieved, and return, and have indignation against the holy covenant: so shall he do, he shall even return, and have intelligence with them that forsake the holy covenant."
(Daniel 11:30)

This is immediately followed by the fruition of his ultimate goal of world worship:
"And arms [forces] shall stand on his part, and they shall pollute the sanctuary of strength and shall take away the daily sacrifice, and they shall place the abomination [image of Antichrist] that makes desolate." (Daniel 11:31)

It appears that the time leading up to the 70th Week of Daniel will be occupied by Elijah's ministry of restoration including the revival of God's people and the restoration of all things regarding the *"holy covenant"*.

The Antichrist will rise to power during this same timeframe eventually confirming the covenant with [the] *"many"* of the nation of Israel (Daniel 9:27) at the beginning of the 70th Week.

Then, the host and regular sacrifice will be given over to the Antichrist with the culmination of his wicked influence coming at the mid-point of the 70th Week of Daniel. That is when his forces stop the regular sacrifice and pollute the sanctuary by setting up his image in the holy place for the remaining 1260 days of the 70th Week which is the renowned *"abomination of desolation"* indicated by the Lord Jesus Christ (Matthew 24:15).

This major religious/political takeover by the Antichrist will also serve to bring peace in the land and across the globe. But, this peace will only come to those who submit to him and take his mark during the days following the mid-point of the 70th Week of Daniel as the Antichrist grasps world rule like the Caesars of old who also were worshipped as god.

Ezekiel, a contemporary of Daniel who also ministered to the Jews in Babylon during their 70 years of captivity, provides key information on the conditions that will exist in the land during the time of the end:

"After many days thou [Gog]: **in the latter years** *thou shall come into the land [Israel] that is brought back from the sword, and is gathered out of many people, against the mountains of Israel, which have always been waste: but it is brought forth out of the nations, and they shall dwell safely all of them. And thou [Gog] shall say, I will go up to the land of unwalled villages [Israel]; I will go to them that are at rest that dwell safely, all of them dwelling without walls, and having neither bars nor gates." (Ezekiel 38:8, 11)*

According to this passage, Israel will be living in a time of peace, without walls for protection from the enemy, as security will abound and there will be no need for barring/locking the door or having gates to keep out unwanted intruders. Later, in the same chapter, the Lord again addresses Gog:

"In that day when My people of Israel dwells safely, shall thou not know it?"(Ezekiel 38:14a)

There will be peace and safety in the land for the unsaved majority who will be living under the Antichrist's oppressive rule, having taken his mark, which supplies them with the ability to buy and sell (Revelation 13:16, 17).

However, this will not be the lot of the faithful, neither in the land nor across the globe, for the Antichrist's world domination will bring the most intensive persecution to the saints ever as spoken by the Lord:

"For then shall be great tribulation, such as was not since the beginning of the world to this time, no, nor ever shall be."
(Matthew 24:21)

An unaware "business as usual" attitude will definitely be evident during the second half of the 70th week just before the Lord's Second Coming to resurrect/rescue/rapture/receive the saints and the **same-day** beginning of the Day of the Lord according to the Lord Jesus Christ's teaching:

"And as it was in the days of Noah, so shall it also be in the days of the Son of man. They did eat, they drank, they married wives, they were given in marriage, until **the day** *that Noah entered the ark, and the flood came, and destroyed them all. Likewise also as it was in the*

34

*days of Lot; they did eat, they drank, they bought, they sold, they planted, they builded; But **the same day** that Lot went out of Sodom it rained fire and brimstone from heaven, and destroyed them all. Even thus shall it be in **the day** when the Son of man is revealed."*
(Luke 17:26-30)

Paul also supplies additional information concerning this time:
*"But of the times and the seasons brethren, ye have no need that I write unto you. For yourselves know perfectly that the day of the Lord so comes as a thief in the night. For when they [unbelievers] shall say **peace and safety**; then sudden destruction comes upon them as travail upon a woman with child; and they shall not escape."*
(I Thessalonians 5:1-3)

The Lord Jesus reveals the attitude of unbelievers during the time just before His Second Coming/Day of the Lord. Paul supplies the reason for their unaware attitude, as it will be a time of *"peace and safety"* just as Ezekiel prophesied in his description of those future days in the land of Israel.

Present-day [2007] Israel is in the midst of a deadly conflict against its age-old enemies, the Islamic Fascists, building walls and strengthening its defense. However, events can and will turn quickly, by the hand of God, to bring to pass these necessary end times conditions clearly outlined by the Lord Jesus Christ, the prophets Daniel and Ezekiel, and the Apostle Paul.

Although those days will be filled with Satan's *"great wrath"* *(Revelation 12:12)* also called *"the great tribulation" (Matthew 24:21; Revelation 7:14)* affecting the faithful, the majority of the world population will be experiencing outward peace under the oppressive-dictatorial rule of the Antichrist after he attains control of Jewry and its world capital Jerusalem at the mid-point of the 70th Week of Daniel. However, prior to that event:
1. The Jews will be a people/nation (Daniel 9:24)
2. They will be in their Promised Land
   (Deuteronomy 30:5; Matthew 24:16)
3. They will occupy their holy city Jerusalem
   (Daniel 9:24)
4. The prophet Elijah will be sent to revive/restore

(Malachi 4:5, 6; Matthew 17:11; Mark 9:12)
5. The *"holy covenant"* will be restored (Daniel 11:28-32)
6. The *"temple of God"* will be rebuilt
   (Daniel 11:31; II Thessalonians 2:1-4; Revelation 11:1, 2)
7. The *"holy place"* included (Matthew 24:15)
8. The *"regular sacrifices"* will be instituted
   (Daniel 8:11, 12, 9:27, 11:31, 12:11)
9. The Jews will worship in *"the temple of God" (Revelation 11:1)*
10. The "*Sabbath" (Matthew 24:20)* will be honored
11. The sending of prophets will occur
    (Malachi 4:5, 6; Revelation 11:3-14)
12. The *"twelve tribes"* of Israel will be recognized and sealed
    (Revelation 7:4-8)

The first three events have already taken place with the remaining events just over the Lord's prophetic horizon. They will definitely come to pass as necessary prerequisites for the unfolding of His plan during the 70th Week of Daniel/time of the end. The subject of the following chapters is those people who appear in Scripture during the end times who are called:

"The People of the Apocalypse"

As the Bible is surveyed, at least twenty individuals or groups are evident:
1. The Lamb of God (John 1:29; Revelation 5:6-8)
2. The Twenty Four Elders (Revelation 4:4)
3. The Four Beasts (Revelation 4:6-8)
4. The Angels (Revelation 5:2, 11)
5. The Prophet Elijah (Malachi 4:5, 6; Matthew 17:11; Mark 9:12)
6. The Martyrs (Daniel 11:33-35; Revelation 6:9-11)
7. The Saints (Daniel 7:18-27; Revelation 13:7, 10)
8. The Earth Dwellers (Revelation 3:10, 6:10)
9. The 144 Thousand (Revelation 7:1-8)
10. The Great Multitude in Heaven (Revelation 7:9-17)
11. The Woman (Revelation 12:1-17a)
12. The Rest of the Woman's Seed (Revelation 12:17b)
    Those Who Understand (Daniel 11:33)
13. The Devil (Revelation 12)
14. The Antichrist (Daniel 7-12; Revelation 13:1-10)
15. The False Prophet (Revelation 13:11-18)
16. The Two Witnesses (Revelation 11:3-14; Zechariah 4:1-14)

17. The Israelites Saved (Isaiah 59:20; Romans 11:25)
18. The Gentiles Saved (Isaiah 19:18-25; Micah 7:15-17)
19. The Ten Kings (Daniel 7:7; Revelation 17:12-14)
20. The Great Whore/Mystery Babylon (Revelation 17,18)

With these prophetic truths in view, it is imperative for today's saints to fully surrender to the Lord, discerning His plan for their lives, during the closing climactic days of this age. The Lord will definitely call out, send and mightily use "The People of the Apocalypse" as He brings to pass His end times plan for His earthly people Israel and the Church of the Lord Jesus Christ.

Like Daniel the prophet who effectually and fervently prayed after he discerned in the Scripture exactly what the Lord was planning to accomplish (Daniel 9:2), the saints likewise, must pray to the Lord in order that He might send forth laborers into His harvest. These laborers must recognize their calling and prayerfully give themselves to Him for His glory in this coming time of unprecedented privilege being willing to: *"Spend and be spent" (II Corinthians 12:15)* as *"living sacrifices unto God." (Romans12: 1)*

2

The Most Prophesied Event in Scripture

When the Lord Jesus' four disciples, James, John, Peter and Andrew, asked Him the following questions, *"When shall these things be? And what shall be the sign of Thy coming, and of the end of the world [age]?" (Matthew 24:3b),* He answered their question with simplicity and great clarity.

However, He addressed the second part of their question first [*"the end of the world [age]"*] because the events leading up to the end of the age are also the signs for His Second Coming. Both events, the end of this age and the Second Coming of Christ, begin on the very same day:
*"And as it was in the days of Noah, so shall it also be in the days of the Son of man. They did eat, they drank, they married, they were given in marriage, until **the day** that Noah entered into the ark, and the flood came, and destroyed them all. Likewise also as it was in the days of Lot; they did eat, they drank, they bought, they sold, they planted, they builded; But **the same day** that Lot went out of Sodom it rained fire and brimstone from heaven, and destroyed them all. Even thus shall it be in the day when the Son of man is revealed."*
(Luke 17:26-30)

The Lord is emphasizing *"the same day"* rescue of His people, then, immediate retribution. This has been His unchanging method through the ages. In other words, this present age, which is the age of grace, will end when the Lord returns to rescue His saints by rapture from Satan's great tribulation, which is immediately followed by His Day of the Lord judgment. His Second Coming will bring an end to this present age, which is also called the Church age.

Man's time on earth started *"In the beginning" (Genesis 1:1)* when God created man (Genesis 1:27) and gave him *"Dominion...over every living thing" (Genesis 1:28)* and therefore, the time since Creation could rightly be called the day of man.

Man's day will be immediately followed by God's Day, which is the eschatological Day of the Lord, "The Most Prophesied Event in Scripture". In that day God will systematically re-take control of His planet through His righteous Day of the Lord judgments. In the process these judgments will also accomplish His purpose of purging and purifying the earth from the ages-long effects of sin's corruption (Psalm 102:25, 26; II Peter 3:10-12). This Day of the Lord judgment period will be preceded by these heavenly wonders:

*"And I will show wonders in the heavens and in the earth, blood, and fire, and pillars of smoke. The sun shall be turned into darkness, and the moon into blood, **before** the great and the terrible day of the Lord come." (Joel 2:30, 31)*

Joel, whose entire book focuses upon the Day of the Lord, is the first to write of this event indicating that these heavenly wonders will be the sign of the Day of the Lord for they will precede the Lord's wrathful judgment in that day.

Isaiah also attests to these same signs in the heavens in connection with the Day of the Lord:

"Behold, the day of the Lord comes, cruel both with wrath and fierce anger, to lay the land desolate: and He shall destroy the sinners thereof out of it. For the stars of heaven and the constellations thereof shall not give their light: the sun shall be darkened in his going forth, and the moon shall not cause her light to shine." (Isaiah 13:9, 10)

The prophet Amos speaks of the darkness during this future event:

"Woe unto you that desire the day of the Lord: to what end is it for you: the day of the Lord is darkness and not light...Shall not the day of the Lord be darkness, and not light? Even very dark, and no brightness in it?" (Amos 5:18, 20)

Zephaniah, whose book theme is the Day of the Lord, records this same darkness along with other defining characteristics:

"The great day of the Lord is near, it is near, and hastes greatly, even the voice of the day of the Lord: the mighty man shall cry there bitterly. That day is a day of wrath, a day of trouble and distress, a day of wasteness and desolation, a day of darkness and gloominess, a day of clouds and thick darkness." (Zephaniah 1:14, 15)

The Lord Jesus Christ links these same heavenly wonders to the end of this age and His return to rescue the saints from Satan's *"great wrath" (Revelation 12:12)* also called the Great Tribulation:

*"**Immediately after** the [great] tribulation of those days shall the sun be darkened, and the moon shall not give her light, and the stars shall fall from heaven, and the powers of the heavens shall be shaken: And **then** shall appear the sign of the Son of man in heaven: and **then** shall all the tribes of the earth mourn, and they shall see the Son of man coming in the clouds of heaven with power and great glory. And He shall send His angels with a great sound of a trumpet, and they shall gather together His elect from the four winds, from one end of heaven to the other." (Matthew 24:29-31)*

Notice the Lord's step-by-step chronological explanation:
1. *Immediately **after** the great tribulation is shortened the heavenly wonders occur (Matthew 24:21, 29) (The entire planet is miraculously darkened)*
2. ***Then** shall appear the sign of the Son of man in heaven. (The entire planet is miraculously illuminated by His "great [Shekinah] glory")*
3. ***And then** shall all the tribes of the earth mourn.*
4. *They shall see the Son of man coming in the clouds of heaven.*
5. *And He shall send His angels*
6. *With a great sound of a trumpet.*
7. *They shall gather together His elect (rapture).*

Mark also records this most significant sequence of prophetic events:

*"But in those days **after** that tribulation, the sun shall be darkened, and the moon shall not give her light, And the stars of heaven shall fall, and the powers that are in heaven shall be shaken. And **then** shall they see the Son of man coming in the clouds with great power and glory. **And then** shall He send His angels, and shall gather together His elect from the four winds, from the uttermost part of the earth to the uttermost part of heaven." (Mark 13:24-27)*

Luke, too, tells of these future signs in each of the books he wrote:

"And there shall be signs in the sun, and in the moon, and in the stars... And I will show wonders in heaven above, and signs in the earth beneath; blood, and fire, and vapor of smoke: The sun shall be

*turned into darkness, and the moon into blood, **before** that great and notable day of the Lord come." (Luke 21:25; Acts 2:19, 20)*

John's record of these supernatural events provides additional descriptive information:
"And I beheld when He had opened the sixth seal, and, lo, there was a great earthquake; and the sun became black as sackcloth of hair, and the moon became as blood; And the stars of heaven fell unto the earth, even as a fig tree casts her untimely figs, when she is shaken of a mighty wind." (Revelation 6:12, 13)

While these passages focus upon the sign that occurs **before** the Day of the Lord, ultimately indicating this sign's prominence in the Lord's end times plan, this is only the sign that **precedes** His Coming and wrath-filled Day of the Lord judgment. This major prophetic sign and its global effects are referred to in at least fourteen different Bible passages: (Isaiah 5:30, 13:10, 24:23; Ezekiel 32:7, 8; Joel 2:2, 10, 30-31; Amos 1:18; 8: 9; Zephaniah 1:15; Matthew 24:29; Mark 13:24, 25; Luke 21:25; Acts 2:20; Revelation 6:12, 13).

The Biblical importance of this event [the sign of the Day of the Lord/Coming of Christ] is clear, for it is the key to understanding the unfolding chronology of the end times as it is the sign that occurs *"after"* the great tribulation (Matthew 24:29), and just *"before" (Joel 2:30, 31) "the same day" (Luke 17:29)* beginning of the Day of the Lord which is initiated by the Second Coming of Christ (Matthew 24:30, 31) to rescue His elect by rapture.

The Day of the Lord is thoroughly described in the seven trumpet plagues (Revelation 8-11), the seven vial plagues (Revelation 15, 16), the destruction of Babylon (Revelation 17, 18) and the culminating battle of Armageddon (Revelation 19:11-21).

There are three Minor Prophets whose books are dedicated wholly to the Day of the Lord: Obadiah, Joel and Zephaniah, while Isaiah 2-5, and major portions of "The Little Apocalypse" (Isaiah 24-27) also focus upon this unparalleled time of God's wrath/judgment.

Although the rapture of the saints continues to be the event that receives the most attention because it is the major occurrence on

God's prophetic timetable clearly effecting the saints, it is not the primary event that the Lord has underlined in His Word, for the rapture itself is scarcely mentioned when compared to the amount of Bible text that is devoted to the eschatological Day of the Lord.

The Bible gives a clear and compelling witness to this future plan of God's time of the end judgment when He will fulfill His three-fold purpose for the Day of the Lord by:
1. Punishing the Peoples (Isaiah 2:10-17; Zephaniah 1:17)
2. Purging the Planet (Micah 1:3, 4; II Peter 3:10, 11)
3. Purifying His People (Isaiah 6:10, 13; Daniel 12:10; Zechariah 13:8, 9; Malachi 3:1-3)

It is during this time called the Day of the Lord that God will utilize a mighty company of 144 Thousand servants (Revelation 7:3) who will be called out, prepared and sealed (Revelation 7:4-8). They will be protected (Revelation 9:4) in order that they might be His servants during this future time of judgment. They are in reality "The Time of the End Israel of God".

They will carry the Redemption Message of the Gospel of grace to those (Daniel 11:32-35, 12:3; Zechariah 13:9) who are written in the Lamb's book of life from the foundation of the world. The chronological sequence of events recorded in Matthew 24:4-31 and Revelation 6-8 indicate:
1. The Beginning of Sorrows
   (Matthew 24:4-8; Revelation 6:1-8)
2. The Great Tribulation
   (Matthew 24:9-28; Revelation 6:9-11)
3. The *Sign* of The Day of the Lord & The Second Coming of Christ
   (Matthew 24:29-30; Revelation 6:12-17)
4. The Sealing of The 144 Thousand (Revelation 7:1-8)
5. The Coming of the Lord to Rescue/Rapture/Receive the Saints
   (Matthew 24:31; John 14:3; Revelation 7:9-17)
6. The Beginning of The Day of the Lord (Revelation 8:1-5)
7. The Day of the Lord Plagues/Judgments
   (Revelation 8:6-11:15, 15, 16)
   a. The Seven Trumpets
      [The first plagues (Revelation 9:20)]
   b. The Seven Vials

[The last plagues (Revelation 15:1)]
c. The Judgment of Babylon (Revelation 17. 18)
d. The Battle of Armageddon (Revelation 19:11-15)

These horrendous cataclysmic Day of the Lord judgments mentioned above, which are sent from God and executed by His angels, are the main elements of God's wrath upon the earth and its inhabitants taking up the majority of the prophetic section of the Revelation of Jesus Christ.

The following events will occur ***before*** the Day of the Lord begins:
1. The Sending of Elijah (Malachi 4:5, 6)
2. The Revival of Hearts (Malachi 4:5, 6)
3. The Restoration of All [Holy Covenant] Things
    (Daniel 11:28-32; Matthew 17:11; Mark 9:12)
    a. The Jews will be in the land (Deuteronomy 30:5; Daniel 9:24;
        Matthew 24:16)
    b. They will occupy Jerusalem (Daniel 9:24)
    c. The temple will be rebuilt (Daniel 11:31;
        I Thessalonians 2:1-4; Revelation 11:1, 2)
    d. The holy place included (Matthew 24:15)
    e. The regular/morning and evening sacrifices will be instituted
        (Daniel 8:11, 12, 9:27, 11:31, 12:11)
    f. The Sabbath will be honored (Matthew 24:20)
    g. The two witnesses/prophets will be sent to God's people
        (Revelation 11:3-17)
    h. The twelve tribes of Israel will be recognized/sealed
        (Revelation 7:3-8)
4. The Awareness of the Believer
    (Matthew 24:32, 33; I Thessalonians 5:1-10)
5. The Falling Away (Daniel 11:30; II Thessalonians 2:1-3)
6. The Man of Sin Revealed
    (Daniel 11:31; Matthew 24:15; II Thessalonians 2:1-10)
7. The Abomination of Desolation
    (Daniel 9:27, 11:31; Matthew 24:15; II Thessalonians 2:3, 4)
8. The Great Tribulation (Daniel 11:31-12:1, 2, 10;
    Matthew 24:15-28; Revelation 13:1-18)
9. The Heavenly Wonders (Joel 2:31; Isaiah 13:10; Matthew 24:29;
    Mark 13:24, 25; Luke 21:25, 26; Revelation 6:12)
10. The Sealing of The 144 Thousand (Revelation 7:1-8)

11. The Last Trump
    (Joel 2:1; Matthew 24:31; I Corinthians 15:52;
    I Thessalonians 4:16)
12. The Second Coming of Christ to Rapture the Saints
    (Matthew 24:29-31; I Thessalonians 4:13-18)

The Day of the Lord is clearly described as God's wrath:
*"Behold, the day of the Lord comes, cruel both with **wrath** and fierce anger, to lay the land desolate; and He shall destroy the sinners thereof out of it...Therefore I will shake the heavens, and the earth shall remove out of her place, in the **wrath** of the Lord of hosts, and in the day of His fierce anger." (Isaiah 13:9, 13)*

*"The great day of the Lord is near, it is near, and hastes greatly, even the voice of the day of the Lord: the mighty man shall cry there bitterly. That day is a day of **wrath**, a day of trouble and distress, a day of wasteness and desolation, a day of darkness and gloominess, a day of clouds and thick darkness."*
(Zephaniah 1:14, 15)

However, God's people will not experience the Day of the Lord, which is God's wrath, for He has promised that they will be delivered from this unparalleled period of judgment:
*"And to wait for His Son from heaven whom He raised from the dead, even Jesus, which delivered us from the **wrath** to come... For God has not appointed us to **wrath**, but to obtain salvation [deliverance] by out Lord Jesus Christ." (I Thessalonians 1:10; 5:9)*

God's people have never been promised deliverance from tribulation. On the contrary, the Scripture teaches *"through much tribulation"* we *"enter into the kingdom of God" (Acts 14:22).*

The Lord Jesus told the eleven disciples the night before He was crucified: *"In the world ye shall have tribulation" (John 16:33)* which the apostle Paul also confirmed:
"For verily, when we were with you, we told you before that we should suffer tribulation; even as it came to pass, and ye know."
(I Thessalonians 3:4)

Tribulation is used by God to produce patience in His people for

44

"Tribulation works patience" (Romans 5:3) as any true child of God will testify, knowing that it is the Lord's working in their life. James, the Lord's half-brother was the first to record this vital truth in the New Testament:

"My brethren, count it all joy when ye fall into divers temptations; Knowing this, that the trying of your faith works patience. But let patience have her perfect work, that ye may be perfect and entire, wanting nothing". (James 1:2-4)

Paul himself gloried *"in tribulation" (Romans 5:3)* and was *"exceeding joyful" (I Corinthians 7:4)* in and through all of the tribulation God allowed him to suffer knowing that the Lord was at work in his life.

This patience building process through tribulation ultimately allows the child of God to *"possess ye your soul" (Luke 21:19)* during the coming and most vicious persecution believers will ever face during the Great Tribulation. (Luke 21:12-18).

The Great Tribulation is carried out by the Antichrist and the false prophet (Revelation 13:1-18) and is also called the *"war against the saints" (Daniel 7:21; Revelation 13:7,)*. It must not be confused with God's wrath for His wrath immediately follows the *"great tribulation" (Matthew 24:29)* and is called the Day of the Lord.

God will definitely rescue the saints before His wrath by cutting off, thereby shortening, this time of *"great tribulation" (Matthew 24:22)* when He sends His Son, the Lord Jesus Christ, to rescue the saints by rapture from this, the most intense tribulation ever experienced by the saints (Matthew 24:21). This glorious supernatural rescue of the people of God is also referred to as *"that blessed hope"*:
"Looking for that blessed hope, and the glorious appearing of the great God and our Saviour Jesus Christ; Who gave Himself for us, that He might redeem us from all iniquity, and purify unto Himself a peculiar people, zealous of good works." (Titus 2:13, 14)

The saints will be taken home to heaven (Revelation 7:9-17) being delivered (I Thessalonians 5:9) from the wrath of God, which is "The Most Prophesied Event in Scripture":
"The great and dreadful day of the Lord." (Malachi 4:5)

45

3

The Nature of the Second Coming of Christ

After the Lord Jesus arose from the dead, He appeared on numerous occasions to His disciples and other followers. He was seen on the road to Emmaus by *"two of them" (Luke 24:13)* and spoke with them and broke bread. The Lord eventually *"vanished out of their sight" (Luke 24:31)* returning to heaven.

Mary Magdalene, on resurrection morning, while visiting the sepulcher where Jesus was buried *"saw Jesus standing, and knew not that it was Jesus" (John 20:14)*. After the Lord called her name she recognized Him and the Lord said, *"Touch me not, for I am not yet ascended to My Father" (John 20:17)* indicating that He had not yet ascended to heaven after His resurrection.

"Then the same day at evening, being the first day of the week, when the doors were shut where the disciples were assembled for fear of the Jews, came Jesus and stood in the midst, and said unto them, Peace be unto you." (John 20:19)

He then showed His followers His hands and His side but one of His disciples, Thomas, was absent. He eventually left them and returned to heaven. Eight days later He appeared unto them again, Thomas included, and showed His wounds to Thomas:
"And Thomas answered and said unto Him, My Lord and My God. Jesus said unto Him, Thomas, because thou has seen Me, thou has believed: blessed are they that have not seen and yet have believed" (John 20:28, 29). The Lord once again returned to heaven.

"After these things Jesus showed Himself again to the disciples at the sea of Tiberias; and on this wise shewed He Himself." (John 21:1)

The account continues with the Lord and the disciples on the seaside and the Lord calls them to *"come and dine"* (John 21:12), followed by the account of the Lord's conversation with Peter concerning feeding His sheep. The Lord then returned to heaven.

Mark 16:9-20 also tells of these appearances of the Lord after His resurrection, to Mary Magdalene, to the two on the road to Emmaus, and to the eleven as they sat eating, eventually ascending into heaven. After each of His post-resurrection appearances He returned to heaven, now being exalted at the right hand of the Father.

He was in His glorified resurrection body and was able to appear on earth at one moment and then vanish, returning to heaven the next. While there are no specific texts indicating exactly where the Lord went when He disappeared during His post-resurrection ministry, it is logical to assume that during the time between appearances He went to His home in heaven where all of those with glorified bodies like His will spend eternity.

So it will be with His Second Coming. He will appear and fulfill what has been written and then return to heaven until the entire work of His Second Coming is complete and He comes to physically rule and reign upon earth for 1,000 years which is known as the Millennium (Revelation 20:1-4). His Second Coming will unfold in these three appearances:
1. The Glorious Reception (Rapture of the Church)
    (John 14:3; Matthew 24:29-31; I Corinthians 15:51, 52
    I Thessalonians 4:13-18)
2. The Grand Redemption (Redemption of Israel)
    (Isaiah 59:20; Romans 11:25, 26; Revelation 14:1)
3. The Great Retribution (Retribution/Gentiles/Armageddon)
    (Daniel 2:44, 7:11, 12; Revelation 19:11-21)

These three appearances will occur when the Lord Jesus Christ physically intervenes on earth and brings a close to the following events:
1. The Glorious Reception/Rapture will end the Great Tribulation
    (Matthew 24:21-31)
2. The Grand Redemption will end the 70th Week of Daniel
    (Psalm 2:6; Revelation 11:15, 14:1)
3. The Great Retribution will end the Day of the Lord
    (Daniel 7:11, 12; Revelation 16:14; 19:11-21)

When God's plan is accomplished, the Lord Jesus Christ will end each major series of end times events and in the process He will complete God's ultimate purpose for each of them:

1. The Great Tribulation prepares the Church for:
   The Glorious Reception (Ephesians 5:27; I John 3:1-3)
2. The 70th Week of Daniel prepares Israel for:
   The Grand Redemption (Daniel 12:10; Zechariah 13:9)
3. The Day of the Lord prepares the Gentiles for:
   The Great Retribution
   Isaiah 13:11-13; Revelation 9:20, 21, 16:9, 11, 19:11-21)

4

The Master's Merging Mentality

The Lord has dealt with men throughout the ages with a "Merging Mentality". When He is about to make a change in the way He deals with mankind He always merges one economy with the next while not making any abrupt changes in His methods or manners.

All six of the major dispensations, or economies, if you will, economy [oikonomia-Gk.] being the Biblical word, Innocence, Conscience, Human Government, Promise, Law and Grace have merged one into the other just as we merge into traffic on the highway and run alongside of another lane for a certain distance. So God and His economies have done the same throughout history.

Innocence shows Eve with a Conscience for some period of time with Adam still innocent. It can be easily demonstrated that Conscience, Human Government, Promise, and Law are also still continuing to run alongside of Grace and are still in effect to varying degrees.

There are those who would even say that Innocence is the condition of an infant at birth, but the Word of God clearly teaches that we are conceived and born in sin (Psalm 51:5; Romans 5:12). Even though there are principles from the previous economies still active, we are presently living in the economy of Grace which is also called the Church Age.

This merging of economies, being the standard method God uses in dealing with men, will continue to be His method at the end of the age. He once again will merge the two, the Old and the New, the Church and the Jew, Grace and Law, with the bridge over this final period of time being that great multitude called *"the servants of our God" (Revelation 7:3)*. They are the 144 Thousand who are sealed from each of the twelve tribes of Israel.

They are born during the New Covenant period, during the economy of Grace. But they are saved, sealed and serve under the Old Covenant, during Daniel's Seventieth Week when God again deals with the nation of Israel. This completes Daniel's prophesied 70 Weeks /490 years (Daniel 9:24), during which time God eventually pours out His Day of the Lord wrath on an unbelieving world with the purpose of purifying the Jew and punishing Jew and Gentile alike.

This bridge group of 144 Thousand Jews is seen on Mt. Zion with the Lamb of God, our precious Redeemer the Lord Jesus Christ, at the end of the 70th Week of Daniel. They already have the Father's name written on their foreheads (Revelation 14:1) similar to those that received a mark on their foreheads in Ezekiel 9 who also were protected. They were the faithful Jews in Ezekiel's vision of Gods judgment of Jerusalem.

The 144 Thousand are seen on a number of occasions in the book of the Revelation. Once at the time they are *"sealed" (7:3)* and again when they appear on *"the mount Zion" (14:1)* with the Lamb having the signature of God in their foreheads as mentioned above. And finally they are again seen *"with Him" (17:14),* the Lamb, the Lord of lords and King of kings, as He goes forth to war at the battle of Armageddon.

This unprecedented time at the end of the age brings with it an unprecedented restoration by Elijah (Matthew 17:11; Mark 9:12) as the Lord will likely revert to the practices of the Old Covenant during this last week, or seven years, of His dealing with the nation of Israel just as He did the first sixty-nine weeks.

Therefore, during the last seven weeks the Jews must be a people (Daniel 9:24); they must be in the land (Deuteronomy 30:1, 5-9; Ezekiel 36:24-26, 37:21ff, 38, Daniel 9:24); they must posses their holy city (Daniel 9:24); the temple of God must be rebuilt (II Thessalonians 2:4; Revelation 11:1, 2); the holy covenant honored (Daniel 11:28-30); the daily sacrifices reinstated (Daniel 8:11, 12, 9:27; 11:31, 12:11); the holy place recognized (Matthew 24:15); the prophet Elijah sent to the people (Malachi 4:5,6); the Sabbath restored (Matthew 24:20), and the twelve tribes recognized (Revelation 7:3-8).

At this point in history [2007] only three of these events have taken place. The Jews are a people, they are in the holy land and the holy city belongs to the Jews which are the first in order of the things required for the Lord to begin this last seven year dispensation for Gabriel told Daniel that [all of] the seventy weeks would be upon his people and his holy city (Daniel 9:24).

The events mentioned above are necessary to begin this last Old Covenant dispensation, for how can the *"holy covenant"* be honored unless there is a *"temple of God"* and *'holy place'*, with *"the regular morning and evening sacrifices"* being offered, along with restoration of *"the Sabbath"* and *"the twelve tribes"* recognized?

All of these Old Covenant necessities will eventually be restored through the ministry of the last Elijah-like prophet as he has been given the duty of restoring all things according to the prophecy of the Lord Jesus Christ: *"Elijah truly shall come first and restore all things." (Matthew 17:11)*

The next event on God's timetable appears to be the sending of Elijah:
"Behold, I will send you Elijah the prophet before the coming of the great and dreadful day of the Lord: And he shall turn the hearts of the fathers to the children, and the heart of the children to their fathers, lest I come and smite the earth with a curse." (Malachi 4:5, 6)

God will of necessity send him before the beginning of the 70th Week for the above mentioned physical and spiritual necessities are precursors of the 70th Week and will be in place before the covenant is confirmed with the many in the nation of Israel by the Antichrist at the beginning of the 70th Week (Daniel 9:27).

The Antichrist will rise to power and world prominence accumulating military clout and political might as he goes forth *"conquering, and to conquer" (Revelation 6:1, 2)* in order to build his eventual global domination (Daniel 7:14, 23; 8:23-25; 11:41) giving him the ability to maneuver politically on the world scene.

The Lord has begun His final merging of economies as He has already put in place the first three prerequisites for the 70th Week of

(Daniel 9:24) and is presently executing His plan in order to bring to pass the remaining events that He might once again begin to deal with His earthly people and fulfill the prophecies recorded in His Word.

As the prophet Daniel saw in the Scripture (Jeremiah 29:10) exactly what God was planning, requiring the necessary prayer of repentance (Leviticus 26:40-46), he prayed confessing his sins, the sins of his fathers, and the sins of his people with deep repentance and contrition requesting God's mercy and forgiveness (Daniel 9:1-19).

So, too, the saints must cry out to God in full surrender, realizing that the seedbed for this bridge group, the 144 Thousand, and Elijah himself, is the Church of Jesus Christ. For God will raise up these, His servants, from among the faithful families of the Body of Christ in order to bring to pass His precious promises as He continues to merge these two economies as we close in on the end of this age.

5

The Covenants in The Book of Daniel

The prophet Daniel was given a clear and concise timeline of certain future events:

"And he [Antichrist] shall __confirm__ [strengthen/cause to prevail] the __covenant__ with [the] many [Israelites] for one week [Daniel's 70th Week]: and in the midst of the week he shall cause the sacrifice and the oblation to cease, and for the overspreading of abominations he shall make it desolate, even until the consummation, and that determined shall be poured upon the desolate." (Daniel 9:27)

The 70th Week of Daniel will begin when the Antichrist confirms an existing covenant with [the] *"many"* in the nation of Israel. The Hebrew word translated *"confirm"* is used 25 times in the Old Testament and emphasizes the act of prevailing or strengthening.

Isaiah used this same word to indicate the Lord's prevailing actions during the coming Day of the Lord:

"The Lord shall go forth as a mighty man, He shall stir up jealousy like a man of war: He shall cry, yea, roar; He shall __prevail__ against His enemies." (Isaiah 42:13)

Zechariah also employed this word on two occasions when he described the Lord's future strengthening of His re-gathered people during the Day of the Lord:

"And I will __strengthen__ the house of Judah, and I will save the house of Joseph...And I will __strengthen__ them in the Lord; and they shall walk up and down in His name, saith the Lord." (Zechariah 10:6, 10)

The word *"confirm"* in Daniel 9:27 focuses upon the strengthening of an existing covenant, thereby causing it to prevail. It can be said that the Antichrist will literally "put teeth into" this existing agreement which is the starting point for the 70th and last week, or seven years, which have been determined by God upon Daniel's people, the Jews and his holy city Jerusalem (Daniel 9:24).

Exactly what this covenant contains is not indicated in the text. However, from the information given in the book of Daniel and the book of the Revelation of Jesus Christ, it is clear that the Antichrist will be a powerful political leader with great military clout capable of making a covenant to guarantee peace for Israel. This has been the prevailing opinion of most students of Bible prophecy.

The fact that the Antichrist confirms an existing covenant at the beginning of the 70th Week of Daniel means that he will have already established this covenant/agreement with Israel during the days, months or years prior to his action of confirming, strengthening, and causing this existing covenant to prevail.

Isaiah indicates the deadly nature of this future covenant:
"Wherefore hear the word of the Lord, ye scornful men, that rule this people which is in Jerusalem, Because ye have said, We have made a covenant with death, and with hell are we at agreement; when the overflowing scourge shall pass through, it shall not come unto us: for we have made lies our refuge, and under falsehood have we hid ourselves...And your covenant with death shall be disannulled, and your agreement with hell shall not stand; when the overflowing scourge shall pass through, then ye shall be trodden down by it." *(Isaiah 28:14, 15, 18)*

The many in Israel will put their trust in this covenant saying: *"When the overflowing scourge [God's Day of the Lord judgment] shall pass through, it shall not come unto us"*. The Lord makes it clear that this will not be the case in that future day:
"From the time that it goes forth it shall take you: for morning by morning shall it pass over, by day and by night: and it shall be a vexation [sheer terror] only to understand the report [what it means] ...For the Lord shall rise up as in mount Perazim, He shall be wroth as in the valley of Gibeon, that He may do His work, His strange work; and bring to pass His act, His strange act. Now, therefore be ye not mockers, lest your bands be made strong: for I have heard from the Lord God of hosts a consumption, even determined upon the whole earth." *(Isaiah 28:19, 21, 22)*

The worldwide judgment of God is here indicated beginning with Israel and going forth being empowered by His wrath when He will *"bring to pass His act, His strange act"* which is described as a *"consumption, even determined upon the whole earth."*

Daniel uses the word ***"covenant"*** six different times. The first time he uses the word it refers to a covenant made by God with His people: *"And I prayed unto the Lord my God, and made my confession, and said, O Lord, the great and dreadful God, keeping the **covenant** and mercy to them that love Him, and to them that keep His commandments." (Daniel 9:4)*

Then follows the 70th Week covenant of Antichrist mentioned above, found in Daniel 9:27. In chapter eleven the word appears again:
*"And in his [king of the north] estate shall stand up a vile person [last king of the north/Antichrist], to whom they shall not give the honor of the kingdom: but he shall come in peaceably, and obtain the kingdom by flatteries. And with the arms [forces] of a flood shall they be overflown [flooded away] from before him [Antichrist], and shall be broken; yea, also the prince [ruler/head] of the **covenant**."*
(Daniel 11:21, 22)

In this verse the Antichrist's forces shatter those who had the power to make him king but did not give him that honor. This destruction includes *"the prince"* or ruler/head of the covenant. The nature of this covenant is also not given in the text but may be an internal agreement within the Antichrist's own country's political structure or the previous covenant with the Jews in Daniel 9:27.

Then the word appears four times in context being described by the word *"holy"* in three of these instances:
*"Then shall he [Antichrist] return into his land with great riches; and his heart shall be against the **holy covenant**; and he shall do exploits and return to his own land. At the time appointed he shall return, and come toward the south; but it shall not be as the former, or as the latter. For the ships of Chittim shall come against him: therefore he shall be grieved, and return, and have indignation against the **holy covenant**: so shall he do; he shall even return, and have intelligence with them [apostate Jews] that forsake the **holy covenant**. And arms [forces] shall stand on his part, and they shall pollute the sanctuary of strength, and shall take away the daily sacrifice, and they shall*

place the abomination that makes desolate. And such as do wickedly [apostate Jews] against the [holy] __covenant__ shall he corrupt by flatteries: but the people that do know their God shall be strong and do exploits." (Daniel 11:28-32)

In this passage the covenant spoken of is not the one which appears earlier in Daniel 9:27 or 11:22. This passage is referring to the covenant which will be restored by the Elijah-like prophet whom God will send *"before the great and dreadful day of the Lord"* to *"turn hearts"* and *"restore all things"* (Malachi 4:5, 6; Matthew 17:11; Mark 9:12).

The two earlier covenants in the book of Daniel are both political agreements. But, the one here in Daniel 11:28-32 is clearly indicated to be *"holy"*, which means it is set apart unto God. The word *"holy"* appears (10) times in the "Jewish" section of the book of Daniel (Chapter 8-12) describing various things that are set apart unto God:

1. *The holy people [Israel] (8:24)*
2. *Thy holy mountain [Jerusalem/Mount Zion] (9:16)*
3. *The holy mountain of my God (9:20)*
4. *Thy holy city [Jerusalem] (9:24)*
5. *The most holy [place] (9:24)*
6. *The holy covenant (11:28)*
7. *The holy covenant (11:30a)*
8. *The holy covenant (11:30b)*
9. *The glorious holy mountain (11:45)*
10. *The holy people (12:7)*

Although, *"holy"* appears 468 times in the Old Testament and 229 times in the New, it is used in the Old Testament only in Daniel 11:28-32 to describe a 'covenant'. There is also just one occurrence in the New Testament where the word covenant is described by the word holy:

"To perform the mercy promised unto our fathers, and to remember His __holy covenant__; The oath which He swore to our father Abraham." (Luke 1:72, 73)

These two *"holy covenant[s]"* are __not__ identical. The one in Daniel 11:28-32 is the restored Old Covenant referred to in Exodus 19:5, 6 and the *"holy covenant"* in Luke 1:72, 73 indicates the covenant that

God made with Abraham in Genesis 12:1-3. However, both of them are described as *"holy"*, being set apart unto God.

The *"holy covenant"* which appears in Daniel 11:28-32 will of a certainty be fully restored in practice prior to the time God has determined upon His holy people and His holy city (Daniel 9:24). For the conditions necessary for the 70th Week of Daniel are the same conditions which prevailed during the first 69 Weeks of Daniel when the Old covenant was in full operation.

These additional 70th Week necessities are also indicated in other Bible texts:
1. The holy people will be a nation. (Deuteronomy 30:5; Ezekiel 36:23-28; Daniel 9:24)
2. They will re-gather in the Holy Land. (Ezekiel 36:23-28; Daniel 9:24; Matthew 24:16)
3. They will occupy their holy city Jerusalem. (Daniel 9:24)
4. The prophet Elijah will be sent to revive hearts and restore all things. (Malachi 4:5, 6; Matthew 17:11)
5. The temple of God will be rebuilt. (II Thessalonians 2:3, 4; Revelation 11:1, 2)
6. The holy place included (Matthew 24:15; Revelation 11:2)
7. The regular [morning and evening] sacrifices will be offered. (Daniel 8:11-14, 9:27, 11:31, 12:11)
8. The Jews will worship in the temple of God. (Revelation 11:1, 2)
9. The Sabbath will be restored. (Matthew 24:20)
10. The twelve tribes will be recognized. (Revelation 7:3-8)

At this present time [2007] the Jews are a people, in the land, occupying their holy city Jerusalem with certain Jews in Israel already practicing limited portions of the Old Covenant.

What appears to be next on God's agenda is the sending of this mighty Elijah-like Hebrew prophet who will *"turn hearts"* and *"restore all things"*. He will prepare the way for the 70th Week of Daniel, which will definitely unfold under the restored *"holy covenant"* when God once again deals with His earthly people, Israel.

6

The Church in Philadelphia
(Revelation 3:10)

"Because thou hast kept the word of My patience, I also will keep thee from the hour of temptation, which shall come upon all the world, to try them that dwell upon the earth." (Revelation 3:10)

This verse, which is found in the midst of the Lord's message to the church in Philadelphia, is one of the most studied prophetic verses in recent times. It is used by some to prove, and by others to disprove, the timing of the rapture which has become a somewhat controversial and often times emotional topic in Christian circles.

Those who hold to the pre-tribulation rapture say that this verse proves their position of the church being promised exemption from *"the hour of temptation"* by the rapture. Those who hold to a post-tribulation rapture say that the church will be protected by being kept out from within the midst of *"the hour of temptation"*.

In order to resolve this highly charged issue, which in fact is separating believers and causing much discord among the brethren, let us define the terms the Lord used by asking a few simple questions:
1. What is the Lord promising?
2. What is *"the hour of temptation"*?
3. Who is being kept from "the hour of temptation"?
4. Who will go through *"the hour of temptation"*?
5. Where will *"the hour of temptation"* take place?

The Lord says He will *"keep thee from the hour of temptation"* which is the same as the Greek grammatical construction in the request He made of the Father in His great high priestly prayer:
"I pray not that Thou shouldest take them out of the world, but that Thou shouldest keep them from the evil [one] `'" (John 17:15)

The Lord Jesus Christ is asking the Father to *"keep"* believers *"from the evil [one]"* while they continue to be in the world in order that the world might believe that God the Father is the One Who sent the Lord Jesus Christ (John 17:21, 23, 25).

The only time the words *"keep...from"* appear together in the New Testament is in these two verses. Being kept from **while in the midst of** the world which is ruled by *"the evil one" (John 17:15)* or being kept from **while in the midst of** the worldwide *"hour of temptation"* is the literal sense of both of these phrases.

Exactly what *"the hour of temptation"* is must then be defined. The word *"hour"* is used ten times in the Revelation and refers to a certain but often short period of time when accompanied with the article *"the"*:
*"the hour of temptation" (*Revelation 3:10)
*"the hour of His judgment is come" (*Revelation 14:7*)
*"the time [hour] is come for Thee to reap" (*Revelation 14:15)

Even though the New Testament word *"temptation"* is usually associated with being tempted to do evil it can also refer to a time of testing or proving in order to determine or improve the quality of those who are being tested.

The Septuagint, which is the Greek translation of the Old Testament completed before the time of Christ, uses this same word to define "an experiment, attempt, trial, proving". New Testament examples include: "The trial made of you by my bodily condition, since this condition served to test the love of the Galatians towards Paul, Gal 4:14...the trial of man's fidelity, integrity, virtue, constancy etc.: I Pet 4:12". (Thayers Greek-English Lexicon of the New Testament p.498)

John, the human author of the Revelation of Jesus Christ, uses the verb form of *"temptation"* five times (John 6:6, 8:6; Revelation 2:2, 2:10, 3:10) and the noun only once (Revelation 3:10) in his writings. In all but one occurrence (John 8:6) he uses the word to describe a test being given to produce a result which will prove or improve the quality of those being tested.

The Lord Jesus Christ when addressing Philip His disciple set before him a simple test using this same word:

59

"And this He said to __prove__ him: for He Himself knew what He would do." (John 6:6)

The Lord also gave the patriarch Abraham a major test that is later recorded in the New Testament:
"By faith Abraham, when he was __tried__, offered up Isaac: and he that received the promises offered up his only begotten son."
(Hebrews 11:17)

James in the classic *"temptation/testing"* passage (James 1:1-15) records this verse:
"Blessed is the man that endureth __temptation__: for when he is __tried__, he shall receive the crown of life, which the Lord hath promised to them that love Him" (James 1:12)

These examples illustrate how this word is used to try or test a person in order to produce a response or outcome from the test being given. The tests were not given in order for the Lord to find out how these two men would respond for He already knows the beginning from the end in every circumstance.

The purpose of the tests was to teach and prove/improve these men in order that they might grow in grace and the knowledge of the Lord with the ultimate purpose being that He might be glorified through it all.

Both the noun *"temptation"* and the verb *"try"* are utilized in Revelation 3:10 and in both instances they are being used to prove the quality of those being tried or tested which brings the focus upon exactly who is being tried in this *"the hour of temptation"*.

Those who are being tried/tested are called *"them that dwell upon the earth"*. This phrase appears numerous times in the Revelation indicating those who are in direct opposition to God and His people:
(1) They are responsible for the martyrdom of God's people:
"And they [martyrs] cried with a loud voice, saying, How long, O Lord, holy and true, dost Thou not judge and avenge our blood on them that dwell on the earth?" (6:10)
(2) They are the focus of the *"three woes"* of judgment sent by God:
"And I beheld, and heard an angel flying though the midst of heaven,

saying with a loud voice, Woe, woe, woe, to the inhabiters of the earth by reason of the other voices of the trumpet of the three angels which are yet to sound!" (8:13)

(3) They rejoice upon the death of God's two prophets:
"And they that dwell upon the earth shall rejoice over them [two prophets], and they stood upon their feet; and great fear fell upon them who say them." (11:10)

(4) They *"worship the beast"* [Antichrist]:
"And all that dwell upon the earth shall worship him [Antichrist], whose names are not written in the book of life of the Lamb slain from the foundation of the world." (13:8)

"And he [false prophet] exerciseth all the power of the first beast [Antichrist] before him, and causeth the earth and them which dwell therein to worship the first beast, whose deadly wound was healed." (13:12)

(5) They *"make an image"* of *"the beast"*
"And deceiveth them that dwell on the earth by the means of those miracles which he had power to do in the sight of the beast, saying to them that dwell on the earth, that they should make an image to the beast which had the wound by a sword, and did live." (13:14)

(6) *"They that dwell on the earth shall wonder [marvel], whose names were not written in the book of life from the foundation of the world, when they behold the beast that was, and is not, and yet is." (17:8).*

These are the people who are the subjects of *"the hour of temptation, which shall come upon all the world, to try **them that dwell upon the earth**."* This *"hour of temptation"* is a global event as it comes upon *"the whole world"*.

And even though there are various theories as to exactly when this time of testing will occur, it can be identified by the fact that it is designed to test *"them that dwell upon the earth"* and not believers.

The *"Day of the Lord"* which comes upon unbelievers or *"them that dwell upon the earth"* is clearly indicated by Paul:
*"But of the times and the seasons, brethren, ye have no need that I write unto you. For yourselves know perfectly that the day of the Lord so cometh as a thief in the night. For when **they** shall say, Peace and safety: then sudden destruction cometh upon **them**, as travail upon a*

*woman with child; and **they** shall not escape. But, ye **brethren**, **are not** in darkness, that that day should overtake you as a thief. Ye are all the children of light, and the children of the day: we are not of the night, nor of darkness. For God hath not appointed us to [the Day of the Lord's] wrath but to obtain salvation by our Lord Jesus Christ." (I Thessalonians 5:1-5, 10)*

Paul continues to instruct the Thessalonian believers in his second letter concerning the timing of the Day of the Lord:

*"Now we beseech you, brethren, by the coming of the Lord Jesus Christ, and by our gathering together unto Him, That ye be not soon shaken in mind, or be troubled, neither by spirit, nor by word, not by letter as from us, as that the day of Christ [the Lord] is at hand. Let no man deceive you by any means: for that day shall not come, except there come a **falling away** first, and that **man of sin be revealed**, the son of perdition; Who opposes and exalts himself above all that is called God, or that is worshipped; so that he as God sits in the temple of God, showing himself that he is God." (II Thessalonians 2:1-4)*

In this passage he indicates two events that will take place **before** the Day of the Lord begins:

1. *"The falling away" [Jewish apostasy] (Daniel 11:30)*
2. *"That man of sin [Antichrist] be revealed"*
   (Daniel 11:31; Matthew 24:15)

The *"Day of the Lord"*, which is the most prophesied event in Scripture, must not be confused with the time of *"great tribulation"* spoken of by the Lord Jesus Christ:

"For then shall be great tribulation such as was not since the beginning of the world to this time, no nor ever shall be. And except those days [of great tribulation] be shortened, there should no flesh be saved: but for the elect's sake those days shall be shortened." (Matthew 24:21, 22)

The time called the Great Tribulation is clearly focused upon *"the elect"* who are God's people, those believers who are on earth when the Antichrist brings to pass the greatest persecution ever experienced by the Church of the Lord Jesus Christ.

This is also indicated in the book of Daniel:

"I beheld and the same horn [Antichrist] made war with the saints, and prevailed against them. And he [Antichrist] shall speak great words against the Most High, and shall wear out the saints of the most High, and think to change times and laws: and they [the saints] shall be given into his hand until a time and times and the dividing of time [3-1/2 years]." (Daniel 7:21, 25)

The Revelation also records this same time of the Antichrist's Great Tribulation against the saints:
"And there was given unto him [Antichrist] a mouth speaking great things and blasphemies and power was given unto him to continue forty and two months [3-1/2 years]. And he opened his mouth in blasphemy against God, to blaspheme His name, and His tabernacle, and them that dwell in heaven. And it was given unto him to make war with the saints, and to overcome them: and power was given him over all kindreds, and tongues and nations." (Revelation 13:5-7)

The glorified saints in heaven are seen before the throne of God having just been rescued by rapture out of the *"great tribulation"*:
"And one of the elders answered, saying unto me, What are these which are arrayed in white robes? And whence came they? And I said unto him, Sir, thou knowest. And he said to me, These are they which came out of [the] great tribulation, and have washed their robes, and made them white in the blood of the Lamb." (Revelation7: 13, 14)

This fierce persecution called *"[the] great tribulation"* is summarized by the Lord in Matthew 24:9-14 then detailed in chronological order (Matthew 24:15-28) in His focused step-by-step response to His disciples questions.

The *"great tribulation"* is not *"the end"* *(Matthew 24:14)* but merely the final act before the beginning of the end for when the Lord shortens/cuts off the Great Tribulation *"the end"*, which is the Day of the Lord, will come as the following verses indicate:
"Immediately after the [great] tribulation shall the sun be darkened and the moon shall not give her light and the stars shall fall from heaven and the powers of the heavens shall be shaken. And then shall appear the sign of the Son of man in heaven: and then shall all the earth mourn, and they shall see the Son of man coming in the clouds of heaven with power and great glory. And he shall send His angels

with a great sound of a trumpet, and they shall gather together His elect from one end of heaven to the other." (Matthew 24:29-31)

The Lord will display this miraculous series of heavenly wonders as a sign and prelude *"before the great and the terrible day of the Lord come" (Joel 2:30, 31).* The earth will be completely darkened just before He sends His Son who arrives *"with power and great [Shekinah] glory"* illuminating the earth so that *"every eye shall see Him" (Revelation 1:7)* when He comes to *"gather His elect"* through the agency of His angels (Matthew 24:30, 31).

Then, immediately after the *"great tribulation"* which focuses on the elect, the sign of the Day of the Lord and the *"same day" (Luke 17:29)* Coming of Christ occur followed by the Day of the Lord judgment which comes upon unbelievers. Paul makes it clear that believers will be delivered from God's wrath, which is the Day of the Lord:
"For God hath not appointed us to wrath but to obtain salvation by our Lord Jesus Christ." (I Thessalonians 5:9)

After the Lord delivers His own by rapture it will be time for God's Day, the long awaited Day of the Lord which will serve to *"try"* the unbelieving earth dwellers through *"the hour of temptation".* Sadly, most of them will refuse His marvelous redemptive grace found in the shed Blood of the Lord Jesus Christ.

The accounts of their rebellious and unrepentant hearts are given in Revelation 9:20, 21 and Revelation 16:9-11 in response to the two major series of events that will occur during the Day of the Lord, the seven trumpet judgments (Revelation 8:1-11:15) and the seven vial judgments (Revelation 15:1-16:21).

The Scripture is clear. There will be many who are *"purified and made white and tried" (Daniel 12:10,)* being *"refined", (Zechariah 13:9)* who turn and call upon the Lord in that day with Jew (Isaiah 59:20; Romans 11:25-27) and Gentile (Isaiah 19:16-25; Micah 7:15-17) alike demonstrating the ageless principle which proceeds from the loving God of eternal mercy: *"For His mercy endureth forever." (Psalm 136:1-26)*

This is one of the purposes for *"the hour of temptation"* from which believers will be exempt. Who are these believers in the church of Philadelphia that receive the promise of being kept from [in the midst of] *"the hour of temptation"*?

Who will be God's servants in that future day of worldwide judgment? Who are those that are not hurt by the Day of the Lord judgment described in Revelation 9:1-12?
"And it was commanded them that they should not hurt the grass of the earth, neither any green thing, neither any tree; but only those men which have not the seal of God in their foreheads."
(Revelation 9:4)

The servants of God who are kept from the sixth seal judgment which occurs during the Day of the Lord called *"the hour of temptation"* by having the seal of God in their foreheads are the 144 Thousand from all the tribes of the sons of Israel.
(Revelation 7:3-8, 14:1).

There are also two other New Testament groups of saints who will have God's name/signature upon them, however, they appear to be glorified saints:
1. The *"overcomers"* of the church in Philadelphia (Revelation 3:12)
2. The *"servants"* of the Lamb in heaven (Revelation 22:4)

There is only one group in the Word of God that have the seal of God physically placed upon them and that is the 144 Thousand. But, this does not necessarily exclude other believers from having God's seal. It may very well be that all who are saved during this future dispensation [The 70th Week of Daniel/Day of the Lord], a.k.a. the last Jewish dispensation, may also have this physical seal of God.

There is another group of faithful Jews who are protected by God during the last half of Daniel's 70th Week:
"And the woman [faithful Israel] fled into the wilderness, where she hath a place prepared of God, that they should feed her there a thousand two hundred and three score days [3-1/2 years]."
"And to the woman were given two wings of a great eagle, that she might fly into the wilderness, into her place, where she is nourished for a time, and times, and half a time [3-1/2 years], from the face of

the serpent." (Revelation 12:6, 14)

Could it be that *"the church in Philadelphia"* represents the time of the end assemblies which will be largely Jewish congregations out of which the 144 Thousand *"servants of our God" (Revelation 7:3),"the woman"* of Revelation 12 and *"the two witnesses" (Revelation 11:3-13)* will serve?

The *"church in Philadelphia"* does have numerous Old Testament/Jewish aspects adding to the possibility that this letter may apply to the end times Jewish church:
1. The Lord Jesus' title of "*holy [one]*" (3:7) hearkens back to one of His Old Testament Titles: "*Holy One*" (Psalm 16:10).
2. The Lord Jesus has "*the key of David*" (3:7; Isaiah 22:22).
3. Those who "*say they are Jews*" (3:9) are present.
4. "*The synagogue of Satan*" (3:9) is also present.
5. The "*temple of God*" (3:12)
6. The "*city of My God, the New Jerusalem*" (3:12)

The faithful suffering sister church of the church in Philadelphia, which is *"the church in Smyrna" (Revelation 2:8-11),* contains some significant parallels to the church of Philadelphia:
1. The command to repent is not given to either of these faithful churches.
2. The people who *"say they are Jews" (2:9, 3:9)* are present in both churches.
3. *"The synagogue of Satan" (2:9, 3:9)* is mentioned in both churches.
4. The Lord commends/gives encouragement to both churches:
   a. "*I know thy works, and tribulation, and [physical] poverty*" *(2:9)*
      "*I know thy works: behold I have set before thee an open door*" *(3:8)*
   b. "*thou art rich [spiritually]*" *(2:9)*
      "*thou hast a little strength*" *(3:8)*
   c. "*Fear none of those things which thou shalt suffer*" *(2:10)*
      "*[thou] hast kept My word*" *(3:8)*
   d. "*be thou faithful unto death and I will give thee a crown of life.*" *(2:10)*
      "*[thou] hast not denied My name*" *(3:8)*

5. The Lord does not correct/rebuke either church

The two definite links that tie these churches together is the appearance of those people *"who say they are Jews"* and *"the synagogue of Satan"*. These two were evident in both first century churches. They existed in the churches throughout the Church age including the present-day Church, and they will continue to be active during the future time of the end Jewish dispensation.

The interpretation of the majority of orthodox Bible students has been that these seven letters apply to all time periods of the Church's existence. When examining *"the church in Philadelphia"*, it must be recognized that it is the only church that has a definite time of the end event mentioned for *"the hour of temptation"* *(3:10)* and the future world judgment of God, called the Day of the Lord, are synonymous terms indicating the same period of time which gives this church a unique and most significant setting.

The faithful church in Smyrna, which contains two parallels to the faithful church in Philadelphia, may also shed light upon the time of the end. The church in Smyrna experiences *"tribulation...tribulation ten days"* *(Revelation 2:9, 10)* at the hand of *"the devil"* *(Revelation 2:10.)* This points to the possibility that the tribulation recorded in the end of the age church in Smyrna is *"[the] great tribulation"(Matthew 24:15-29; Revelation 7:21)* which is also described as the devil's *"great wrath"* *(Revelation 12:12)* ultimately resulting in the martyrdom of many of God's people including many Jewish believers. (Daniel 11:33, 35; Revelation 6:10, 11, 12:10, 11, 20:4).

Who are these people *"who say they are Jews, and are not, but do lie"* and what is *"the synagogue of Satan"*? It is an historical fact that the 1st century church was plagued with intense persecution from the Jews.

The church in Smyrna was the most persecuted church of the seven churches. The Jews without sanction of the Roman authorities martyred Polycarp, the bishop of Smyrna.

It is said that these zealous Christian-hating Jews violated their own Sabbath in order to gather the wood for the fire that burned

Polycarp. His grave remains in Smyrna to this day.

As we near the return of the Lord, there are a number of possibilities concerning those *"who say they are Jews, and are not, but do lie."* At this present time there are a few different groups claiming to be Jews. The immigrants from Ethiopia who say they are Jews and those from India claiming to be from the tribe of Manasseh are two groups that have come to Israel in recent times.

While there is an advantage to being a Jew, there also will be a great disadvantage. They will be the focus of Satan's *"great wrath" (Revelation 12:12)* during the last half of the 70th Week of Daniel, while the Satanically energized Antichrist and his false prophet will zero in on the Church world wide (Revelation 13).

Only those who know the prophetic Scripture understand these truths, for at the moment it evidently appears to be an advantage to be a Jew. These people who are not Jews will *"come and worship before thy feet" (Revelation 3:9)* as has been written by the prophet Isaiah:
*"Egypt...Ethiopia and of the Sabeans, men of stature shall "come over, and **they shall fall down unto thee**, they shall make supplication unto thee, saying, Surely God is in thee; and there is none else, there is no God." (Isaiah 45:14)*
*"Arise, shine; for thy light is come, and the glory of the LORD is risen upon thee. For, behold, the darkness shall cover the earth, and gross darkness the people; but the LORD shall arise upon thee, and His glory shall be seen upon thee. And the Gentiles shall come to thy light, and kings to the brightness of thy rising...the sons also of them that afflicted thee shall come bending unto thee; and **all they that despised thee shall bow themselves down at the soles of thy feet**; and they shall call thee, The city of the LORD, the Zion of the Holy One of Israel." (Isaiah 60:1-3, 14)*
*"For I am the LORD thy God, the Holy One of Israel, thy Saviour: I gave Egypt for thy ransom, Ethiopia and Seba for thee. Since thou was precious in My sight, thou has been honorable, and **I have loved thee**: therefore will I give men for thee, and people for thy life. Fear not: for I am with thee: I will bring thy seed from the east, and gather thee from the west; I will say to the north, Give up; and to the south, Keep not back: bring My sons from far, and My daughters from the ends of the earth; Even every one that is called by My name: for I*

have created him for My glory, I have formed him; yea, I have made him." (Isaiah 43:3-7)

These time of the end passages in Isaiah also foretell those very events that the Lord Jesus Christ spoke of in His promises to the church in Philadelphia:
*"Behold, I will make them of the synagogue of Satan, which say they are Jews, and are not, but do lie, **behold I will make them to come and worship before thy feet, and to know that I have loved thee.**" (Revelation 3:9)*

As the Lord's return draws ever closer there will continue to be those who claim to be from the twelve tribes of Israel. However, only the Lord knows those who truly are His earthly people from which He will definitely call *"the servants of our God" (Revelation 7:3).*

7

The Chronological Structure of the Revelation

While lightning is spectacular and draws us to wonder at the great power of God in the heavenlies, it is the ground-shaking, ear-rattling effect of thunder that is the real attention-getter as the power of a fierce and furious thunderstorm passes by, when the majestic might of God Himself seems to fill the landscape.

So it was, as indicated in the book of Job 36:26-37:5 the first [in time] book written in the Bible and it will be again when God unveils His time of the end program for the earth and its inhabitants in the last book written, the book of the Revelation of Jesus Christ.

The Revelation of Jesus Christ chapter four opens a door into heaven for the Apostle John to experience the thundering throne room of God as all of heaven's glory is brought before him:
"And immediately I was in the Spirit; and, behold, a throne was set in heaven, and one sat on the throne. And He that sat was to look upon like a jasper and a sardine stone: and there was a rainbow round about the throne, in sight like unto and emerald. And round about the throne were four and twenty seats; and upon the seats I saw four and twenty elders sitting, clothed in white raiment; and they had on their heads crowns of gold. ***And out of the throne proceeded lightnings and thunderings and voices****." (Revelation 4:2-5a)*

The Scripture continues for the remainder of the chapter describing the rest of the heavenly throne room scene including those who are present worshipping God in this grand and glorious opening chapter of *"the things which must be hereafter" (Revelation 1:19).*

The underlined phrase above is found three other times in the course of the book of the Revelation of Jesus Christ. This heavenly sequence serves to indicate the progressive and chronological nature of this final book of Scripture.

These occurrences will also show the increasing activity of God and His Day of the Lord wrath/judgment upon the entire world in order that He might purify His people, the Jews, and punish the rest of those who have openly rebelled against Him and continually refuse to repent.

In chapters five, six and seven much takes place in the unfolding drama of end time events. Chapter five is coupled to chapter four continuing the throne room scene. This chapter emphasizes the heavenly coronation of the Lord Jesus Christ and His worthiness as the Lamb of God to take the book which contains God's Day of the Lord wrath/judgment, and to open the seals which are on the outside of the book [scroll].

The seven seals are opened sequentially conditioning the earth for God's wrath. The first four center upon the Antichrist's actions during Daniel's 70th Week with the last three seals focusing upon the Day of the Lord's wrath:
1. The martyrs in the fifth seal are inquiring of God, wanting to know when His wrath/judgment is going to come.
2. The sign given in the sixth seal indicates His wrath/judgment is impending or just about to occur.
3. The seventh seal initiates His wrath/judgment after silence overwhelms heaven for thirty minutes. Then, the Day of the Lord begins with the first trumpet judgment.

But, right before the Day of the Lord begins, "The Passing of the Torch" (Revelation 7:1-8) takes place when the 144 Thousand Jews are sealed and the saints are raptured (Revelation 7:9-17) between the opening of the sixth and seventh seal.

The key point in all of that which has transpired in Revelation 4-7 to this point in time is what is ALLOWED by God vs. what is AUTHORED by God. The great tribulation has just ended indicated by the heavenly wonders (Matthew 24:29; Revelation 6:12, 13). They occur just **before** the Day of the Lord (Joel 2:30, 31) which is now about to begin.

The wrath of God has just been given a hefty introduction through the fifth and sixth seal with this summary statement, *"For the great day of His wrath is come" (Revelation 6:17).* It shows that we are on the threshold of the most prophesied event in Scripture, the eschatological Day of the Lord.

After the "Passing of the Torch" from the Church saints to the 144 Thousand Sons of Israel, the time has come for God to bring about His work of judgment.

The throne of God is the source of the lightnings and thunderings and voices. And, at this point in time, nothing has been authored by God to effectively bring His wrath/judgment upon the earth.

With the next occurrence of these heavenly events (Revelation 8:5) there is a significant change. The preceding verses in chapter eight show that we are still in the throne room of God and at this point He is about to intervene with His Day of the Lord wrath/judgment upon the earth through the agency of His angel:
*"And the angel took the censer, and filled it with fire of the altar, and cast it into the earth; **And there were voices and thunderings, and lightnings, AND AN EARTHQUAKE.**"*

At this point in God's program of end time events His wrath/judgment has begun. Not only do these events originate in heaven but now the earth experiences the beginning of God's direct judgment through the addition of this earthquake. This throne room sequence marks the beginning of the seven trumpet judgments, which is the initiation of God's wrath/judgment on earth.

The next time this sequence appears is in Revelation 11:19 at the end of the seven trumpet judgments. But, there is an additional effect upon the earth as the progressive nature of God's increasing judgment is seen:
*"And the temple of God was opened in heaven, and there was seen in His temple the ark of His testament: **And there were lightnings, and voices, and thunderings, and an earthquake, AND GREAT HAIL.**"*

At this time multiple major events have taken place as described in verses fifteen though eighteen. While this is a point in God's program with many ramifications, the emphasis here is to show the repetition of this sequence from the throne of God and how it underlines the progressive nature of God's wrath/judgment. It also indicates the beginning and the ending of His wrath/judgment upon mankind by punctuating the beginning and the ending of the trumpet judgments.

In the next sequence, the beginning and ending of the vial judgments are also highlighted, for out of the seventh trumpet judgment proceeds the first vial judgment. The above sequence not only marks the end of one series of judgments but it also punctuates the beginning of the next.

In Revelation 16 the Bible says:
*"And the seventh angel poured out his vial into the air; and there came a great voice out of the temple of heaven, from the throne, saying, It is done. **And there were voices, and thunderings, and lightnings; and there was A GREAT EARTHQUAKE, SUCH AS WAS NOT SINCE MEN WERE UPON THE EARTH, SO MIGHTY AND EARTHQUAKE, AND SO GREAT...AND THERE FELL UPON MEN A GREAT HAIL OUT OF HEAVEN, EVERY STONE ABOUT THE WEIGHT OF A TALENT.**"*
(Revelation 16:17, 18, 21)

The **global** wrath/judgment of God upon mankind is done. The grand finale, as it were, is this progressive and punctuating sequence of events authored by God, executed by His angels, and experienced by all mankind, with all of it proceeding from the thundering throne room of God.

In addition to this progressive chronological sequence of events sent from the throne room in heaven, there are also textual indicators that divide the book of the Revelation according to the unfolding of time indicating the beginning and ending of other major series of events.

The brief but definitive time indicating phrase *"**After these things**"* is found in the prophetic section of the book of the Revelation, (Revelation 4:1-22:21) six times. The first and second occurrences are in the very first verse:
*"**After these things** I looked, and, behold, a door standing open in heaven; and the first voice which I had heard, like the sound of a trumpet speaking with me; said, Come up here, and I will show you*

73

*what must take place **after these things**." (Revelation 4:1) NASV*

John is given the first sequence of the prophetic vision in Revelation 4:1-7:8 where a similar phrase *"**After this**"* appears (Revelation 7:1) which is used to divide the events in heaven (Revelation 4:1-6:17) from the events occurring on earth (Revelation 7:1-8) within the first section.

"The things which shall be hereafter" (Revelation 1:19c), indicates this large prophetic section (Revelation 4:1-22:21). It is divided into five major divisions by this key time indicating phrase: *"**After these things**"* developing the following outline:

"After these things" (Revelation 4:1)
I. The Earth's Preparation for The Day of the Lord's Wrath (Revelation 4:1-7:8)
   A. The Throne Room Scene (Chapter 4, 5)
   B. The Six Seals Opened (Chapter 6)
      [Beginning 70th Week of Daniel]
"After this" (7:1)
   C. The Preservation of True Religion/The 144 Thousand Sealed (7:1-8)

"After these things" (Revelation 7:9)
II. The Events of the Day of the Lord's Wrath to the end of the 70th Week of Daniel (Revelation 7:9-15:4)
   A. The Saints of the Ages in Heaven (Chapter 7:9-17)
   B. The Seventh Seal Opened/The Beginning of the Day of the Lord (8:1-5)
   C. The Six Trumpet Judgments/The Little Book/The Two Witnesses (8:6-11:14)
   D. The Seventh Trumpet Judgment/The World Kingdoms become the Lord's/End 70th Week (11:15-19)
   E. The Interlude/Events of the Last 3-1/2 Years of the 70th Week of Daniel (Revelation 11, 12, 13, 14)
      1. The Witnesses Testimony (11:3-14)
      2. The Woman [Faithful Israel] Protected (12:1-6)
      3. The War in Heaven (12:7-12)
      4. The War on Earth[Great Tribulation (12:13-12:17)
      5. The Wild Beast [Antichrist] (13:1-10)

6. The Worship Leader [False Prophet] of The Wild Beast (13:11-18)
7. The Worship Leaders of God [End of 70th Week](14:1-5)
   a. The 144 Thousand Sons of Israel
   b. The Harpers in Heaven
   c. The Four Beasts
   d. The Twenty-four Elders
8. The Three Angels of Mercy (14:6-13)
9. The Son of Man [The Lord Jesus Christ] (14:14)
10. The Three Angels of Judgment (14:15-20)
F. The Heavenly Prelude before The End of the Day of the Lord (15:1-4)

"After these things" (Revelation 15:5)
III. The Events of the Day of the Lord's Wrath *after* The 70th Week of Daniel (Revelation 15:5-17:18)
   A. The Preparation for the Seven Vial Judgments (Revelation 15:5-8)
   B. The Seven Vial Judgments (Revelation 16:1-21)
   C. The Preparation for Judgment of Babylon the Great Whore (Revelation 17:1-18)

"After these things" (Revelation 18:1)
IV. The Punishment of False Religion (Revelation 18:1-24)
   A. The Destruction of Babylon the Great Whore Announced (Revelation 18:1-8)
   B. The Kings of the Earth Lament Her Destruction (Revelation 18:9, 10)
   C. The Merchants of the Earth Lament Her Destruction (Revelation 18:11-17a)
   D. The Merchants of the Sea Lament Her Destruction (Revelation 18:17b-19)
   E. The Destruction of Babylon the Great Whore Realized (Revelation 18:20-24)

"After these things" (Revelation 19:1)
V. The Concluding Events of the Day of the Lord
   A. The Rejoicing in Heaven for the Destruction of Babylon (Revelation 19:1-6)

B. The Marriage Supper of the Lamb (Revelation 19:7-10)
C. The Great Retribution at Armageddon (Revelation 19:11-21)
D. The Binding of Satan (Revelation 20:1-3)
E. The First Resurrection and Millennium (Revelation 20:4
F. The Final Rebellion (Revelation 20:7-10)
G. The Great White Throne Judgment (Revelation 20:11-15)
H. The New Heaven, Earth & Jerusalem Described
   (Revelation 21:1, 21:9-27-22:1-5)
J. The Heavenly Conclusion (Revelation 22:6-21)

Two major occurrences are singled out by time indicating phrases. The first appears at 7:1-8 which is called: 'The Preservation of True Religion' with the second, 'The Punishment of False Religion' recorded in chapter 18.

These notable end times events are the only two actions of the Lord in the book of the Revelation that are clearly set off by these time indicating phrases. This underlining by the Word of God points to His time of the end priority to preserve His testimony by sealing the 144 Thousand Sons of Israel (Revelation 7:1-8) and His most certain and severe punishment of false religion (Revelation 18:1-24).

The Lord seals His servants just before the beginning of His Day of the Lord judgment and then after His global judgment is complete the punishment of false religion occurs through the destruction of the Great Whore Babylon.

Just before the sealing of the 144 Thousand, the text utilizes the singular *"After this" (7:1)* instead of *"After these things"* which is the plural form of this time indicating phrase. Here the Lord is underlining the sealing of the 144 Thousand, which occurs right after the sign of the Day of the Lord (6:12, 13).

This is the only place this time indicating phrase is found in the singular form within the book of the Revelation emphasizing a number of truths:
1. The significance of the sealing of the 144 Thousand (7:1-8)
2. Their sealing immediately follows (7:1-8) the sign Day of the Lord
3. Their sealing is the final step in God's preparation of Earth for the Day of the Lord (4:1-7:8)

This key group of *"servants of our God" (Revelation 7:3)* are protected by God from His judgment (Revelation 9:4) in order that they might continue to serve Him during the Day of the Lord when they will testify to those who will be redeemed when:

"The Redeemer [Lord Jesus Christ] shall come to Zion...And so all Israel shall be saved." (Isaiah 59:20; Romans 11:25, 26)

These two textual indicators, the progressive sequence of *"voices and thunderings and lightnings"* from the throne of God, and the time indicating phrase *"after these things"* clearly illustrate the progressive and chronological unfolding of the Revelation of Jesus Christ.

8

<u>The Lamb of God</u>

The Lord Jesus Christ is the main Person of the Apocalypse with His preferred title the *"Lamb"* appearing (28) times in the book of the Revelation. Although He is seen by John in Revelation 1-3 as the glorified Lord of glory, the first appearance of the Lord as the **"<u>Lamb</u>"** occurs at Revelation 5:6-8 where He is introduced in the throne room of God at His heavenly coronation:

*"And I beheld, and, lo, in the midst of the throne and of the four beasts, and in the midst of the elders, stood a <u>**Lamb**</u> as it had been slain, having seven eyes, which are the seven Spirits of God sent forth into all the earth. And He came and took the book out of the right hand of Him that sat upon the throne. And when He had taken the book, the four beasts and four and twenty elders fell down before the Lamb having every one of them harps and golden vials full of odors, which are the prayers of the saints."*

The magnificent praise and worship scene that follows in 5:9-14 reveals that this is the main event of the Apocalypse as the Lord Jesus Christ, the Lord of Glory, is the only One worthy to take the scroll from the Father which begins end-time events on planet earth.

The Lord Jesus, who alone is the Righteous Judge (John 5:27-29), is now prepared to loose the seals on the outside of the scroll in order to begin the events of the 70th Week of Daniel. It is only as the Lord Jesus starts the unfolding of events at the end of the age that *"The things which shall be hereafter" (Revelation 1:19)* will occur in His perfect timing and sovereign control.

Now it is His day that is about to happen, for the LORD Jehovah is making the enemies of the Lord Jesus Christ *"His footstool"* *(Psalm 110:1)* and the time has now come for God the Father to bring this promise He made to the Lord Jesus Christ to complete fruition.

At the end of this glorious praise scene in Revelation 5:9-14, which occurs in heaven, the time-clock of the end times begins to tick as *"the Lamb"* opens the seals on the outside of the scroll He has just taken from God the Father's hand:

*"And I saw when **the Lamb** opened one of the seals, and I heard, as it were the noise of thunder, one of the four beasts saying, Come and see. And I saw, and behold a white horse: and he that sat on him had a bow; and a crown was given unto him; and he went forth conquering and to conquer." (Revelation 6:1, 2)*

The Lamb who is in complete control of the events of the 70th Week of Daniel, allows the Antichrist to begin conquering when he will *"subdue three kings" (Daniel 7:24, 7:20, 7:8)* of *"the ten kings that shall arise" (Daniel 7:24; Revelation 17:12)* in that day.

The next time *"the Lamb"* is mentioned occurs in Revelation 6:16, 17:

*"And said to the mountains and rocks, Fall on us, and hide us from the face of Him that sits on the throne, and from the wrath of **the Lamb**: For the great day of His wrath is come; and who shall be able to stand?"*

After the events which occur from the opening of the first five seals by the Lamb, the opening of the sixth seal causes the men of the earth to recognize that God is about to send His Day of the Lord judgment from heaven. They realize that no one will be able to bear the Lamb's great wrath. Then, after the sealing of the 144 Thousand (Revelation 7:1-8), the Lamb appears *"before the throne"* in heaven when the resurrected and raptured saints arrive in heaven:

*"After this I beheld, and, lo, a great multitude, which no man could number, of all nations, and kindreds, and people, and tongues, stood before the throne, and before **the Lamb**, clothed with white robes, and palms in their hands. And cried with a loud voice, saying, Salvation to our God which sits upon the throne, and unto **the Lamb**."*
(Revelation 7:9, 10)

This great victory celebration goes forth in view of *"the blessed hope" (Titus 2:13)* now a reality for the millions, yea, billions of innumerable resurrected and raptured saints who have just arrived in heaven. This glorious heavenly scene continues to unfold:

"And one of the elders answered saying unto me, What are these

*which are arrayed in white robes? And whence came they? And I said unto him, Sir, thou knowest. And he said to me, These are they which came out of [the] great tribulation, and have washed their robes, and made them white in the blood of **the Lamb**." (Revelation 7:13, 14).*

The resurrected and raptured saints are clearly identified by one of the elders in heaven, for the Lord shortens the great tribulation (Matthew 24:22) by rescuing His elect/saints from the Antichrist's persecution by the rapture just before He pours out His wrath on an unbelieving world (I Thessalonians 1:10, 5:9).

At the close of this marvelous scene in heaven the Lamb is once again at the forefront:
*"For **the Lamb** which is in the midst of the throne shall feed them, and shall lead them unto living fountains of waters: and God shall wipe away all tears from their eyes." (Revelation 7:17)*

The Lord Jesus Christ will continue to minister to His resurrected, raptured and glorified saints for eternity in heaven as will God the Father. The next place the word Lamb is seen is in Revelation 12:11:
*"And they overcame him [Satan] by the blood of **the Lamb** and by the word of their testimony; and they loved not their lives unto the death."*

The power of *"the blood of the Lamb",* along with an impeccable testimony demonstrated by their willingness to give their lives for the Lord, provides certain and clear victory over Satan's vicious assault during his *"great wrath" (Revelation 12:12).*

The Lord Jesus Christ is shown to be the Owner of the book of life for He has given His life in order that the eternal life of God can be given to those who will turn from their sin and trust Him as their Savior (John 6:35, 8:12, 10:10, 11:35, 14:6). Unfortunately many will reject His free gift of salvation as this verse indicates for the vast majority will worship the Antichrist in that day.

*"And all that dwell upon earth shall worship him [the Antichrist] whose names are not written in the book of life of **the Lamb** slain from the foundation of the world" (Revelation 13:8).*

The Lamb, the Lord Jesus Christ, is an integral part of the next passage being mentioned (3) times:

*"And I looked, and, lo, a **Lamb** stood on the mount Zion, and with Him an hundred forty and four thousand, having His Father's name written in their foreheads. And I heard a voice from heaven, as the voice of many waters, and as the voice of a great thunder: and I heard the voice of harpers harping with their harps: And they sung a new song before the throne, and before the four beasts and the elders: and no man could learn that song but the hundred forty and four thousand, which were redeemed from the earth. These are they which were not defiled with women; for they are virgins. These are they which follow **the Lamb** whithersoever He goes. These were redeemed from among men being the first fruits unto God and to **the Lamb**." (Revelation 14:1-4)*

This scene is filled with a holy heavenly aura, as it is unique to Scripture with heaven and earth joining in a harmonious praise song before the throne of God.

It is now the end of the 70th Week of Daniel and the Lord has redeemed Israel. It is this event that is being celebrated on earth and in heaven. The Lord Jesus Christ receives *"the kingdoms of this world"* *(Revelation 11:15).*

The 144 Thousand are standing *"with Him"* demonstrating their continuing action of physically following the Lamb throughout the Day of the Lord when they will continue to carry on their ministry.

The writing upon the foreheads of the 144 Thousand includes His name [The Lamb] and the name of His Father. There are others in Scripture who have the Lord's name inscribed on their foreheads (Revelation 3:12, 22:3, 4). These young men are unique for they have both the name of the Father and the name of the Lamb and are thereby protected in the midst of the Day of the Lord judgments when they will continue to serve the Lord (Revelation 9:4).

The 144 Thousand represent the Old and New Covenant having full benefit of the knowledge of the Lord Jesus Christ and the New Covenant but serving as *"servants of our God"* *(Revelation 7:3)* during the seven-year restored *"holy covenant"* *(Daniel 11:28-32)* period [70th Week of Daniel].

The title given the 144 Thousand in this passage is also unique to this group of men. They are called *"the first fruits unto God and to the Lamb" (Revelation 14:4)* indicating that they are the first of God's earthly people the Jews to be redeemed during this restored holy covenant dispensation.

*"And the third angel followed them, saying with a loud voice, If any man worship the beast and his image, and receive his mark in his forehead, or in his hand, The same shall drink of the wine of the wrath of God, which is poured out without mixture in the cup of His indignation; and he shall be tormented with fire and brimstone in the presence of the holy angels, and in the presence of **the Lamb**." (Revelation 14:10)*

This important angelic announcement is global in scope along with the two previous angelic announcements in Revelation 14:6-9 as all three are being directed to *"them that dwell on the earth, and to every nation, and kindred, and tongue, and people" (Revelation 14:6).*

The penalty for worshiping the beast by receiving his identifying mark is clear and concise having eternal consequences. Although not specified directly in this passage, the announcement includes the eternal name of *"**the Lamb**"* (Revelation 21:9, 14, 22, 23, 27, 22:1, 3) and the eternal *"holy angels"*. Therefore, this *"fire and brimstone"* is most likely referring to the eternal torment of hell itself. (Revelation 19:20, 20; 11-15)

*"And I saw as it were a sea of glass mingled with fire: and them that had gotten the victory over the beast, and over his image, and over his mark, and over the number of his name, stand on the sea of glass, having the harps of God. And they sing the song of Moses the servant of God, and the song of **the Lamb**, saying, Great and marvelous are Thy works, Lord God Almighty; just and true are Thy ways, Thou King of saints. Who shall not fear Thee, O Lord, and glorify Thy name? For Thou only are holy: For all nations shall come and worship before Thee; For Thy judgments are made manifest." (Revelation 15:2-4)*

The *"song of **the Lamb**"* is focused upon in this passage along with

82

the victory *"song of Moses the servant of God"* which is found in Exodus 15:1-19 having been sung by Moses and the children of Israel who celebrated the Lord's victory over the Egyptians.

The lyrics to *"the song of **the Lamb**"* are set forth here in this text being derived from the announcement given by the angel in Revelation 14:6, 7. Four specific points are recorded in both passages:
1. The Fear of God
2. The Glorifying of God
3. The Worship of God
4. The Judgment of God

In Revelation 14:6, 7 a global angelic warning is given as the Antichrist begins his control over humanity *"unto them that dwell on the earth, and to every nation, and kindred, and tongue and people"* before the judgment of God comes.

Notice the statement *"for the hour of His judgment is [about to] come"* *(Revelation 14:7)*. It utilizes the same grammatical construction as *"for the great day of His wrath is [about to] come"* *(Revelation 6:17)* indicating the judgment of God had not yet occurred but was now impending or just about to happen.

This warning will be given some time after the mid-point of the 70th Week of Daniel, but before the judgment of God is executed when the Day of the Lord begins (Revelation 8:1).

In Revelation 14:6, 7 the warning is given. In Revelation 15:3, 4 *"the song of **the Lamb**"* initially praises the Father followed by a rhetorical question and declaration of the future world worship of the Lord God Almighty after His final *"judgments [the seven vials] are made manifest"*.

This heavenly throne room scene (Revelation 15:3, 4) on the *"sea of glass"* *(Revelation 4:6)* where both the Old and New Covenant victory songs are being sung depicts those martyrs who have gotten *"the victory over the beast"* as recorded earlier:
*"And they overcame him [Satan] by the blood of **the Lamb** and the word of their testimony; and they loved not their lives unto the death"* *(Revelation 12:11)*.

This indicates the three keys to victory over Satan regardless of when he attacks:
1. The [Blood] of the Lamb
2. The word of their testimony [Blamelessness]
3. They loved not their lives unto the death
   [Being spent (II Corinthians 12:15) for the Master's glory]

The next passage mentioning *"**the Lamb**"* moves forward to the end of the Day of the Lord:

*"And the ten horns which thou saw are ten kings, which have received no kingdom as yet; but receive power [authority] as kings one hour with the beast. These have one mind, and shall give their power and strength [authority] unto the beast. These shall make war with **the Lamb**, and **the Lamb** shall overcome them: for He is Lord of lords and King of kings: and they that are with Him [144 Thousand (Revelation 14:4)] are called, and chosen, and faithful." (Revelation 17:12-14)*

The ten kings will eventually give their full allegiance to the Antichrist near the end of the Day of the Lord to perform primarily two specific duties. First of all, they will be the instrument God uses to destroy Babylon theGreat [Rome/Romanism:World False Religion] (Revelation 17:16, 17).

Secondly, they will become part of the Antichrist's global army that goes forth to war at Armageddon ultimately being destroyed by the Lamb, the Lord Jesus Christ (Revelation 19:11-21). This is also indicated in the passage when they *"shall make war with **the Lamb**, and **the Lamb** shall overcome them: for He is Lord of lords and King of kings"*.

The last end times *"**Lamb**"* passage occurs just before Jesus comes as *"King of kings and Lord of lords"*:

*"Let us be glad and rejoice, and give honor to Him: for the marriage of **the Lamb** is come, and His wife has made herself ready. And to her was granted that she should be arrayed in fine linen, clean and white: for the fine linen is the righteousness of saints. And he said unto me, Write, Blessed are they which are called unto the marriage supper of **the Lamb**. And he said unto me, These are the true sayings of God." (Revelation 19:7-9)*

This passage shows that all of God's redeemed have the blessed promise of attending this great celebration in heaven. The wedding garment is described as *"fine linen clean and white...the righteousness of the saints"*.

This garment is promised to every saint when they are justified by faith as described by Isaiah:
"I will greatly rejoice in the LORD, my soul shall be joyful in my God; for He has clothed me with the garments of salvation, He has covered me with the robe of righteousness, as a bridegroom decks himself with ornaments, and as a bride adorns herself with her jewels." (Isaiah 61:10)

The martyrs also are given these same white robes of righteousness:
"And white robes were given unto every one of them [martyrs]; and it was said unto them, that they should rest yet for a little season, until their fellow servants also and their brethren (Revelation 12:11, 15:3, 4, 20:4) that should be killed as they were, should be fulfilled." (Revelation 6:11)

The raptured saints and the resurrected saints of the ages will also be clothed with these same beautiful white and glorious *"garments of salvation...robes of righteousness"*:
"After this I beheld, and, lo, a great multitude, which no man could number, of all nations, and kindreds, and people, and tongues, stood before the throne, and before the Lamb, clothed with white robes, and palms in their hands." (Revelation 7:9)

The remaining occurrences of the Lamb are seen after the Apocalypse, the Day of the Lord, ends. However, the Lamb, who is the Price and Person of redemption, continues to be the Lord's favorite title throughout eternity as the following seven passages affirm:
*"And there came unto me one of the seven angels which had the seven vials full of the seven last plagues, and talked with me, saying, Come hither, I will show thee the bride, **the Lamb's** wife." (Revelation 21:9)*

"And the wall of the city [The Heavenly Jerusalem] had twelve

*foundations, and in them the names of the twelve apostles of **the Lamb.**" (Revelation 21:14)*

*"And I saw no temple therein: for the Lord God Almighty and **the Lamb** are the temple of it." (Revelation 21:22) And the city had no need of the sun neither of the moon, to shine in it: for the glory of God did lighten it, and **the Lamb** is the light thereof." (Revelation 21:23)*

*"And there shall in no wise enter into it any thing that defiles, neither whatsoever works abomination, or makes a lie: but they which are written in **the Lamb's** book of life." (Revelation 21:27)*

*"And he showed me a pure river of water of life, clear as crystal, proceeding out of the throne of God and of **the Lamb**."*
(Revelation 22:1)

*"And there shall be no more curse: but the throne of God and of **the Lamb** shall be in it; and His servants shall serve Him."*
(Revelation 22:3)

The angel also confirms exactly who is the Lamb's wife during his heavenly showing to the apostle John:
1. The nations of them which are saved (21:24)
2. They which are written in the Lamb's book of life (21:27)
3. The servants of the Lamb (22:3)

While the Lamb's Redemption of mankind is the major underlying theme of the Revelation with persecution and judgment only being utilized to purify and draw men to the Lord Jesus Christ, the Lord's Second Coming will unfold in three distinct phases:
1. The Glorious Reception (Revelation 7:9-17)
   [When the Saints are resurrected and raptured]
   (I Thessalonians 4:13-18)
2. The Grand Redemption (Revelation14:1)
   [When 'The Redeemer comes to Zion']
   (Isaiah 59:20; Romans 11:25, 26)
3. The Great Retribution (Revelation 19:11-21)
   [When Jesus comes as King of kings and Lord of Lords at the Battle of Armageddon]

He will come to receive the saints *"in the clouds" (Matthew 24:30; Acts 1:9-11; I Thessalonians 4:17; Revelation 1:7)* ending the great tribulation. Then He will redeem the nation of Israel at the end of the 70th Week of Daniel. And finally He will appear as King of kings and Lord of lords bringing retribution upon the Antichrist and the nations at Armageddon ending the Day of the Lord.

Every major series of events of the end times, the Great Tribulation, the 70th Week of Daniel, and the Day of the Lord, will be concluded by the certain intervention of the Lord Jesus Christ.

He will not only author the conclusion of these events, but He will also initiate the beginning of the end of the age when He systematically opens the seven sealed scroll, preparing the world for the Day of the Lord judgments which are contained within the scroll.

All facets of the end times will be in His hands. He, the Lamb of God, the Redeemer, has been given all *"power [authority] in heaven and in earth" (Matthew 28:18)* and for that may all the praise, honor and glory be given to Him, Amen and Amen!

9

<u>The Twenty Four Elders</u>

This section of "The People of the Apocalypse" focuses upon the first group of people described in the prophetic section of the book of the Revelation:

"I saw four and twenty elders sitting, clothed in white raiment: and they had on their heads crowns of gold." (Revelation 4:4)

This group of heavenly elders has been somewhat of a mystery to Bible commentators over the years. There are at least thirteen different interpretations given for their identity, so we cannot be dogmatic concerning just who they are or what they represent.

They are an important heavenly group during the time of the end being mentioned twelve different times in the Revelation. Their importance is shown by their position *"round about the throne"* *(Revelation 4:4)* having access to God, located in close proximity to the Lord of the universe.

Although they are not mentioned in any other book of the Bible, they do serve as worship leaders in heaven for they are repeatedly seen falling down before the throne *"and cast their crowns before the throne" (Revelation 4:10)* causing some to identify them with the Church.

There is nothing in the Bible text to support this theory, for the Church saints are still on earth at this time having been promised to be *"delivered from the wrath to come" (I Thessalonians 1:10, 5:10)* which has not yet begun. The word *"wrath"* does not appear in the book of the Revelation until *"the great day of His wrath is come" (Revelation 6:17)* indicating that God's wrath is just about to begin at that point in the chronological unfolding of the book.

The identity of the twenty-four elders may be rooted in the Old Testament for the Revelation is full of Old Testament parallels, and:

1. Twenty-four is the number of courses of Old Testament priests. (I Chronicles 24:1-24)
2. Their vocation was to minister in the presence of God. (Exodus 40:15)
3. They wore gold crowns. (Exodus 29:30; Zechariah 6:11)
4. There were elders of the priests. (II Kings 19:2)
5. They receive [white] robes of righteousness/garments of salvation. (Isaiah 61:10)

This same earthly group of old could well be represented here in the heavens. It is the interpretation containing the most Biblical parallels thereby providing a possible identity based upon the Word. Their leading in the worship of God appears at key points in the unfolding of the Revelation.

They are the first to be seen in heaven after God Himself is described (Revelation 4:4). As this same scene continues to unfold they are mentioned again:
"The four and twenty elders fall down before Him that sat on the throne, and worship Him that lives for ever and ever and cast their crowns before the throne saying, Thou art worthy, O Lord, to receive glory and honor and power for Thou hast created all things and for Thy pleasure they are and were created." (Revelation 4:10)

In Revelation 5:5 one of them consoles the Apostle John saying:
"Weep not: behold, the Lion of the tribe of Judah, the Root of David, hath prevailed to open the book, and to loose the seven seals thereof."
This elder has the privilege of heralding the entrance of the Lord Jesus Christ as His title *"the Lion of the tribe of Judah"* is only mentioned this one time in all of Scripture.

Then they appear again as a group:
"And I beheld, and in the midst of the throne, and of the four beasts, and in the midst of the elders, stood a Lamb as it had been slain, having seven horns and seven eyes, which are the seven Spirits of God sent forth into the earth." (Revelation 5:6)

Their importance is emphasized here, for they are present at the introduction and coronation of the central figure of the Revelation and all of Scripture itself, the Lamb of God, the King of glory, the Lord

Jesus Christ. They are involved in heavenly praise and worship when the Lamb takes the book [seven-sealed scroll] from the right hand of God the Father:

"And when He had taken the book, the four beasts and four and twenty elders fell down before the Lamb having every one of them harps and golden vials full of odors, which are the prayers of saints. And they sung a new song." (Revelation 5:8, 9)

The next time they appear they are part of the heavenly chorus which includes *"many angels round about the throne and beasts and the elders"* (Revelation 5:11,12) once again proclaiming the worthiness of the Lamb and giving Him praise.

The last time they are mentioned in this opening heavenly throne room scene which encompasses chapter four and five, their now familiar action of full worship to the God of heaven is repeated:

"And the four and twenty elders fell down and worshipped Him that lives for ever and ever." (Revelation 5:14)

In Revelation 7:11 they join the four beasts standing around the throne as the angels *"fell down before the throne on their faces, and worshipped God"* in direct response to the praise given by *"the great multitude"* who have just appeared in heaven.

Then a single elder once again addresses John:

"One of the elders answered, saying unto me, What are these which are arrayed in white robes? And whence came they? And I said unto him, Sir, thou knowest. And he said to me, These are they which came out of great tribulation, and have washed their robes, and made them white in the blood of the Lamb." (Revelation 7:13, 14)

These references indicate that the elders respond as single individuals and are not just a collective group acting only as a unit, but in fact they are real people whom God has chosen to minister to Him around His heavenly throne.

After this, the twenty-four elders are only seen three times, each of which marks a vital and important point in the unfolding chronology of the Revelation:

"And the four and twenty elders, which sat before God on their seats,

fell upon their faces, and worshipped God, Saying, We give Thee thanks, O Lord God Almighty, which are, and was, and are to come; because Thou has taken to Thee Thy great power, and has reigned." (Revelation 11:16, 17)

This time they worship God for His mighty act of taking the rule of earth and giving it to His Son, the Lord Jesus Christ:
"And the seventh angel sounded; and there were great voices in heaven, saying, The kingdoms of this world are become the kingdoms of our Lord and of His Christ; and He shall reign for ever and ever." (Revelation 11:15)

At this point in time we have come to a major, climactic point in history. The 70th Week of Daniel has ended 3-1/2 days earlier when the two witnesses were killed (Revelation 11:11, 12). *"A great earthquake"* has occurred:
"The tenth part of the city [Jerusalem] fell, and in the earthquake were slain of men seven thousand, and the remnant [rest] were affrighted, and gave glory to the God of heaven. The second woe is past; and, behold, the third woe cometh quickly."
(Revelation 11:13, 14)

"The nations were angry, and Thy wrath is come, and the time of the dead, that they should be judged, and that Thou should give reward unto Thy servants the prophets, and to the saints, and them that fear Thy name, small and great; and should destroy them which destroy the earth." (Revelation 11:18)

These twenty-four elders, without the accompaniment of any other heavenly group or being, mark this momentous time when they alone are seen falling down before God and praising Him for His great power in bringing about these major events in the history of mankind.

Chapter fourteen records still another significant event when the elders are present as *"a Lamb stood on Mount Zion, and with Him an hundred and forty and four thousand." (Revelation 14:1)*. This scene is split between heaven and earth with the Lamb and the 144 Thousand standing on earth on Mount Zion, and *"the...harpers"* singing in heaven *"a new song before the throne and before the four beasts, and the elders" (Revelation 14:3)*.

This marks the first time the Lamb is seen upon earth with the 144 Thousand. They are accompanied by a heavenly chorus of harpers in heaven who sing the new song which occurs at the end of the 70th Week of Daniel when the Lord Jesus Christ redeems the nation of Israel (Romans 11:26).

The last time the twenty-four elders are seen occurs during the now famous Hallelujah Chorus that is sung by *"much people in heaven."* *(Revelation 19:1.* They are once again performing their now familiar act of worship with the four beasts:
"And the four and twenty elders and the four beasts fell down and worshipped God that sat on the throne, saying, Amen; Alleluia." (Revelation 19:4)

Here the record of their ministry as heavenly worship leaders ends, just as it began, in the throne room of God worshipping with the four beasts. Now they are celebrating God's judgment of Babylon, just prior to the Lord Jesus Christ's return to bring an end to the Day of the Lord at the battle of Armageddon.

10

The Four Beasts

This group of beings or living creatures is called *"the four beasts"*. They, like *"the twenty-four elders"*, are also found in the throne room of God in the very beginning of the prophetic section of the Revelation and they are thoroughly described:

"And round about the throne, were four beasts full of eyes before and behind. And the first beast was like a lion, and the second beast like a calf, and the third beast had a face as a man, and the fourth beast was like a flying eagle. And the four beasts had each of them six wings about him; and they were full of eyes within: And they rest not day and night, saying, Holy, holy, holy, Lord God Almighty, which was, and is, and is to come." (Revelation 4:6-8)

This description is similar to the heavenly vision of Ezekiel recorded in Ezekiel 1:5-10. The beasts, or living creatures as they are called in Ezekiel, are supernatural heavenly beings created for the express purpose of worshipping the God of heaven. In the Revelation they appear on seven different occasions and perform a variety of necessary ministry services to the Lord.

Their pronouncement of *"Holy, holy, holy, Lord God Almighty, which was and is and is to come" (Revelation 4:7)* is also similar to the heavenly seraphim's declaration in Isaiah 6:3: *"Holy, holy, holy, is the LORD of hosts: the whole earth is full of His glory."*

This opening panoply of praise to the Lord God of heaven are the first words of praise to be uttered in heaven, emphasizing His unique essence of holiness, the characteristic for which He is the most well known and the one characteristic by which He most desires to be remembered.

This threefold praise of *"Holy, holy, holy"* ascribed to God continues:
"And when those beasts give glory and honor and thanks to Him that

sat on the throne, who lives for ever and ever, The four and twenty elders fall down before Him that sat on the throne, and worship Him that lives for ever and ever, and cast their crowns before the throne, saying, Thou art worthy, O Lord, to receive glory and honor and power, for Thou hast created all things and for Thy pleasure they are and were created." (Revelation 4:9-11)

The four living creatures team up with the twenty-four elders as a second group of worship leaders in the throne room of God. These two groups are seen together on four separate occasions in the Revelation and each time they join in full adoration and worship of God, which seems to be their primary purpose for being created.

After their introductory appearance to bring praise to God the Father in the throne room, they appear in chapter five when the Lamb of God, the Lord Jesus Christ, makes His entrance into the heavenly throne room:

"And I beheld, and, lo, in the midst of the throne and of the four beasts, and in the midst of the elders, stood a Lamb as it had been slain, having seven eyes, which are the seven spirits of God sent forth into all the earth." (Revelation 5:6)

The importance of the four beasts and the twenty-four elders is underlined, as they are present when the Lamb is introduced at His heavenly coronation. He is the central figure of all of history. He now takes His place in the throne room at the closing stage of time and continues to serve His Father by taking the scroll and eventually breaking each seal, opening the scroll which reveals the judgments of God's wrath also known as the eschatological Day of the Lord.

"And when He had taken the book (scroll), the four beasts and four and twenty elders fell down before the Lamb having every one of them harps and golden vials full of odors which are the prayers of the saints. And they sung a new song saying, Thou art worthy to take the book and to open the seals thereof: for Thou was slain, and hast redeemed us (men) to God by Thy blood out of every kindred, and tongue, and people, and nation; And hast made us (them) unto our (their) God kings and priests and we (they) shall reign on the earth." (Revelation 5:8-10)

The four beasts' ministry of praise to the Lamb continues:
"And I beheld and I heard the voice of many angels round about the throne and the beasts and the elders and the number of them was ten thousand times ten thousand, and thousand of thousands; Saying with a loud voice, Worthy is the Lamb that was slain to receive power, and riches, and wisdom, and strength, and honor, and glory, and blessing." (Revelation 5:11, 12)

This opening throne room scene is the most glorious and majestic praise and worship scene in all of Scripture. It first of all ascribes holiness and praise to the Father in chapter four. Then the Lamb that is slain, the Lord Jesus Christ, is introduced as the only One worthy to open the book, the One Who now ushers in the events of the time of the end. The four beasts bring this magnificent throne room scene to a close:
"And every creature which is in heaven, and on the earth, and under the earth, and such as are in the sea, and all that are in them, heard I saying, Blessing, and honor, and glory, and power, be unto Him that sitteth upon the throne, and unto the Lamb for ever and ever. And the four beasts said, Amen. And the four and twenty elders fell down and worshipped Him that lives for ever and ever." (Revelation 5:13, 14)

Their ministry continues as they play an introductory part in the opening of the first four seals that are located on the outside of the book (scroll). While the four beasts previously acted as a group involved in worshipping the Lord, now, in Revelation chapter six they perform individual duties as each one is identified with one of the first four seals located on the outside of the scroll.

When the Lamb opens the seal they simply say *"come and see"* inviting all present to observe the activities and outcome of each event. These first four seals are set apart from the last three as they are introduced by the four beasts and are symbolized by four horsemen.

The events of the seals are authored by the Antichrist who is the symbolic rider on each of the four horses. The seals comprise the Satanically sourced preparation of the earth for the final cataclysmic events of the Day of the Lord's wrath is contained inside the scroll.

The last three seals focus upon the Day of the Lord judgment. The martyrs of the fifth seal are inquiring of God's wrath. The sixth seal is the sign indicating the Day of the Lord wrath/judgment is impending, and the seventh seal introduces the Day of the Lord wrath/judgment beginning with the seven trumpet and vial judgments.

The four beasts play an important part in this sequence as their appearances in the Revelation demonstrate. The next scene they are involved in is found in chapter seven:

"And all the angels stood round about the throne, and about the elders, and the four beasts, and fell before the throne on their faces, and worshipped God, Saying, Amen: Blessing, and glory, and wisdom, and thanksgiving, and honor, and power, and might, be unto our God for ever and ever. Amen." (Revelation 7:11)

In this heavenly scene, which occurs between the sixth and seventh seal, the 144 Thousand have been sealed (Revelation 7:3-8), the saints of the ages have been resurrected, raptured and received into heaven (Revelation 7:9, 10). This is followed by the praising response of all the inhabitants of heaven (Revelation 7:11, 12) with the resurrected saints being identified in Revelation 7:13-17.

These four beasts are once again an integral part of the heavenly worship scene of celebration when the redeemed of the ages experience the final phase of their redemption by the Lamb and appear in the throne room before God.

Their next place of activity and worship is in heaven with the twenty-four elders as the Lamb and the 144 Thousand Israelites appear on earth on Mt. Zion:

"And they (the harpers) sung as it were a new song before the throne, and before the four beasts, and the elders: and no man could learn that song but the hundred and forty four thousand, which were redeemed from the earth." (Revelation 14:3)

Here the four beasts appear with the twenty-four elders at another major event in the throne room and now the harpers also are with them singing *"a new song"* in the presence of God the Father. The Lamb makes His first time of the end appearance on earth as the Redeemer that comes to Zion (Isaiah 59:20) to accomplish the redemption of the nation of Israel represented by the 144 Thousand from each of the twelve tribes of Israel.

When God's Day of the Lord judgment draws to a close, one of the four beasts takes part in the final stages:
"And one of the four beasts gave unto the seven angels seven golden vials full of the wrath of God, Who lives for ever and ever." *(Revelation 15:7)*

This seemingly minor detail involving one of the four beasts demonstrates the continuity and progressive nature of the Revelation. It also supports the chronological sequence of the book as these heavenly creatures are seen in the throne room of God Almighty in a supporting role during the progressive outpouring of God's judgment at the end of the age.

The last time they appear is in chapter nineteen:
"And the four and twenty elders and the four beasts fell down and worshipped God that sat on the throne, saying, Amen; Alleluia." *(Revelation 19:4)*

They join their throne room companions, the twenty-four elders, in the three-fold Hallelujah Chorus of praise to God Almighty for His judgment of the great whore Babylon just prior to the King of king's return to earth to *"smite the nations"* at the battle of Armageddon (Revelation 19:11-21).

The four beasts presence on this momentous occasion underscores their ongoing ministry to God the Father and the Lamb as praise and worship leaders in heaven along with their direct involvement in the administration of God's program of judgment during the eschatological Day of the Lord.

11

The Angels

The Angels are key players in God's overall end times plan. He uses them mightily throughout the book of Daniel, the Old Testament parallel to the book of the Revelation. And, even though almost 2600 years have passed since the time Daniel's book was written, the angels continue to be the same powerful messengers of God today as they fulfil their role as merciful ministers unto His people:

"Bless the LORD, ye His angels, that excel in strength, that do His commandments, hearkening unto the voice of His word. Bless ye the LORD, all ye His hosts; ye ministers of His, that do His pleasure." (Psalm 103:20, 21)

They will be used mightily in the unfolding of the end times. They appear repeatedly as the servants that God uses to bring forth both of the major series of judgments, the seven trumpets and the seven vials, during the Day of the Lord as recorded in the book of the Revelation of Jesus Christ.

Before the Revelation is considered, the book of Daniel must be surveyed as it also reveals much vital angelic activity affecting the time of the end:

"I, Daniel, was grieved in my spirit in the midst of my body, and the visions of my head troubled me. I came near unto one of them that stood by, and asked him the truth of all this. So, he told me, and made me know the interpretation of the things." (Daniel 7:15, 16)

Daniel has just received a vision (Daniel 7:1-14) containing near future events involving *"Four great beasts" [four kingdoms] (Daniel 7:3-7)* and far future events (Daniel 7:7-14) which will occur during the end times. He receives the interpretation of this vision from an angel referred to as *"one of them that stood by" (Daniel 7:16).*

Although Daniel had received a vision from God previously (Daniel 2:19) in order to interpret king Nebuchadnezzar's first vision, this vision in chapter seven is the first one he was given which required the interpretation of an angel. This complex vision is the first of four end times visions given to Daniel requiring angelic interpretation.

Notice, Daniel *"came near unto one of them that stood by"* *(Daniel 7:16)* indicating that there was more than one angel attending this event. Daniel was able to physically come near one of them revealing that they were in his presence during the interpretation. The vision was *"a dream and visions of his head...the visions of my head troubled me" (Daniel 7:2, 15)* being supernaturally revealed to the mind of Daniel.

The angel gave Daniel a brief interpretation (Daniel 7:16-18) causing him to want more information concerning the fourth beast [end times 8th beast empire (Revelation 17:3, 8-11], the ten horns [the ten kings (Revelation 17:12-14], and the little horn [the Antichrist] (Daniel 7:19-22). He then receives a lengthy, more specific response from the interpreting angel (Daniel 7:23-27).

The next vision given to Daniel is revealed in chapter eight:
"In the third year of the reign of King Belshazzar a vision appeared unto me, even unto me Daniel, after that which appeared unto me at the first. And I saw in a vision; and it came to pass, that I was at Shushan in the palace, which is in the province of Elam; and I saw in a vision, and I was by the river of Ulai." (Daniel 8:1, 2)

The vision is then given (Daniel 8:3-14) followed by Daniel seeking for the meaning:
"And it came to pass, when I, even I Daniel, had seen the vision, and sought for the meaning, then, behold, there stood before me as the appearance of a man. And I heard a man's voice between the banks of Ulai, which called, and said, Gabriel, make this man to understand the vision. So he [Gabriel] came near where I stood: and when he came, I was afraid, and fell upon my face: but he said unto me, Understand, O son of man: for at the time of the end shall be the vision." (Daniel 8:15-17)

Once again, Daniel receives instruction from an angel whose name is Gabriel. He, Gabriel, is told to *"make this man understand"* and

physically comes near to Daniel causing him to be afraid and fall upon his face. Nevertheless, Gabriel continues his detailed interpretation of the vision (Daniel 8:19-26). Then, Daniel responds:
"And I Daniel fainted, and was sick certain days; afterward I rose up, and did the king's business; and I was astonished [astounded] at the vision, but none understood it." (Daniel 8:27)

Although Daniel did not fully understand this vision at the time, its time of the end content has been invaluable in determining:
1. The Rise of the Antichrist (Daniel 8:9, 10),
2. The Rule of the Antichrist (Daniel 8:11, 12 23-25a)
3. The Ruin of the Antichrist (Daniel 8:25b)

This vision also includes the first mention of the most significant event of the Antichrist's wicked rule, the abomination of desolation (Daniel 8:11).

Daniel's third vision in chapter nine once again involves the angel Gabriel:
"And whiles I was speaking, and praying, and confessing my sin and the sin of my people Israel, and presenting my supplication before the LORD my God for the holy mountain of my God; Yea, whiles I was speaking in prayer, even the man Gabriel, whom I had seen in the vision at the beginning, being caused to fly swiftly, touched me about the time of the evening oblation. And he informed me, and talked with me, and said, O Daniel, I am now come forth to give thee skill and understanding. At the beginning of thy supplications the commandment came forth, and I am come to show thee; for thou art greatly beloved: therefore understand the matter and consider the vision." (Daniel 9:20-23)

Daniel's detailed prayer of confession and supplication (Daniel 9:3-19) is the prelude to this personal appearance by the angel Gabriel. He gives Daniel, in three succinct verses, the entire panorama of Israel's future:
"Know therefore and understand, that from the going forth of the commandment to restore and build Jerusalem [445 B.C.-Nehemiah 2:5-7] unto Messiah the Prince shall be seven weeks and three-score and two weeks [69 weeks/483 years] ...And after three-score and two weeks shall Messiah be cut off [Jesus' Death on the Cross] but not for

Himself...And he [Antichrist] shall confirm the covenant with many for one week [70th Week of Daniel] and in the midst of the week he shall cause the sacrifice and the oblation to cease, and for the overspreading of abominations he shall make it desolate [abomination of desolation (Matthew 24:15)], even unto the consummation, and that determined shall be poured upon the desolate [desolator/Antichrist]." (Daniel 9:25-27)

These verses are some of the most studied and quoted time of the end Scriptures containing a complete time frame for the coming events during the time of the end. This passage reveals that there is one remaining week [7 years] of time on God's prophetic calendar of events when He will once again deal with Israel as a nation. These seven years will begin when the Antichrist confirms a covenant with [the] many of Israel. Then, after 3-1/2 years he will bring to pass the abomination of desolation.

His eventual destruction is also recorded at the close of this remarkable passage, with all of this key information spoken directly to Daniel by the angel Gabriel. The last vision of Daniel is the grand culmination of the visions given to the aged prophet for it unfolds in the last three chapters of the book (Daniel 10-12).

It is the direct result of this man of God's willingness to put aside for a time the physically enjoyable things and concentrate totally on spiritually preparing himself to receive this glorious revelation from the Lord:
"In the third year of Cyrus king of Persia a thing was revealed unto Daniel, whose name was called Belteshazzar; and the thing was true, but the time appointed was long: and he understood the thing, and had understanding of the vision. In those days I Daniel was mourning three full weeks. I ate no pleasant bread, neither came flesh nor wine in my mouth, neither did I anoint myself at all, till three whole weeks were fulfilled." (Daniel 10:1-3)

After receiving the three previous visions, with the third (Daniel 9:20-27) coming during Daniel's prayer, he is fully given over to seeking the Lord and is duly rewarded for his lengthy all-consuming spiritual preparation:
"And in the four and twentieth day of the first month, as I was by the

side of the great river, which is Hiddekel; Then I lifted up my eyes, and looked, and behold a certain Man clothed in linen whose loins were girded with fine gold of Uphaz: His body also was like the beryl, and His face as the appearance of lightning, and His eyes as lamps of fire, and His arms and His feet like in color to polished brass, and the voice of His words like the voice of a multitude." (Daniel 10:4-6)

This vision of the Lord Himself is similar to His appearance to the Apostle John in Revelation 1:12-16. Daniel reveals the effects of this great vision:

"And I Daniel alone saw the vision: for the men that were with me saw not the vision, but a great quaking fell upon them, so that they fled to hide themselves. Therefore I was left alone, and saw this great vision, and there remained no strength in me; for my comeliness was turned in me into corruption, and I retained no strength. Yet heard I the voice of His words: and when I heard the voice of His words, then was I in a deep sleep on my face, and my face toward the ground." (Daniel 10:7-9)

Those with Daniel did not see the vision. But the holy presence of the Lord caused them to quake and run away, hiding themselves. Daniel himself turned pale and lost all physical strength causing him to go into *"a deep sleep"* falling prostrate on his face, but a messenger from God intervenes and ministers to Daniel:

"And, behold, an hand touched me, which set me upon my knees and upon the palms of my hands. And he said unto me, O' Daniel, a man greatly beloved, understand the words that I speak unto thee, and stand upright: for unto thee am I now sent. And when he had spoken this word unto me, I stood trembling. The said he unto me, Fear not, Daniel: for from the first day that thou didst set thy heart to understand, and to chasten thyself before thy God, thy words were heard, and I am come for thy words. But the prince of the kingdom of Persia with stood me one and twenty days: but, lo, Michael, one of the chief princes, came to help me; and I remained there with the kings of Persia." (Daniel 10:10-13)

The very touch of this angel caused Daniel to arise to his knees. Then, the angel spoke comforting words to him telling him to *"stand upright" (Daniel 10:11)*. The angel knew of Daniel's spiritual preparation when he began to *"chasten" (Daniel 10:12)* himself. He also said that Daniel's *"words were heard" (Daniel 10:12)* indicating Daniel prayed to God during that twenty-one day period (Daniel 10:3) although his prayer is not recorded. He then explains that the three-week delay in answering Daniel was due to a heavenly conflict with "The prince of the kingdom of Persia [Satan's angelic leader in Persia]."

Michael, the archangel of Israel, came to help him while he was with the kings of Persia. Then the angel begins to tell Daniel the details of the vision:

"Now I am come to make thee understand what shall befall thy people in the latter days: for yet the vision is for many days. And when he had spoken these words unto me, I set my face toward the ground, and I became dumb. And, behold, one like the similitude of the sons of men touched my lips: then I opened my mouth, and spoke, and said unto him that stood before me, O my lord, by the vision my sorrows are turned upon me, and I have retained no strength. For how can the servant of this my lord talk with this my lord? for as for me, straightway there remained no strength in me, neither is there breath left in me." (Daniel 10:14-17)

Once again, Daniel turns his face toward the ground, speechless, being weakened and breathless from the words spoken to him by the angel. The angel touches him, allowing Daniel to tell of his great humility in the presence of the angel, but he still is without strength.

This repeated weak condition of Daniel causes another encounter from the heavenly messenger:

"Then there came again and touched me one like the appearance of a man, and he strengthened me, And said, O man greatly beloved, fear not: peace be unto thee, be strong, yea, be strong. And when he has spoken unto me, I was strengthened, and said, Let my lord speak; for thou has strengthened me." (Daniel 10:18, 19)

Daniel is again ministered to by the angel and the repeated words *"greatly beloved" (Daniel 9:23, 10:11, 23),* which is the third time they are spoken to Daniel, point to the possibility that Gabriel is the angel that God sent to minister to Daniel during this last most magnificent vision:

"Then said he, Know thou wherefore I come unto thee? And now I

will return to fight with the prince of Persia: and when I am gone forth, lo, the prince of Greece [Satan's angelic leader in Greece] shall come. But I will show thee that which is noted in the scripture of truth: and there is none that holds with me in these things, but Michael, the archangel (Jude 9) your prince. Also, I in the first year of Darius the Mede, even I, stood to confirm and to strengthen him. And now will I show thee the truth." (Daniel 10:20, 21, 11:1)

This passage in Daniel is the most informative section of Scripture concerning the angels, their ministry to man, and their ongoing heavenly communication and warfare. Notice a number of significant facts given in these verses:

1. God sends his angels to those who are prepared. (Daniel 10:2, 3)
2. God's angels appear physically. (Daniel 10:10-21)
3. God's angels minister to His people. (Daniel 10:10, 16, 18)
4. God's angels know His people specifically by name (Daniel 10:11, 12, 19)
5. Satan has angels over certain countries. (Daniel 10:13, 20)
6. God's angels are in direct conflict with Satan's angels (Daniel 10:13)
7. Satan's angels are able to delay God's message but do not stop God's angels (Daniel 10:13)
8. God's angels minister to kings over certain countries (Daniel 11:1)
9. The importance of God's message is evidenced by the amount of Satan's resistance to its delivery.
10. The importance of the receiver is evidenced by those whom God sends to minister.

Remember, during the days of Daniel, Persia and Greece were countries that contained many of God's chosen people after the captivity and dispersion of the Israelites when they were taken to all parts of the known world. These countries received angelic attention from the Lord and His heavenly host, most likely due to their importance and the likely presence of many of His people.

This same truth applies to the countries and leaders of today. There are countless accounts of God's miraculous assistance, even outright miracles being performed by Him on behalf of His people in the centuries that have passed since this marvelous record in Daniel was penned.

The angel goes on to give Daniel the most complete vision of the time of the end in the two remaining chapters. Once again, the major emphases of this vision are:
1. The Rise of the Antichrist (Daniel 11:20, 21)
2. The Rule of the Antichrist (Daniel 11:22-45a)
3. The Ruin of the Antichrist (Daniel 11:45b)

The first verse of chapter twelve records the last mention of the archangel Michael in the book of Daniel:
"And at that time shall Michael stand up, the great prince which stands for the children of thy people: and there shall be a time of trouble, such as never was since there was a nation even to that same time: and at that time thy people shall be delivered, every one that shall be found written in the book." (Daniel 12:1)

The time of this event is revealed in the preceding verse as the Antichrist makes his center of military operations in the temple at Jerusalem *"in the glorious holy mountain" (Daniel 11:45)*. This refers to Mt. Zion where he brings to pass the renowned abomination of desolation (Daniel 8:11, 12, 9:27, 11:31, 12:11; Matthew 24:15; II Thessalonians 2:4).

Michael will *"stand up"*, which is the translation of the Hebrew word "amad", which is sometimes translated: "To stand still, stop (moving or doing) to cease" as Strong's lexicon records. It also appears in other places being translated with this same meaning:
*"When I had waited, (for they spoke not, but **stood still** [amad]), and answered no more" (Job 32:16)*
*"Hearken unto this, O Job: **stand still** [amad] and see the wondrous works of God." (Job 37:14)*

This is the sense of the Hebrew word "amad" in this verse as Revelation 12 also supports. Michael and his angels are active in heaven winning the war with the devil and his angels who are subsequently cast out of heaven into the earth. But, Michael and his angels do not actively intervene on the behalf of Israel by restraining Satan's evil plan on earth (Revelation 12:7-9).

Even though Satan attacks Israel, *"the woman"* of Revelation 12, she is not once helped by Michael her prince, instead she is given: *"Two wings of a great eagle that she might fly into the wilderness, into her place, where she is nourished for a time, and times, and half a time, from the face of the serpent. And the serpent cast out of his mouth water as a flood after the woman, that he might cause her to be carried away of the flood. And the earth helped the woman, and the earth opened her mouth, and swallowed up the flood which the dragon cast out of his mouth." (Revelation 12:14, 15)*

These passages, coupled with II Thessalonians 2:6, 7 support the theory that Michael is the restrainer:
"And now ye know what withholds [restrains] that he [Antichrist] might be revealed in his time. For the mystery of iniquity does already work: only he [Michael] who now lets [restrains] will let [restrain], until he be taken out of the way."

The restraining influence of Michael the archangel, Israel's prince, continues today as it did in Daniel and Paul's day. But, in order *"that he [the Antichrist] might be revealed in his time"* there is coming a time, at the mid-point of the 70th Week of Daniel, when he, the Antichrist, will be revealed when Michael, the one who now restrains, *"stands still"* as recorded in Daniel 12:1.

God's purpose for the persecution that Satan inflicts upon His people is to purge and purify (Daniel 12:10; Zechariah 13:9) them during this time, preparing them for their Redeemer when He comes to Zion *"when all Israel shall be saved" (Romans11: 26)*. He does not utilize Michael to restrain, instead Michael *"stands still"* during this time of Israel's purification.

The last appearance of an angel is in the closing scene of the book of Daniel:
"Then I Daniel looked, and, behold, there stood other two, the one on this side of the bank of the river, and the other on that side of the bank of the river: And one said to the Man clothed in linen, which was

upon the waters of the river, How long shall it be to the end of these wonders? And I heard the Man clothed in linen, which was upon the waters of the river, when He held up His right hand and His left hand unto heaven, and swore by Him that lives for ever that it shall be for a time, times, and an half; and when he shall have accomplished to scatter the power of the holy people, all these things shall be finished." (Daniel 12:5-7)

Two more angels, in addition to the one giving him the substance of the vision (Daniel 11:2-12:4), are seen by Daniel, one on each side of the river. One of them spoke to the Lord Jesus Christ, Who is the *"Man clothed in linen" (Daniel 10:5, 12:6)*. The angel is inquiring of the length of time *"to the end of these wonders"*.

The Lord indicates a 3-1/2 year time period, which is the last half of the 70th Week of Daniel. At this point He will physically intervene, coming to earth as the Redeemer/Deliverer of Israel (Isaiah 59:20; Romans 11:25, 26; Revelation 14:1) at the same time taking control of *"the kingdoms of this world" (Revelation 11:15)*.

The book of the Revelation begins and ends with major appearances by these heavenly messengers of God for the word *"angel"* appears over seventy times beginning with the opening verse: *"The Revelation of Jesus Christ which God gave unto Him, to show unto His servants things which shortly come to pass, and He sent and signified it by His angel unto His servant John." (Revelation 1:1)*

Although, *"All Scripture is given by inspiration of God" (II Timothy 3:16)* this is the only book specifically *"sent and signified by His angel"*. In the last chapter this same significant fact is underlined after the Revelation has been given: *"I Jesus have sent My angel to testify unto you these things in the churches. I am the Root and the Offspring of David, and the bright and Morning Star." (Revelation 22:16)*

The importance of this book can not be overemphasized! It brings to life the ancient prophecies of Scripture spelling out those *"things to come" (John 16:13)* in vivid detail. The Lord's most significant players, next to the Lord Himself, are His angels whom He utilizes to accomplish His supernatural work on earth.

107

The angels are active throughout the three opening chapters which cover "the things which thou has seen, and the things which are" (Revelation 1:19a,b) with the word "angel" appearing (10) times. It is "the things which shall be hereafter" (Revelation 1:19c) that are focused upon in this study which are covered in the prophetic section (Revelation 4:1-22:21) of the Revelation.

The first appearance of an angel in the prophetic section occurs during the opening heavenly throne room scene:
"And I saw in the right hand of Him that sat on the throne a book written within and on the backside, sealed with seven seals. And I saw a strong angel proclaiming with a loud voice, Who is worthy to open the book, and to loose the seals thereof?" (Revelation 5:2)

This is the first time a *"strong angel"* is seen in the book of the Revelation and the first time an angel speaks with *"a loud voice"*. This significant proclamation is given to emphasize the unique qualifications of the Lamb, the Lord Jesus Christ, as He alone is worthy to take the book from God His Father and open the seals on the outside of the scroll in order to reveal the contents within.
"And I beheld, and I heard the voice of many angels round about the throne and the beasts and the elders: and the number of them was ten thousand times ten thousand, and thousands of thousands; Saying with a loud voice, Worthy is the Lamb that was slain to receive power, and riches, and wisdom, and strength, and honor, and glory, and blessing." (Revelation 5:11, 12)

The magnificent praise and worship of the Lamb is enjoined by the angels after *"the beasts and the elders"* sing a new song of praise with the same emphasis:
"Thou art worthy to take the book, and to open the seals thereof: for Thou was slain, and has redeemed men to God by Thy Blood out of every kindred, and tongue, and people, and nation; And has made them unto our God kings and priests: and they shall reign upon on the earth." (Revelation 5:9, 10)

Then, *"every creature which is in heaven, and on the earth, and under the earth, and such as are in the sea, and all that are in them, heard I saying, Blessing, and honor, and glory, and power, be unto Him that sits upon the throne, and unto the Lamb for ever and ever."*

(Revelation 5:13) also join the beasts, elders and angels in this most magnificent worship scene ever recorded in the pages of Scripture. It concludes with the continued worship by the beasts and elders:
"And the four beasts said, Amen. And the four and twenty elders fell down and worshipped Him that lives for ever and ever."
(Revelation 5:14)

This marvelous worship scene marks the beginning of the end as the Lord Jesus Christ, the Lamb, has taken the seven sealed book from His Father which contains the judgments of the most prophesied event in all of Scripture, *"the great and dreadful Day of the Lord" (Malachi 4:5)*. The next time angels are seen is just before the Day of the Lord begins:
"And after these things I saw four angels standing on the four corners of the earth, holding the four winds of the earth, that the wind should not blow on the earth, nor on the sea, nor on any tree. And I saw another angel ascending from the east, having the seal of the living God: and he cried with a loud voice to the four angels, to whom it was given to hurt the earth, and the sea, Saying, Hurt not the earth, neither the sea, nor the trees, till we have sealed the servants of our God in their foreheads." (Revelation 7:1-3)

This event begins with these three words: *"after these things"* which is a time indicating phrase used only five times (Revelation 4:1, 7:9, 15:5, 18:1, 19:1) to divide major phases of the book of the Revelation.

The angels are seen continuing the preparation of earth, which includes six of the seven seals, before the seventh is broken (Revelation 8:1) allowing the book to open beginning God's Day of the Lord judgment.

These four angels are delayed from beginning their work of judgment until the 144 Thousand (Revelation 7:4) are sealed. This sealing provides them with protection (Revelation 9:4) during this devastating time of God's wrath upon the earth and its inhabitants.

Now it is time for the Day of the Lord to begin:
"And when He had opened the seventh seal, there was silence in heaven about the space of half and hour. And I saw the seven angels

which stood before God; and to them were given seven trumpets. And another angel came and stood at the altar, having a golden censer; and there was given unto him much incense, that he should offer it with the prayers of all saints upon the golden altar which was before the throne. And the smoke of the incense, which came with the prayers of the saints, ascended up before God our of the angel's hand. And the angel took the censer, and filled it with fire of the altar, and cast it into the earth: and there were voices, and thunderings, and lightnings, and an earthquake." (Revelation 8:1-5)

This scene contains the seven angels who are given the seven trumpets. Then another angel comes and initiates the judgment by first creating smoke from the incense he put upon the fire of the altar in order that the fragrance of the incense might ascend up into God's presence. This occurs prior to the beginning of this major event, the great and dreadful Day of the Lord.

Then, six of the seven angels proceed to sound their trumpets in somewhat of a rapid succession with the first four being grouped together bringing God's judgment upon 1/3 of the trees, green grass, sea, sea creatures, rivers and fountains of waters, sun, moon and stars (Revelation 8:6-13).

The last three trumpet judgments, also called *"woes"*, are more complex, bringing additional and increasingly devastating effects upon the earth's inhabitants with the sixth trumpet killing one third of the planet's population (Revelation 9:1-21).

Between the sixth and seventh trumpet another angel appears:
"And I saw another mighty angel come down from heaven, clothed with a cloud: and a rainbow was upon his head, and his face was as it were the sun, and his feet as pillars of fire: And he had in his right hand a little book open: and he set his right foot upon the sea, and his left foot upon the earth, And cried with a loud voice, as when a lion roars: and when he had cried, seven thunders uttered their voices." (Revelation 10:1-3)

When the *"seven thunders had uttered their voice"* John was told to *"seal up those things which the seven thunders uttered, and write them not." (Revelation 10:4)* However, he does record the words of

110

the mighty angel:

"And the angel which I saw stand upon the sea and upon the earth lifted up his hand to heaven And swore by Him that lives for ever and ever, Who created heaven, and the things that therein are, and the earth, and the things that therein are, and the sea, and the things which are therein, that there should be time [delay] no longer: But, in the days of the voice of the seventh angel, when he shall begin to sound, the mystery of God should be finished, as He has declared to His servants the prophets." (Revelation 10:5-7)

John is then told to take the little book from the mighty angel and the angel told him to literally:

"Take it and eat it up; and it shall make thy belly bitter, but it shall be in thy mouth sweet as honey." (Revelation 10:9)

John obeys, experiencing those same inward results, and is told:

"And he [the mighty angel] said unto me, Thou must prophesy again before many peoples, and nations, and tongues, and kings."
(Revelation 10:11)

This refers to the remainder of the Day of the Lord judgments which includes the seventh trumpet and the seven vials, the judgment of Babylon, and the climactic battle of Armageddon. Chapter eleven begins with an angel directing the Apostle John:

"And there was given me a reed like unto a rod: and the angel stood, saying, Rise, and measure the temple of God, and the altar, and them [Jews] that worship therein. But the court which is without the temple leave out, and measure it not; for it is given unto the Gentiles: and the holy city [Jerusalem] shall they tread under foot forty and two months [3-1/2 years]." (Revelation 11:1, 2)

This chapter, along with chapters twelve, thirteen and fourteen, provide details that will occur during the last half of Daniel's 70th Week. John is told to measure the temple. Then, after the ministry of the *"two witnesses"* is recorded (11:3-14), the seventh trumpet is sounded:

"And the seventh angel sounded, and there were great voices in
heaven, saying, THE KINGDOMS OF THIS WORLD ARE BECOME
THE KINGDOMS OF OUR LORD AND OF HIS CHRIST; AND HE
SHALL REIGN FOR EVER AND EVER." (Revelation 11:15)

This seventh trumpet marks the end of the 70th Week of Daniel bringing about numerous major events on God's timetable. The most significant event is announced by the great voices in heaven, which indicates the physical return of Christ the King to begin His eternal rule over *"THE KINGDOMS OF THIS WORLD."*

Then, another appearance of Michael the archangel occurs:
"And there was war in heaven: Michael and his angels fought against the dragon; and the dragon fought and his angels, And prevailed not; neither was their place found any more in heaven. And the great dragon was cast out, that old serpent, called the Devil, and Satan, which deceives the whole world: he was cast out into the earth, and his angels were cast out with him." (Revelation 12:7-9)

Michael's victory in heaven, having cast out the devil and his angels into the earth, brings about a most intensive spiritual conflict called the great tribulation: (Matthew 24:21)
"Woe to the inhabitants of the earth and of the sea! For the devil is come down unto you, having great wrath, because he knows that he has but a short time." (Revelation 12:12)

Chapter thirteen introduces and details the Antichrist and false prophet's activities with chapter fourteen revealing God's mighty overshadowing response to Satan's two henchmen. In the process, the sealed of God, the 144 Thousand, appear with the Lord, and six angels are sent forth bringing with them powerful messages to the earth's inhabitants:
(1) *"And I saw another angel fly in the midst of heaven, having the everlasting gospel to preach to them that dwell on the earth, and to every nation, and kindred, and tongue, and people, Saying with a loud voice, Fear God, and give glory to Him; for the hour of His judgment is come: and worship Him that made heaven, and earth, and the sea, and the fountains of waters." (Revelation 14:6, 7)*

This global announcement given to the earth dwellers is *"the everlasting gospel"* which is heralded prior to God's judgment the Day of the Lord. They are given the opportunity to turn to God before they take the fatal identifying mark of the beast as the following verses (Revelation 14:9-11) indicate.

Notice, they are commanded to do three things in view of God's coming judgment:
1. Fear God [Faith must be exercised before one can fear God]
2. Give Him glory [Glorifying God is the result of repenting (Revelation 16:9) being in a right relationship to God]
3. Worship Him [True worship can only be accomplished through faith and repentance, worshipping in spirit and in truth]

(2) *"And there followed another angel, saying, Babylon is fallen, is fallen, that great city, because she made all nations drink of the wine of the wrath of her fornication." (Revelation 14:8)*

The destruction of false world religion is foretold here, and is described later in chapter eighteen. God's purpose in announcing this event at this point in time is to warn those who are involved in this false religious system. First, He gives opportunity for true worship, then, He warns of the coming destruction of false worship.

(3) *"And the third angel followed them, saying with a loud voice, If any man worship the beast and his image, and receive his mark in his forehead, or in his hand, The same shall drink of the wine of the wrath of God, which is poured out without mixture into the cup of his indignation; and he shall be tormented with fire and brimstone in the presence of the holy angels, and in the presence of the Lamb." (Revelation 14:9, 10)*

This third angel also deals with the consequences of false worship underlining the eternal penalty of torment in the lake of fire (Revelation 19:20, 20:15). These three worship announcements by the angels of God will be given prior to the Day of the Lord judgment of God some time during the last half of the 70th Week of Daniel.

But, before the fourth angel appears, John sees the Lord Himself: *"And I looked, and behold a white cloud, and upon the cloud one sat like unto the Son of man, having on His head a golden crown, and in His hand a sharp sickle." (Revelation 14:14)*

While the first three angels brought messages of mercy, the Lord Jesus Christ divides the two sets of three angels, being seen as the Divine Judge, for God has:

"Given Him authority to execute judgment also, because He is the Son of man." (John 5:27) as *"He hath appointed a day, in the which He will judge the world in righteousness by that Man [the Lord Jesus Christ] whom He hath ordained; whereof He hath given assurance unto all men, in that He has raised Him from the dead." (Acts 17:31)* That day has now come!

(4) *"And another angel came out of the temple, crying with a loud voice to Him that sat on the cloud, Thrust in Thy sickle, and reap: for the time is come for Thee to reap; for the harvest of the earth is ripe. And He that sat on the cloud thrust in His sickle on the earth; and the earth was reaped." (Revelation 14:15, 16)*

Notice the chain of command: God the Father formally sends His divine message from His heavenly temple by His angel, to God the Son, in order to begin the execution of His divine judgment upon the earth for: *"The harvest of the earth is ripe"*. The three global angelic announcements extending God's mercy have already been given.

Now, it is time for the final judgment of God to begin. All three of these angels of judgment proceed *"out of the temple/altar"* in heaven, directly from God the Father where all authority resides, which authority has been given to His Son:
'All power [authority] is given unto Me in heaven and in earth' (Matthew 28:18) spoken by the Lord Jesus Christ at the beginning of this age. Now, at the end of the age, He, as the Divine Judge is formally given the command from His Father, by His angel, to begin the most prophesied event in all of Scripture: The great and dreadful Day of the Lord!

(5) *"And another angel came out of the temple which is in heaven, he also having a sharp sickle.*
(6) *And another angel came out from the altar, which had power over fire; and cried with a loud cry to him that had the sharp sickle, saying, Thrust in thy sharp sickle, and gather the clusters of the vine of the earth; for her grapes are fully ripe. And the angel thrust in his sickle into the earth, and gathered the vine of the earth, and cast it into the great winepress of the wrath of God." (Revelation 14:18, 19)*

These two angels perform as a team, with one bringing the

114

message from God and the other gathering the clusters of the vine of the earth casting them into the winepress. The last verse in this section indicates that the angels are working to prepare the final judgment for the Lord Jesus Christ:

"And the winepress was trodden without the city, and blood came out of the winepress, even unto the horse bridles, by the space of a thousand and six hundred furlongs." (Revelation 14:20)

The treading of the winepress will be accomplished by the Lord Jesus Christ at the end of the Day of the Lord (Revelation 19:15) at the battle of Armageddon which will bring about the gruesome mega-flow of blood mentioned above. The distance given for the blood flow is about 184 miles, which also approximates the north-south length of the Holy Land.

Isaiah also refers to this same event:
Question:
"Who is this that comes from Edom, with dyed garments from Bozrah? This that is glorious in His apparel, traveling in the greatness of His strength?"
Answer:
"I [the Lord Jesus Christ] that speak in righteousness, mighty to save."
Question:
"Wherefore [Why] are Thou red in Thy apparel, and Thy garments like him that treads the winefat?"
Answer:
"I have trodden the winepress alone; and of the people there was none with Me: for I will tread them in My anger, and trample them in My fury; and their blood shall be sprinkled upon My garments, and I will stain all My raiment. For the day of vengeance [Day of the Lord] is in My heart, and the year of My redeemed is come." (Isaiah 63:1-4)

"And I saw another sign in heaven, great and marvelous, seven angels having the seven last plagues; for in them is filled up the wrath of God." (Revelation 15:1)

This chapter, which serves as an introduction to the seven vial judgments, also provides key information concerning God's wrath:
1. The seven vials are *"the seven last plagues"* indicating the

necessity of first plagues which are the seven trumpets. (Revelation 9:20).

2. The global wrath of God is *"filled up"* or finished with these seven last plagues.

3. These two sets of plagues/judgments were all sent from God and administered by His angels.

However, the seven seals are not called *"plagues"* nor were they sent from God or administered by His angels. They are not considered to be part of His Day of the Lord wrath. Remember that God has promised the saints that they will be delivered from His wrath (I Thessalonians 1:10, 5:9), not the tribulation of the Antichrist.

This is exactly what the seven seals encompass for they end with the sign of the coming Day of the Lord's wrath (Revelation 6:12-17) which sign occurs *"after that [great] tribulation"* (Matthew 24:29) and just **before** the Day of the Lord begins:
*"And I will show wonders in the heavens and in the earth, blood, fire, and pillars of smoke. The sun shall be turned into darkness, and the moon into blood, **before** the great and terrible day of the Lord come." (Joel 2:30, 31)*

"And after that I looked, and, behold, the temple of the tabernacle of the testimony in heaven was opened: And the seven angels came out of the temple, having the seven plagues, clothed in pure and white linen, and having their breasts girded with golden girdles. And one of the four beasts gave unto the seven angels seven golden vials full of the wrath of God, who lives for ever and ever. And the temple was filled with smoke from the glory of God, and from His power; and no man was able to enter into the temple, till the seven plagues of the seven angels were fulfilled." (Revelation 15:5-8)

This is God's heavenly preparation for the grand finale of His global judgment. The temple, tabernacle and testimony are all mentioned. The angels are uniquely clothed. The four beasts are involved as God's heavenly temple messengers to bring His seven golden vials to His seven angels and the heavenly temple is filled with the smoke of God's presence, power and glory like in the days of Solomon (II Chronicles 5:13, 14) when the first most glorious earthly temple was dedicated.

This magnificent heavenly preparation has all the earmarks of the global finale of the Day of the Lord being staged as God's Day nears its close…but, not before these *"seven last plagues"* are executed by His holy angels. Chapter sixteen is taken up with these seven angels pouring out the seven vials of final judgment.

"And the seventh angel poured out his vial into the air; and there came a great voice out of the temple of heaven, for the throne, saying, It is done. And there were voices, and thunders, and lightnings; and there was a great earthquake, such as was not since men were upon the earth, so mighty and earthquake, and so great. And the great city [Jerusalem] was divided into three parts, and the cities of the nations fell: and great Babylon came in remembrance before God, to give unto her the cup of the wine of the fierceness of His wrath. And every island fled away, and the mountains were not found. And there fell upon men a great hail out of heaven, every stone about the weight of a talent: and men blasphemed God because of the plague of the hail; for the plague thereof was exceeding great." (Revelation 16:17-21)

The Lord proclaims three simple words: *"It is done"*. This brings about the closing **global** supernatural phenomena including the greatest earthquake ever. It causes the city of Jerusalem to be divided in three parts, all the cities on earth to fall, the islands and mountains to literally disappear, followed by hailstones from heaven weighing 75 pounds falling upon men eliciting their blasphemy of God.

Although God's program of global judgment upon the earth and its inhabitants has formally ended, He turns His attention to *"Great Babylon"* as it has come *"in remembrance before God"*.

Chapter seventeen and eighteen focus upon this event with God's angels continuing to be the instruments He uses to accomplish His work of judgment:

"And there came one of the seven angels which had the seven vials, and talked with me, saying unto me, Come hither; I will show unto thee the judgment of the great whore that sits upon many waters: With whom the kings of the earth have committed fornication, and the inhabitants of the earth have been made drunk with the wine of her fornication. So he carried me away in the spirit into the wilderness: and I saw a woman sit upon a scarlet colored beast, full of names of blasphemy, having seven heads and ten horns. And the woman was

arrayed in purple and scarlet color, and decked with gold and precious stones and pearls, having a golden cup in her hand full of abominations and filthiness of her fornication: And upon her forehead was a name written, MYSTERY, BABYLON THE GREAT, THE MOTHEER OF HARLOTS AND ABOMINATIONS OF THE EARTH.' And I saw the woman drunken with the blood of the saints, and with the blood of the martyrs of Jesus: and when I saw her, I wondered with great admiration." (Revelation 17:1-6)

John is given a supernatural tour in the wilderness revealing two symbolic enemies of God, the great whore representing false religion, indicated by the title written upon her forehead, and the scarlet colored beast which is the 8th beast kingdom, the revived Roman ten king empire of the Antichrist.
"And the angel said unto me, Wherefore didst thou marvel? I will tell thee the mystery of the woman, and of the beast that carries her, which has the seven heads and ten horns." (Revelation 17:7)

In the remainder of chapter seventeen the angel gives John a thorough explanation of exactly who and how these two entities will intertwine, with the whore eventually being destroyed by God utilizing the *"ten horns/kings"* as His instruments of judgment upon the whore (Revelation 17:16, 17).

Chapter eighteen begins by introducing another angel:
"And after these things I saw another angel come down from heaven, having great power; and the earth was lightened with his glory. And he cried mightily with a strong voice, saying, Babylon the great is fallen, is fallen, and is become the habitation of devils, and the hold of every foul spirit, and a cage of every unclean and hateful bird. For all nations have drunk of the wine of the wrath of her fornication, and the kings of the earth have committed fornication with her, and the merchants of the earth are waxed rich through the abundance of her delicacies." (Revelation 18:1-3)

This pronouncement reveals the corrupt and wicked nature of this false religious system as it has effected all nations and their leaders both in politics and business. The majority of chapter eighteen records the lament over the destruction of Babylon by these three groups of men:

1. The kings of the earth (Revelation 18:9, 10)
2. The merchants of the earth (Revelation 18:11-17a)
3. The merchants of the sea (Revelation 18:17b-19)

"And a mighty angel took up a stone like a great millstone, and cast it into the sea, saying, Thus with violence shall that great city Babylon be thrown down, and shall be found no more at all."
(Revelation 18:21)

Here, the mighty angel illustrates how violent the overthrow and destruction of Babylon will be when the ten kings turn upon her and bring about her devastating demise. This will occur near the end of the Day of the Lord, just before the battle of Armageddon.

"And I saw an angel standing in the sun; and he cried with a loud voice, saying to all the fowls that fly in the midst of heaven, Come and gather yourselves together unto the supper of the great God; That ye may eat the flesh of kings, and the flesh of captains, and the flesh of mighty men, and the flesh of horses, and of them that sit on them, and the flesh of all men, both free and bond, both small and great."
(Revelation 19:17)

The battle of Armageddon is about to take place. The Lord Jesus Christ has appeared on His white horse as *"King of kings, and Lord of lords" (Revelation 19:11-16)*. God's angel invites all the birds of heaven, before the battle begins, to God's supper spelling out specifically the flesh of all kinds of different men and their horses that will make up the horrendous carnage at the end of the battle.

The rest of the chapter records exactly what the angel prophesied. The Apocalypse has ended and God's angels have performed their major role of executing His Day of the Lord judgment.

12

<u>The Prophet Elijah</u>

*"And Jesus answered and said unto them, Elijah truly shall **<u>first</u>** come, and restore all things. But I say unto you, that Elijah is come already, and they knew him not, but have done unto him whatsoever they listed. Likewise shall also the Son of man suffer of them. Then the disciples understood that He spoke unto them of John the Baptist." (Matthew 17:11-13)*

The event He is referring to when He said: *"Elijah truly shall **<u>first</u>** come, and restore all things"* is recorded in the last prophecy of the Old Testament:
*"Behold I will send you Elijah the prophet **<u>before</u>** the coming of the great and dreadful day of the Lord:*
And he shall turn the heart of the fathers to the children, and the heart of the children to their fathers, lest I come and smite the earth with a curse." (Malachi 4:5, 6)

One of the major events on God's agenda is the sending of this last Elijah-like prophet. He will be given a two-fold ministry. First of all, he will be an integral part of the Lord's preparation of His people, turning the hearts of both Jew and Gentile.

The second facet of his ministry will be to *"restore all things"* pertaining to the *"holy covenant" (Daniel 11:28-32)* because the first 69 weeks of Daniel were under the Old Covenant. Elijah will be responsible to not only revive the hearts of God's people but also to restore those necessary Old Covenant *"things"* prior to the 70th Week of Daniel as spoken by the Lord Jesus Christ.

He will be sent **<u>before</u>** the climactic and unparalleled time of judgment of the earth and its population called the Day of the Lord, which begins during the last half of the 70th Week of Daniel.

His ministry will begin some time prior to the mid-point of the 70th

Week when the *"abomination of desolation"* occurs stopping the regular sacrifice. This regular sacrifice will have begun earlier (Daniel 8:14) through the *"restore all things"* ministry of this last Elijah-like prophet.

Indeed, the Lord will, once again, be sending prophets to His people the Jews. These prophets will not just be affecting the land of Israel as in Old Testament days for, like *"the two prophets"* of Revelation 11:3-14, this last Elijah will likely have a worldwide ministry during his time of the end tenure as he ministers to the hearts of God's people.

It would not have been necessary for the Lord to send this last Elijah-like prophet had the Jews received John the Baptist, as the Lord Jesus Christ indicated:
"For all the prophets and the law prophesied until John [the Baptist]. And if ye will receive it, this is Elijah, which was for to come." (Matthew 11:13, 14)

But, they did not receive him. If they had, the Lord would have continued with His Day of the Lord program as already spelled out in the Old Testament. Instead their rejection of John and the Christ he was heralding, has brought Jew and Gentile alike to this very time in the plan of God.

During the close of the end of the age and before the beginning of the Day of the Lord, God will surely send this last Elijah to *"restore"* those things that He requires which *"restitution"* Peter also spoke of in his second sermon:
*"And He shall send Jesus Christ, which before was preached unto you: Whom the heaven must receive **until** the times of restitution [restoration] of all things, which God hath spoken by the mouth of all His holy prophets since the world began." (Acts 3:20, 21)*

Here Peter indicates the return of the Lord Jesus Christ will not occur *"until the times of restitution of all things"* confirming that the Lord Jesus Christ's Second Coming will not occur **until** this last Elijah-like prophet restores those necessary things and is ministering to the hearts of men.

This word *"restitution"*, a noun only used this one time in the New Testament, also contains the Greek root of the verb *"restore"* the Lord Jesus used in Matthew 17:11 meaning "to restore to its former state" indicating the restoration of certain things.

This same Greek root is found in the word translated *"shall turn again"* of Malachi 4:5:
"And behold I will send to you Elias the Thesbite, before the great and glorious day of the Lord comes; who shall turn again the heart of the father to the son, and the heart of a man to his neighbor, lest I come and smite the earth grievously."

This verse is found in the Septuagint, the Greek Old Testament, a translation of the Hebrew that was the people's Bible before and during New Testament times and is still actively used by certain orthodox Christians in eastern Europe.

Over 90% of the Old Testament quotations in the New Testament find their source in this translation, which the Lord Jesus Himself utilized when He spoke of Elijah's future ministry of restoration in Matthew 17:11 that will occur:
1. Before the Return of the Lord (Acts 3:20, 21)
2. Before the Day of the Lord (Malachi 4:5, 6)

The Lord will send His prophet, the Elijah mentioned above, who will definitely *"restore all things"* indicating his ministry will not be unlike the original Elijah. He in God's wisdom set the stage for the coming of the second Elijah, John the Baptist, who in like manner has accomplished the same for the third.

The Holy Spirit of God, knowing and announcing God's plan as it unfolds will direct him, like the first and second Elijah. The first Elijah knew with absolute certainty exactly where, when and what God was planning in order to accomplish His will for His people as he gave the now famous ultimatum to king Ahab concerning the 3-1/2 year drought (I Kings 17:1)

His preparation for this notable day caused him to have earth shaking faith as he immersed himself in the Word of God thereby receiving the Holy Spirit's understanding that the Lord was about to bring a period of drought upon the earth in response to the idolatrous conduct of His people (Deuteronomy 11:16, 17).

He later made another great ultimatum to Gods people, *"How long halt ye between two opinions? If the Lord be God, follow Him: but if Baal, then follow him" (I Kings 18:21)* followed by the renowned contest between God and Baal (I Kings 18:22-40).

His mighty prayer is recorded near the end of this contest:
"Lord God of Abraham, Isaac, and of Israel, let it be known this day that Thou art God in Israel, and that I am Thy servant, and that I have done all these things at Thy word. Hear me, O LORD, hear me, that this people may know that Thou art the LORD God, and that Thou hast turned their heart back again." (I Kings 18:36, 37)

This brought down the all-consuming fire of God from heaven eliciting the submission and worship of the people. This Holy Spirit filled prayer by God's servant was what it took for God to turn their hearts, which in like manner is what it will take at the end of the age when the last Elijah will accomplish his service to God.

John the Baptist, the second Elijah, after preaching repentance preparing the hearts of God's people, announced the arrival of God's Lamb when Jesus approached on the banks of Jordan the day He was made known publicly at His baptism:
"Behold the Lamb of God Who takes away the sin of the world." (John 1:29)

In the three days recorded in John 1:19-36 John the Baptist would experience the culmination of his ministry when the first day the unbelieving Jews asked him, *"Art thou Elijah?"* and the second day saw *"Jesus coming unto him, and said, Behold the Lamb of God which takes away the sin of the world"* and the third day *"looking upon Jesus as He walked, he said, Behold the Lamb of God."*

John knew who Jesus was, and exactly what He came to do for all of mankind long before the Lord Jesus Christ died on the Cross of Calvary for our sins. He was completely accurate in his proclamations concerning the Christ, the Jewish Messiah, Who came to save His people from their sin.

It was John, like Elijah before him, who preached repentance to God's people, turning their hearts, preparing them for the Coming of the Lord. In like manner, this last Elijah-like prophet will follow the example of the two Elijahs before him preaching repentance to the people of God.

With two Elijahs now past, some conclusions can be drawn from the Biblical record concerning the third and last Elijah. This powerful Hebrew prophet will come during the end of the age, before the coming of Christ/Day of the Lord to *"restore all things"* in the spirit and power of his two predecessors.

If God continues to be *"the same yesterday, today and forever" (Hebrews 13:8)* this prophet's ministry will multiply in a progressive manner. The scope of his ministry will increase from being strictly to the Jews in the land of Israel to include all the saints of the existing church worldwide.

In addition, these (12) Characteristics of John the Baptist's ministry, recorded in Matthew 3:1-12, provide valuable insight into the future ministry of this last Elijah-like prophet:
1. He stood in a difficult place and time (v.1)
2. He preached an unpopular message (v.2)
3. He stood alone (v.3)
4. He was a Biblical separatist/non-conformist (v.4)
5. He had God-given magnetism (v.5)
6. He got results in his ministry (v.6)
7. He spoke out against God's enemies (v.7)
8. He was confident in his life changing message (v.8)
9. He denounced religious tradition (v.9)
10. He proclaimed God's judgment (v.10)
11. He announced the coming of Christ (v.11)
12. He described the ministry of Christ (v.12)
[Source: Sermon by Pastor Al Dickerson]

We can look to the Scripture with strong confidence and great expectation concerning this mighty prophet of God, for he, too, will:
1. Call God's people to repentance
2. Confront the political leader, the Antichrist
3. Condemn the false religious leader, the false prophet

He definitely will be the instrument God uses to restore the *"holy covenant" (Daniel 11:28-32)*. He will also be the likely leader of those who will evangelize the Jews (Daniel 11:33, 12:3) as *"all Israel shall be saved" (Romans 15:26)* when their Deliverer, the Lord Jesus Christ, will *"bring in everlasting righteousness" (Daniel 9:24)* at the end of the 70th Week of Daniel.

Restoration/revival of the nation of Israel, will be his focus, like the day when they said, *"The LORD, He is the God; The LORD HE is the God." (I Kings 18:39)* in response to God's all consuming fire. The revival of God's people, which was the result of the first and second Elijah's ministry, will also be one of the primary goals of this last Elijah.

The Lord's sending of the third Elijah spoken of in Malachi 4:5, 6; Mathew 17:11; Mark 9:12 appears to be on the very doorstep of His prophetic plan that must occur during *"the beginning of sorrows" (Matthew 24:4-8)*. This happens prior to *"the great tribulation" (Matthew 24:9-28)* when the faithful of the nation of Israel will be scattered (Matthew 24:15-28) during the Antichrist's global war with the church saints (Daniel 7:21-25; Revelation 13:1-18). Satan's primary focus will be centered upon the faithful Jews in the nation of Israel (Daniel 11:21-12:1; Revelation 12:1-17).

Like the successful evangelists of old and his two forerunnners (Elijah & John the Baptist) whom the Lord sent to His people, his emphasis will be upon repentance providing the Lord with the opportunity to *"turn the hearts"* of His people, the Jews and Gentiles, within the Church.

Exactly when the restoration of the *"holy covenant" (Daniel 11:28-32)* takes place is not clearly specified. However, it will be part of the ministry of this prophet to *"restore all things"* which will have to take place prior to the last 3-1/2 years of the 70th Week of Daniel. And it is likely to be in effect before the beginning of the 70th Week, as, the Antichrist's involvement with the *"daily sacrifice"* begins after he makes a covenant with the Jews at the beginning of the 70th Week and continues 2300 days or *"evenings and mornings" (Daniel 8:14)*.

The time leading up to the 70th Week of Daniel will be occupied by Elijah's ministry of restoration including:
1. The revival of God's people
2. The restoration of all things regarding the *"holy covenant"*

The Antichrist will rise to power during this same timeframe, confirming a covenant with the many of the nation of Israel (Daniel 9:27) at the beginning of the 70th Week of Daniel. Then, after 220 days, the host and regular sacrifice will be given over (Daniel 8:12) to the Antichrist lasting for the next 1040 days.

The culmination of his wicked influence occurs at the mid-point of the 70th Week of Daniel. His forces will stop the regular sacrifice and pollute the sanctuary by setting up his image in the holy place for the remaining 1260 days of the 70th Week which is the renowned *"abomination of desolation"* indicated by the Lord (Matthew 24:15).

The sending of Elijah to *"restore all things"* (Matthew 17:11; Mark 9:12) will include:
1. The building of "*the temple of God*"
   (II Thessalonians 2:4; Revelation 11:1, 2)
2. The "*the holy place*" included
   (Matthew 24:15; Revelation 11:1)
3. The restoration of the "*holy covenant*" (Daniel 11:28-32)
4. The institution of the "*regular sacrifice*"
   (Daniel 8:11-13, 9:27, 11:31, 12:11)
5. The implementation of "*the Sabbath*" (Matthew 24:20)
6. The recognition of "*the twelve tribes*" (Revelation 7:3-8)
7. The "*turning of the hearts*" of the people of God
   (Malachi 4:5, 6)

He will make ready a people prepared for the coming of the Lord in order:
*"That He [The Lord Jesus Christ] might present it to Himself a glorious church, **not having spot or wrinkle or any such thing; but that it should be holy and without blemish**." (Ephesians 5:27)*
*"And the very God of peace sanctify you wholly; and I pray God your whole spirit and soul and body **be preserved blameless unto the coming of our Lord Jesus Christ.**" (I Thessalonians 5:23)*

*"For the grace of God that brings salvation has appeared to all men, Teaching us that denying ungodliness and worldly lusts, we should live soberly, righteously, and godly, in this present world; Looking for that blessed hope, and the glorious appearing of the great God and our Savior Jesus Christ; Who gave Himself for us, that He might redeem us from all iniquity, and **purify unto Himself** a peculiar people, zealous of good works."* *(Titus 2:12-14)*

*"Beloved, now are we the sons of God, and it does not yet appear what we shall be: but we know **that when He shall appear, we shall be like Him**; for we shall see Him as He is. And every man that has this hope in **him purifies himself, even as He is pure."** (I John 3:3)*

*"Now unto Him that is able to keep you from falling and **to present you faultless before the presence of His glory** with exceeding joy, To the only wise God our Savior, be glory and majesty, dominion and power, both now and ever. Amen."* *(Jude 24, 25)*

Although the above verses contain exhortations for God's people to live holy lives during the present day, they also imply the condition of God's people when He returns. This last Elijah will preach repentance/revival as those two before him and thereby make ready a people prepared for the return of the Lord.

God's sending of this mighty Elijah-like Hebrew prophet is on the Lord's prophetic horizon and will take place in due course as a necessary prerequisite for the unfolding of God's plan during the 70th Week of Daniel and the Day of the Lord.

13

The Martyrs

Throughout the history of the faithful, martyrdom was prevalent as "Foxes Book of Martyrs" accurately chronicles, for the Church of Jesus Christ has experienced an almost countless number of saints being put to death for their unwavering faith in the Lord Jesus Christ.

As the end of the age draws near, martyrdom of God's people is increasing. As Daniel 11:32-35 indicates, after the abomination of desolation (Matthew 24:15) when the Antichrist demands world worship (Revelation 13), there will be many who will not take the mark of the beast and will consequently be put to death for their faithfulness to the Lord:

"And they that understand among the people shall instruct many: yet they shall fall by the sword, and by flame, by captivity, and by spoil many days." (Daniel 11:33)

"And when He had opened the fifth seal, I saw under the altar the souls of them that were slain for the word of God, and for the testimony which they held." (Revelation 6:9)

These specific martyrs are inquiring of the Lord:
"How long, O Lord, holy and true, dost Thou not judge and avenge our blood on them that dwell on the earth?" (Revelation 6:10)

They want to know how long it will be until the Lord judges those who are responsible for their deaths indicating that God's Day of the Lord judgment of those responsible, who are still alive, had not yet begun.

That one of the seven seals is fully devoted to these end of the age martyrs, reveals the prominence of martyrdom during the close of this age when the Antichrist has his way in the world causing God's people to be slaughtered for their obedience to the Word of God, and their Christian testimony.

The Lord's response to these martyrs supplies additional information concerning end of the age martyrs:
"And white robes were given unto every one of them, that they should rest yet for a little season, until their fellow servants also and their brethren, that should be killed as they were, should be fulfilled." *(Revelation 6:11)*

According to this text, they are given a three-fold response:
1. They are given white robes like their brethren the raptured and resurrected saints who also appear in heaven (Revelation 7:9, 13, 14).
2. They are told to rest yet for a little [brief] season.
3. They are told that there is a certain predetermined number of their *"fellow servants"* who will have the high privilege of being martyred for the cause of the Lord Jesus Christ, just as most of the apostles and many prophets and saints of past ages have accomplished in their service for their Lord.

The book of the Revelation records the Holy Spirit-filled warfare principles of these end of the age martyrs:
"For the accuser of our brethren [Satan] is cast down, which accused them before our God day and night. And they overcame him by the blood of the Lamb and the word of their testimony, and they loved not their lives unto the death." *(Revelation 12:10b, 11)*

There are three key elements to having victory over Satan:
1. The overcoming warrior will rely totally upon the atoning sacrificial Blood of the Lamb which supplies the necessary cleansing power (I John 1:9) to give the saint the required personal holiness needed to stand blameless before the throne of God victorious over the accusations of Satan.
2. The word of their testimony is the result of personal holiness which provides the saint with access into the very presence of the Lord (Hebrews 12:14).
3. They loved not their lives unto the death describes their attitude of complete selflessness totally giving themselves as *"Sheep unto the slaughter"* for the glory of their Lord as was the Apostle Paul's

desire:

"That I may know Him and the power of His resurrection and the fellowship of His suffering being made conformable unto His death."
(Philippians 3:10)

The next incident of martyrdom in Scripture supplies much detail and is a most graphic incident of martyrdom as the *"two witnesses"* of (Revelation 11:3-13) are killed by the Antichrist after their ministry on earth is complete:

"The beast...shall make war with them, and shall overcome them, and kill them. And their dead bodies shall lie in the street of the great city, which spiritually is called Sodom and Egypt, where also our Lord was crucified." (Revelation 11:7, 8)

Although they will have a powerful ministry of judgment in the earth during the last half of Daniel's 70th week, they will come to a violent end as they die at the hands of *"the beast"* being martyred and subsequently left lying in the streets of Jerusalem:

"And they of the people and kindreds and tongues and nations shall see their dead bodies three days and an half, and shall not suffer their dead bodies to be put in graves. And they that dwell upon the earth shall rejoice over them, and make merry, and shall send gifts one to another; because these two prophets tormented them that dwelt on the earth." (Revelation 11:9, 10)

At this point it appears that *"the beast"* has won the day. All the world is viewing the corpses of these mighty prophets of God as the electronic media beams around the globe the literal proof of this supposed victory of their ruthless leader, the Antichrist.

There is a worldwide party atmosphere including the almost unthinkable *"sending of gifts"* as though the most celebrated event of that time has taken place. But, as the Scripture records, God always has the last word and He is not finished with His two servants just yet.

"And after three days and an half the Spirit of life from God entered into them, and they stood upon their feet; and great fear fell upon them which saw them. And they heard a great voice from heaven saying unto them, Come up hither, And they ascended up to heaven in a cloud; and their enemies beheld them."(Revelation 11:11, 12)

The Lord miraculously resurrects His servants and *"Great fear fell upon them which saw them"* indicating the world will also witness the climactic ending of this event with the natural response of fear. They in essence have shown their approval of the deaths of these two servants of God demonstrated by their worldwide celebration during the previous 3-1/2 days.

"And the same hour there was a great earthquake, and the tenth part of the city fell, and in the earthquake were slain of men seven thousand: and the remnant [remainder] were affrighted, and gave glory to the God of heaven." (Revelation 11:13)

The Lord concludes this most significant episode of martyrdom in Scripture by sending an earthquake that destroys a tenth of the city of Jerusalem resulting in the deaths of seven thousand people.

The word translated *"remnant"* literally means remainder indicating that those who were not killed *"were affrighted"*, or terrified, which means thrown into a state of great fear.

Later, during the Day of the Lord, just before the *"seven last plagues"* (Revelation 15:1) which are the seven vial judgments, there are more martyrs seen in heaven:

"And I saw as it were a sea of glass mingled with fire: and them that had gotten the victory over the beast [the Antichrist], and over his image, and over his mark, and over the number of his name, stand on the sea of glass, having the harps of God. And they sing the song of Moses the servant of God, and the song of the Lamb, saying, GREAT AND MARVELLOUS ARE THY WORKS, LORD GOD ALMIGHTY, JUST AND TRUE ARE THY WAYS, THOU KING OF SAINTS. WHO SHALL NOT FEAR THEE, O Lord, AND GLORIFY THY NAME? FOR ALL NATIONS SHALL COME AND WORSHIP BEFORE THEE; for Thy judgments are made manifest." (Revelation 15:2-4)

These glorified saints appear in heaven during the time the Antichrist and his minions are still active in the earth. The great tribulation is over and the 70th Week of Daniel has ended with the sounding of the seventh trumpet and these glorified saints *"stand on the sea of glass"* which is *"before the throne" (Revelation 4:6)* of God. They are singing *"The song of Moses"* which was first sung by Moses and the children of Israel (Exodus 15:1-19) after the Lord miraculously wrought the victory over Pharaoh and his army.

At this juncture in God's plan, the Lord Jesus Christ has redeemed Israel:
"And the Redeemer shall come to Zion and unto them that turn from transgression in Jacob, saith the LORD." (Isaiah 59:20)

The redeemed are singing *"the song of the Lamb"* with the lyrics to this song being listed here in Revelation 15:3, 4 tying together and harmonizing the Old and New Covenant. The words are the expected responses to the *"everlasting gospel"* heralded by an angel to:
"Them that dwell on the earth...Fear God, and give glory to Him; for the hour of His judgment is come: and worship Him that made heaven, and earth, and the sea, and the fountains of waters." (Revelation 14:6, 7)

Three specific commands are given in the *"everlasting gospel"*:
1. Fear God
2. Give glory to Him
3. Worship Him

These martyrs singing *"the song of the Lamb"* sing those three expected responses:
1. *Who shall not fear Thee O Lord?*
2. *Who shall not give glory to Thy name?*
3. *For all nations shall come and worship before Thee*

Many of those who experience the supernatural judgment of God, when given the opportunity to repent, instead, do the exact opposite remaining openly defiant, rebellious and unrepentant:
"And the rest of the men which were not killed by these plagues yet repented not of the works of their hands, that they should not worship devils, and idols of gold, and silver, and brass, and stone, and of wood; which neither can see, nor hear, nor walk; Neither repented they of their murders, nor of their sorceries, nor of their fornication, nor of their thefts." (Revelation 9:10, 11)

Although the martyrs of Revelation 15:2-4 are not specifically identified, they are considered to be 70th Week Jewish martyrs because they appear at the end of the 70th Week immediately after

132

Israel is redeemed and they are singing the Old Covenant victory song of Moses which celebrates the deliverance of Israel.

After the seven trumpets end, which are the first series of plagues or judgments, those who dwell upon the earth are unrepentant and the last series of plagues/judgments, the seven vials, begins. The focus now turns to the judgment of those who are responsible for martyring the faithful:

"The men which had the mark of the beast, and upon them which worshipped his image." (Revelation 16:1)
"And the third angel poured out his vial upon the rivers and fountains of waters; and they became blood. And I heard the angel of the waters say, Thou art righteous, O Lord, which art, and was, and shall be, because Thou hast judged thus, For they have shed the blood of saints and prophets, and Thou hast given them blood to drink; for they are worthy. And I heard another out of the altar say, Even so, Lord God Almighty, true and righteous are Thy judgments." (Revelation 16:4-7)

But the earth dwellers do not respond favorably to these last plagues:

"And men were scorched with great heat, and blasphemed the name of God, which hath power over these plagues: and they repented not to give Him glory...And blasphemed the God of heaven because of their pains and their sores, and repented not of their deeds." (Revelation 16:9, 11)

They have now been given three opportunities to turn to God:
1. After the Great Tribulation the angel preaches the everlasting Gospel to the world (Revelation 14:6, 7)
2. After the seven trumpets at the end of Daniel's 70th Week they are unrepentant (Revelation 9:10, 11)
3. After the seven vials at the end of the Day of the Lord they remain unrepentant (Revelation 16:9, 11)

The next Scripture that refers to martyrs is found in Revelation 17:
"And I saw the woman [MYSTERY BABYLON THE GREAT, THE MOTHER OF HARLOTS AND ABOMINATIONS OF THE EARTH] drunken with the blood of the martyrs of Jesus: and when I saw her I wondered with great admiration." (Revelation 17:6)

The woman in this passage most likely represents the false religious system of Romanism/Roman Catholicism, which has been responsible for martyring countless saints throughout the 1600 years of its existence. Notice, these are specifically called *"The martyrs of Jesus"* which refers to those saints who are part of His body, the Church.

The woman in Revelation 17 is introduced and described, along with her willing partner in crime *"the beast"*, upon which she is sitting who is the means of her transport. The beast represents those political kingdoms who were and are willing accomplices in the martyrdom of the faithful and the coming mega-beast kingdom, the Antichrist and his ten nation empire.

The woman's destruction is prophesied and in the concluding verse of chapter eighteen this fitting summary is recorded:
"And in her was found the blood of prophets, and of saints, and of all that were slain upon the earth."

This underscores and fully belies the justifiable cause for her violent destruction. But, the Lord is not finished condemning her murderous acts:
"After these things I heard a great voice of much people in heaven, saying, Alleleuia; Salvation, and glory and honor, and power, unto the Lord our God. FOR TRUE AND RIGHTEOUS ARE HIS JUDGMENTS: for He hath judged the great whore, which did corrupt the earth with her fornication, and HATH AVENGED THE BLOOD OF HIS SERVANTS AT HER HAND." (Revelation 19:1, 2)

The multitudes in heaven, the glorified saints, now take part in the rejoicing after this number one enemy of God's children has been judged. This heavenly celebration continues as all of heaven joins in proclaiming the now famous Alleluia chorus found in this passage (Revelation 19:1-4).

Not only are those men who take the identification of the beast responsible for the martyrdom of God's end of the age servants, but the established world religious system, Romanism or Roman Catholicism, is justifiably destroyed for her part in the killing of God's servants during the Church age.

The last time martyrs are seen in the Scripture occurs at the very beginning of the Millennium:

"And I saw thrones, and they sat upon them, and judgment was given unto them: and I saw the souls of them that were beheaded for the witness of Jesus, and for the word of God, and which had not worshipped the beast, neither his image, neither had received his mark upon their foreheads, or in their hands; and they lived and reigned with Christ a thousand years." (Revelation 20:4)

One of the methods of martyrdom used during the end of the age, beheading, is presently [2007] being used by another religious enemy of Christianity, the radical Muslims. This may well be the religious system in control after Roman Catholicism is destroyed by God, through the agency of the *"ten horns [kings]"* indicated in Revelation 17:16.

As the prophetic Scripture is surveyed, it becomes clear that the martyrdom of the faithful will be commonplace during the end of the age becoming the rule rather than the exception. While martyrdom is the outworking of Satan's murderous minions on earth, in reality, it results in the most glorious and victorious home-going of the saint as they faithfully give all to the Lord by *"spending and being spent"* *(II Corinthians 12:15)* for the glory of God.

14

The Earth Dwellers

This certain people group called *"them that dwell upon the earth"* *(Revelation 3:10, 6:10, 11:10, 13:8, 12, 14, 14:6)* are also known as *"people and kindreds and tongues and nations" (Revelation 10:11, 11:9, 13:7)*. These two vivid descriptions identify those who are spiritually lost and act in direct opposition to the Lord and His people during the end times.

(1) The first time they appear in the book of the Revelation is when the church in Philadelphia is given this promise:
"Because thou hast kept the word of My patience, I also will keep thee from the hour of temptation, which shall try them that dwell upon the earth." (Revelation 3:10)

While some apply this verse to teach that the time of Great Tribulation (Matthew 24:21) will not come upon the Church saints it must be remembered that it (the Great Tribulation) will not be focused upon *"them that dwell upon the earth"*. Instead, the Great Tribulation is in fact described as Satan's *"great wrath"* or *"war with the saints"* *(Daniel 7:21; Revelation 12:12; 13:7)*.

According to the Apostle Paul those who are lost, the earth dwellers, will be saying *"peace and safety"* when *"the day of the Lord" (I Thessalonians 5:2)* overtakes them as *"as a thief"* *(I Thessalonians 5:3, 4)*.

While the Great Tribulation upon the saints is in process, the earth dwellers will be experiencing relative peace and safety until *"the hour of temptation"* God's wrath, the Day of the Lord *"comes upon them"* *(I Thessalonians 5:3)*.

Revelation 3:10 provides an assuring promise to the church in Philadelphia of being kept from God's wrath, which agrees with the Lord's multiple promises given by the Apostle Paul:

"Much more then, being now saved by His blood, we shall be saved from [the] wrath through Him." (Romans 5:9)

"And to wait for His Son from heaven, whom He raised from the dead, even Jesus, which delivered us from the wrath to come."
(I Thessalonians 1:10)

"For God hath not appointed us to wrath, but to obtain salvation [deliverance from the Day of the Lord] by our Lord Jesus Christ."
(I Thessalonians 5:9)

The saints will be raptured/rescued out of the Great Tribulation and received into heaven:
"After this I beheld, and, lo, a great multitude, which no man could number...these are they [raptured saints] which came out of [the] great tribulation." (Revelation 7:9, 14)

(2) The earth dwellers are also seen as the ones responsible for martyring God's people:
"And when He had opened the fifth seal, I saw under the altar the souls of them that were slain [martyrs] for the Word of God, and for the testimony which they held: And they cried with a loud voice, saying, How long, O Lord, holy and true, dost Thou not judge and avenge our blood on them that dwell on the earth?"
(Revelation 6:9, 10)

Those who presently dwell upon the earth have killed these martyrs who appear in heaven. They, the fifth seal martyrs, are calling for God's judgment upon those responsible. They want to know exactly how long is it going to be before He executes their deserved judgment. This question is asked prior to the Day of the Lord judgment, during the last half of the 70th Week of Daniel.

The time of their inquiry is determined by the next event, the opening of the sixth seal which reveals the sign of the Day of the Lord (Revelation 6:12-17) that occurs just *"before"* (Joel 2:30, 31) the Lord begins His Day of the Lord wrath. His wrath begins when the seventh seal is opened (Revelation 8:1) revealing the contents of the scroll which contains the seven trumpet judgments and the seven vial judgments (Revelation 8, 9, 15, 16).

(3) Then, after the first series of judgments, the seven trumpets, are almost complete, John is told:

"And he [the voice from heaven] said unto me, Thou must prophesy again before many peoples, and nations, and tongues, and kings." *(Revelation 10:11)*

Although intense global devastation has been poured out upon the earth and its inhabitants (over 1/3 of world population has died), John is told that he will have to continue his prophesying as he oversees the full and complete Day of the Lord judgments. This includes the seven vial judgments (Revelation 15, 16), the judgment of Babylon (Revelation 17, 18) and the final climactic conflict of the Day of the Lord, the battle of Armageddon (Revelation 19:11-21).

(4) *"And they of the people and kindreds and tongues and nations shall see their dead bodies [two witnesses] three days and a half, and shall not suffer their dead bodies to be put in graves. And they that dwell upon the earth shall rejoice over them, and make merry, and shall send gifts one to another; because these two prophets tormented them that dwell upon the earth." (Revelation 11:9, 10)*

After the death of the *"two witnesses"* a worldwide holiday/party atmosphere breaks out including the almost unthinkable act of "*sending of gifts*" as though the most celebrated event of that time has taken place (Revelation 11:10). But, as the Scripture records, God always has the last word and He is definitely not finished with His two witnesses just yet.

"And after three days and an half the Spirit of life from God entered into them, and they stood upon their feet; and great fear fell upon them which saw them. And they heard a great voice from heaven saying unto them, Come up hither, And they ascended up to heaven in a cloud; and their enemies beheld them." (Revelation 11:11, 12)

The Lord miraculously resurrects His two witnesses and *"great fear fell upon them which saw them"* indicating the climactic ending of this supernatural event. They, the earth dwellers, in essence, know they have participated in this horrendous event by showing their approval of the deaths of these two prophets of God, which is demonstrated by their grandiose worldwide celebration during the previous 3-1/2 days.

(5) *"And it was given unto him [Antichrist] to make war with the saints, and to overcome them: and power [authority] was given him over all kindreds, and tongues and nations. And all that dwell upon the earth shall worship him, whose names are not written in the book of life of the Lamb slain from the foundation of the world."* (Revelation 13:7, 8)

Two distinct facts concerning the earth dwellers are underlined in these verses:

1. Satan gives his authority to the Antichrist to rule over them (Revelation 13:7)
2. They subsequently fall in line and worship the Antichrist (Revelation 13:8)

This clearly indicates the global influence the Antichrist will have over the earth dwellers. He receives full and unfettered authority from Satan who is *"the god of this world"* (II Corinthians 4:4). In response, the earth dwellers give their complete devotion to this Satanically possessed world ruler thereby demonstrating their belief that he is divine, their god, whom they willingly worship.

(6) *"And I beheld another beast [the false prophet] (Revelation 16:13, 14) coming up out of the earth and he had two horns like a lamb. And he exercises all the power of the first beast [the Antichrist] before him, and causes the earth and them that dwell therein to worship the first beast, whose deadly wound was healed. And he does great wonders, so that he makes fire come down from heaven on the earth in the sight of men. And deceives them that dwell on the earth by the means of those miracles which he had power to do in the sight of the beast; saying to them that dwell on the earth, that they should make and image to the beast, which had the wound by a sword and did live."* (Revelation 13:11-14)

The introduction of the false prophet reveals that he is the author and enforcer of global Antichrist worship. It is through his agency that miracles are done causing the earth dwellers to be deceived. The false prophet also calls for the earth dwellers to make an image of the Antichrist. These two archenemies of God are vitally linked together for the false prophet only has power to do these deceptive miracles *"in the sight of the beast [Antichrist]."*

Three more facts emerge concerning the earth dwellers:
1. They worship the Antichrist under the direct enforcement of the false prophet (Revelation 13:12)
2. They are deceived by the miracles of the false prophet (Revelation 13:14a)
3. They make an image of the Antichrist by direct order from the false prophet (Revelation 13:14b)

(7) *"And I saw another angel fly in the midst of heaven, having the everlasting gospel to preach unto them that dwell on the earth, and to every nation, and kindred, and tongue, and people, Saying with a loud voice, Fear God, and give glory to Him; for the hour of His judgment is come: and worship Him that made heaven, and earth, and the sea, and the fountains of waters." (Revelation 14:6, 7)*

This global announcement given to the earth dwellers is *"the everlasting gospel"* which is heralded worldwide prior to God's judgment the Day of the Lord. They are given the opportunity to turn to God before they take the fatal identifying mark of the beast as the following verses (Revelation 14:9-11) indicate.

Notice, they are commanded to do three things in view of God's coming judgment:
1. Fear God [Faith must be exercised first before one can fear God]
2. Give Him glory [Glorifying God is the result of repenting (Revelation 16:9) being in a right relationship to God]
3. Worship Him [True worship can only be accomplished by faith and repentance, worshipping in spirit and in truth

"And the third angel followed them, saying with a loud voice, If any man worship the beast and his image, and receive his mark in his forehead, or in his hand, The same shall drink of the wine of the wrath of God, which is poured out without mixture into the cup of His indignation; and he shall be tormented with fire and brimstone in the presence of the holy angels, and in the presence of the Lamb. And the smoke of their torment ascends up for ever and ever: and they have no rest day or night, which worship the beast and his image, and whosoever receives the mark of his name." (Revelation 14:9-11

The first angel in this series gives the earth dwellers three positive

140

commands for worshiping God in view of His coming judgment. The second foretells God's judgment of the false worship system of Babylon, and the third gives the negative aspect of worshiping the beast. All three of these angels are giving global announcements concerning worship to the earth dwellers prior to the Day of the Lord.

However, the great majority of the earth dwellers will not heed God's gracious warnings:

"And the rest of the men which were not killed by these plagues [The Six Trumpet Judgments] **yet repented not** *of the works of their hands, that they should not worship devils, and idols of gold, and silver, and brass, and stone, and of wood: which neither can see, nor hear, nor walk:* **Neither repented they** *of their sorceries, nor of their fornications, nor of their thefts." (Revelation 9:20, 21)*

"And men were scorched with great heat, and blasphemed the name of God who has power over these plagues [The Seven Vial Judgments]: and **they repented not** *to give Him glory. And blasphemed the God of heaven because of their pains and their sores,* **and repented not of their deeds**. *And there fell upon men a great hail out of heaven, every stone about the weight of a talent [75 lb.]: and men blasphemed God because of the plague of the hail; for the plague thereof was exceeding great." (Revelation 16:9, 11, 21)*

These passages reveal the effect God's judgment will have upon the earth dwellers, even though He graciously gave clear warnings to all men worldwide. Notice, they had opportunity to repent, but, *"they repented not"*. Instead, they deliberately choose to continue their blasphemous rebellion against God, willingly worshiping *"the god of this world"* and sealing their fate in the process.

Their eternal doom will eventually be meted out when all those who refuse to repent and receive the Lord Jesus Christ will stand before God at the final judgment. This will occur at God's *"great white throne judgment"* when all those who have refused to receive the Lord Jesus Christ, including these earth dwellers, will be judged *"according to their works"*. They will then experience *"the second death"* which is eternal separation from God in the lake of fire. (Revelation 20:11-15)

The prophet Isaiah in the very beginning of his eschatological Day of the Lord prophecy called "The Little Apocalypse", which is found in Isaiah 24-27, tells of the coming judgment of these same earth dwellers/inhabitants of the earth:

*"Behold, the LORD makes the earth empty, and makes it waste, and turns it upside down, and scatters abroad the inhabitants thereof. And it shall be, as with the people, so with the priest; as with the servant, so with his master; as with the maid, so with her mistress; as with the buyer, so with the seller; as with the lender, so with the borrower; as with the taker of usury, so with the giver of usury to him. The land shall be utterly emptied, and utterly spoiled: for the LORD has spoken this word. The earth mourns and fades away, the world languishes and fades away, the haughty people of the earth do languish. The earth also is defiled under the inhabitants thereof; because they have transgressed the laws, changed the ordinances, broken the everlasting covenant. Therefore has the curse devoured **the earth, and they that dwell therein are desolate**: therefore **the inhabitants of the earth** are burned, and few men left." (Isaiah 24:1-6)*

Isaiah makes it crystal clear that God's judgment is universal, covering the entire earth, and every single inhabitant who is proud and has transgressed God's laws, changed His ordinances and broke His covenant will be judged.

F.C. Jennings in his commentary "Studies in Isaiah" p.279 writes on Isaiah 24:1-3:
"God will judge the world by that Man whom He hath appointed." It is true that from a human point of view, it was very far off in the day the prophet wrote; but it has come very near now, for that very same Spirit has taught us to *"see the day approaching"*. Does not the book of Revelation also tell the Churches of that *"hour of trial that is to come on all the world to try the earth-dwellers,"* precisely as does Isaiah?"

Isaiah later in this same chapter continues his Day of the Lord prophesy focusing on the earth dwellers:
*"But, I said, My leanness, my leanness, woe unto me! The treacherous dealers have dealt treacherously; yea, the treacherous dealers have dealt very treacherously. Fear, and the pit, and the snare, are upon thee, O **inhabitant of the earth**. And it shall come to pass, that he who*

flees from the noise of the fear shall fall into the pit; and he that comes up our of the midst of the pit shall be taken in the snare: for the windows from on high are open, and the foundations of the earth do shake." (Isaiah 24:16b-18)

Isaiah proclaims this horrific pronouncement upon the end times earth dwellers indicating there will be no escape from the all-consuming judgment of Jehovah God. He closes this powerful section of apocalyptic prophetic judgment upon the earth dwellers at the end of chapter twenty-six:

"For, behold, the LORD comes out of His place to punish __the inhabitants of the earth__ for their iniquity: the earth also shall disclose her blood and shall no more cover her slain." (Isaiah 26:21)

15.a

The 144 Thousand:
Their Ministry Overview

In Revelation 7:1-8 the New Testament introduces a most significant group of *"servants of our God" (Revelation 7:3)* also known as the 144 Thousand Sons of Israel.

They are from the twelve tribes of Israel and are sealed by the name of the Father and the name of the Lamb which are written on their foreheads (Revelation 7:3-8, 14:1).

These choice servants are somewhat of a mystery, especially concerning their end of the age purpose and spiritual condition at the time of their sealing. The actual time of their sealing is clearly fixed for it immediately follows the sign of the Second Coming of Christ and the Day of the Lord (Revelation 6:12-17; Matthew 24:29-31).

They are sealed by God's signature just before Christ's Coming occurs (Revelation 7:9-17; Matthew 24:30, 31) and the Day of the Lord begins (Revelation 8:1, 2). The Church saints that have been *"sealed [by the Holy Spirit] unto the day of redemption" (Ephesians 4:30)* will be raptured when He comes.

The day of redemption refers to the day the rapture occurs, for the church saints will not experience the great and dreadful Day of the Lord's wrath (I Thessalonians 1:9, 5:10). But, the 144 Thousand, who are sealed by the signature of God (Revelation 14:1) will be protected and remain active on earth, serving the Lord, after the rapture during the Day of the Lord (Revelation 9:4, 14:1-5, 17:14).

Just before the Church saints are raptured, they will "Pass the Torch" as it were, to these 144 Thousand servants of God in order that the priesthood and testimony of the Lord Jesus Christ continue throughout the coming Day of the Lord.

This Redemption Ministry in effect will be their primary charge during the Day of the Lord when they will evangelize those Jews (Daniel 11:32-35, 12:3) and Gentiles (Isaiah 19:16-25; Micah 7:15-17) whom God will redeem during that time.

One of the important questions concerning the 144 Thousand is their spiritual condition at the time they are sealed, and there are only two options, are they saved or unsaved when they are sealed? This significant group of "The People of the Apocalypse", the 144 Thousand *"of all the tribes of the children [sons] of Israel" (Revelation 7:4)*, are physically marked by the Lord.

Although there are others upon whom the Lord puts His mark described in the pages of Scripture, this group, appearing numerous times in the Word of God, is the most notable. They are called *"servants of our God"* **before** they are sealed and as the end times are studied they also appear a number of other places supplying indicators of their spiritual condition at the time they are sealed in Revelation 7:3-8.

Determining the exact point in time that they are sealed is also important to note in order to discern just exactly what it is that the Lord has for them to accomplish. The text isolates their sealing by utilizing time indicating phrases to set off this major event: *"And after these things" (Revelation 7:1)*, *"After this" (Revelation 7:9)*, demonstrating the uniqueness and importance of what takes place between these two phrases.

Their sealing occurs immediately after the sign of the Second Coming of Christ and the Day of the Lord (Revelation 6:12-6:17) and just before the rapture of the saints (Revelation 7:9-7). Both of these events occur on the same day as taught by the Lord in Luke 17:22-37. The Lord will surely deliver the saints before He initiates His wrath-filled judgment just as He has done in the past and just as He promised to do in the future (I Thessalonians 1:10, 5:9).

Therefore, the 144 Thousand are sealed just before the Day of the Lord begins since they appear with the Lord Jesus Christ later, during the Day of the Lord in Revelation 14:1-5, 17:14. They also are referred to in Revelation 9:4 and 12:17 with all of these texts

145

supplying additional information concerning this key end of the age group of servants.

Their background prior to their sealing must be considered for they most certainly will have paths similar to those other servants listed throughout the Old and New Testaments. This question must be answered: "Are they saved before or after they are sealed?" Although it surely is possible that they are not saved before they are sealed, it is highly unlikely for a number of reasons.

First of all they are called "*servants of our God" (Revelation 7:3)* which is a title reserved for those who have attained a certain level of spiritual maturity and dedication to the Lord:
"The Revelation of Jesus Christ which God gave unto Him to show unto His servants things which must shortly come to pass." (Revelation 1:1)

This opening verse designates a group of people to whom the Lord Jesus Christ would *"show"* His vital end of the age truths contained in the Apocalypse, and that group of people are called *"His servants"* (Revelation 1:1). His servants include select men and women who were and are willing to *"spend and be spent" (II Corinthians 12:15)* for the cause and glory of the Lord Jesus Christ.

This word translated servant is the Greek word *"doulos"* meaning bondservant or slave, indicating one who is totally given over to the will of his master. It is found in the New Testament over 120 times. Although there are a number of different Greek words translated servant in the KJV, with various meanings such as attendant, minister, household worker, hired employee and under rower, the Greek word *"doulos"* is the one that refers to the ultimate servant with respect to the total giving of oneself to the service of their master.

This is the word chosen by the Apostle Paul to describe his own position in relationship to his Lord a number of times (Romans 1:1; Philippians 1:1; Titus 1:1). The epistles reveal the *"doulos"* or *"servants of the Lord Jesus Christ"* which also include Timothy, Epaphras, Peter, James, John, and Jude.

In the book of the Revelation the same word also describes Moses and the prophets as servants of God (Revelation 10:7, 15:3). But, the most significant occurrences of this word describe the Lord Jesus Christ Himself:

*"Behold, My **Servant** Whom I have chosen, My Beloved in Whom My soul is well pleased, I will put My Spirit upon Him and He will show judgment to the Gentiles." (Matthew 12:18)*

*"Let this mind be in you which was also in Christ Jesus: Who, being in the form of God, thought it not robbery to be equal with God: But made Himself of no reputation, and took upon Him the form of a **servant** and was made in the likeness of men." (Philippians 2:5-7)*

Those *"servants of our God",* or bond slaves of God, in Revelation 7:3 must also be considered to be of this same Biblically defined caliber:

*"Hurt not the earth till we have sealed **the servants** of our God in their foreheads. And I heard the number of them which were sealed an hundred and forty and four thousand of all the tribes of the children of Israel." (Revelation 7:3, 4)*

These 144 Thousand Sons of Israel are definitely classified as *"doulos"* or bondservants along with the Lord, and those Apostles and other saints used mightily of the Lord. This specific word was chosen by the Holy Spirit to describe this select group of men in order to indicate their advanced spiritual condition and relationship to God at the time they are sealed, for they are called *"the servants of our God"* by the angel **before** they are sealed.

This unique group of God's servants are key end times saints and some of the most thoroughly described in the Word of God. They are seen or referred to numerous times in Psalm 110:3, the book of Daniel the prophet: 11:32-35, 12:3, 10 and the book of the Revelation of Jesus Christ: 7:1-8, 9:4, 12:17, 14:1-5, 17:14, 19:19.

Secondly, their decision to be *"undefiled by women" (Revelation 14:4)* reveals their level of dedication to the Lord early in manhood, prior to their sealing. This major decision indicates that they are men of God who have set themselves apart having discerned a certain calling of God upon their lives prior to making this important decision.

They literally will give up the natural desire to marry and have a wife and children in order to give themselves totally to the Lord. By doing this they will greatly limit the effect sexual temptation can have upon their lives and thereby remove the ever increasing pressure from the world, the flesh and the devil to fall into sex sin. Also, remaining unmarried will give them additional opportunity for focused service to the Lord as clearly recommended and practiced by the Apostle Paul (I Corinthians 7:8, 26, 32).

Number three, and definitely one of the most compelling affirmations concerning their spiritual condition at their sealing, is revealed by asking this question: "Would God literally put His name and the name of His Son, The Lamb (Revelation 14:1) upon someone who is an unbelieving depraved sinner, not having experienced Bible salvation by grace through faith in the Blood of Christ?"

The answer to this question must be a definite NO! In addition to these three facts indicating their spiritual condition at the time they are sealed, there are three other Bible examples of the Lord putting His identification or mark upon men:

"Him that overcomes will I make a pillar in the temple of My God, and he shall go no more out: and I will write upon him the name of My God and the name of the city of My God, which is new Jerusalem, which cometh down out of heaven from My God: and I will write upon him My new name." (Revelation 3:12)

These overcomers of the church of Philadelphia are given a number of blessed promises by the Lord Jesus Christ reserved only for those who attain an overcoming level of victory during their time on earth:
1. *"I will make him a pillar in the temple of My God*
2. *He shall go no more out [remains in the temple]*
3. *I will write upon him the name of My God*
4. *I will write upon him the name of the city of My God, Which is New Jerusalem*
5. *I will write upon him My new name."*

These saints are promised some of the most valuable and privileged rewards ever spoken of in the Scripture. Being a pillar in the heavenly temple of Jehovah rings of a highly exalted heavenly position, however, this reward is given the added blessing of being eternal.

These overcomers will have three different inscriptions upon them and not one of them is trivial. All three are truly to be cherished for the incomparable recognition given to those who overcome during their days upon earth, for these names are the three most honorable identities in all of heaven.

The next example is found in the last chapter of the book of Revelation:
"And there shall be no more curse: but the throne of God and of the Lamb shall be in it; and His servants shall serve Him: And they shall see His face; and His name shall be in their foreheads."
(Revelation 22:3, 4)

Notice, these glorified servants of God have the honored privilege of seeing the face of the Lord Jesus Christ, and they also will have the Lamb's name in their foreheads, similar to the 144 Thousand. However, the 144 Thousand have both the Father's name and the name of the Lamb in their foreheads (Revelation 14:1) showing their dual branches of service, being *"servants of our God" (Revelation 7:3)* while also physically serving on earth *"with"* the Lamb during the Day of the Lord. (Revelation 14:1-5, 17:14, 19:19).

In these two instances, the overcomers of the church in Philadelphia and the servants in glory, both having God's identification, are clearly believers, fully redeemed, belonging to the Lord. In order for the Lord to put His name on men, it is evident by these passages that they are definitely children of God when they receive this glorious inscription upon them.

This sets a high standard by which to measure these 144 Thousand sons of Israel, for they will be given God's identification when they are still mere mortals. This underlines the significance of the Lord's bestowal of His signature upon those whom He knows will be worthy of His name during their subsequent earthly service during the Day of the Lord.

In Ezekiel's vision of chapter nine a third example is recorded:

"And the Lord said unto him, Go through the midst of the city, through the midst of Jerusalem, and set a mark upon the foreheads of the men that sigh and that cry for all the abominations that be done in the midst thereof." (Ezekiel 9:4)

These men who are marked by God are those who openly express their disgust and sorrow over the sinful condition of Jerusalem demonstrating their allegiance to the Lord. They are given God's saving protection from the impending slaughter of His coming judgment (Ezekiel 9:1-11).

These marked saints in Ezekiel are similar to the 144 Thousand for those who have His seal in their foreheads in that day will also be spared from God's judgment during the Day of the Lord:
"And it was commanded them [locusts] that they should not hurt the grass of the earth, neither any green thing, neither any tree; but only those men which have not the seal of God in their foreheads." (Revelation 9:4)

The information above indicates the 144 Thousand are surrendered saints who have duly earned their title as *"servants of our God"* before they are sealed. They have willingly surrendered themselves to the Lord to be sealed just prior to the Day of the Lord having become mature believers before that time, being worthy to have the holy name of the Father and the Lamb written in their foreheads.

This seal not only provides protection, but the seal can also indicate ownership, for these have unconditionally and sacrificially given themselves to their Master for His service. Approximately when they are redeemed is indicated in Revelation 14:3, 4:
"The hundred and forty four thousand, which were redeemed from the earth." (Revelation 14:3)

The Greek participle translated *"which were redeemed"* is in the perfect tense indicating their redemption has already taken place at a given point in the past with continuing effect into the present. The act of redemption is not continuing, but the results of this past action of redemption are continuing.

The 144 Thousand are shown to be *"redeemed from the earth.*

...redeemed from among men" the two phrases indicating:
1. Where they are from: The earth
2. What they are: Men, from among men

They are not heavenly angelic beings. They are in fact men of like passions, as we are, whom God will raise up from across the planet just as He has raised up His faithful servants throughout the history of mankind.

The second time the word *"redeemed"* appears (Revelation 14:4) in this passage it is a verb in the aorist tense, which indicates a completed action at one point in past time. The mood of this verb is passive indicating the act of redemption was not accomplished by those who were redeemed but by someone else, namely the Lord.

They are also entitled *"the firstfruits"* showing they are the first of an additional "more of the same" [Jews from the twelve tribes] future harvest who also will be *"redeemed from the earth...redeemed from among men"*. This oft-quoted verse specifies those Jews of this future harvest:
"When all Israel shall be saved: as it is written, There shall come out of Zion the Deliverer [Redeemer], and shall turn away ungodliness from Jacob." (Romans 11:26)

This future national redemption is the very event being celebrated in Revelation 14:1-3 at the end of the 70th Week of Daniel (Revelation 11:15). In addition, there are other Jews who are saved and remain on earth after the rapture, namely *"the two witnesses"* of Revelation 11 and *"the woman"* [faithful Israel] of Revelation 12.

These saints will also continue on earth throughout the last 3-1/2 years of Daniel's 70th Week as the rapture occurs some time after the mid-point of this seven year period, but before the beginning of God's wrath which is the Day of the Lord.

This prophetic timeline follows the Lord Jesus Christ's end of the age chronology found in Matthew 24:3-31, which shows the rapture (Matthew 24:30, 31) shortening the great tribulation (Matthew 24:29a) followed by the sign of the Second Coming of Christ and the impending Day of the Lord (Matthew 24:29b).

"The woman" also is supernaturally protected during this time:
"And the woman fled into the wilderness where she hath a place prepared of God, that they should feed her there a thousand two hundred and threescore days. And to the woman were given two wings of a great eagle, that she might fly into the wilderness, into her place, where she is nourished for a time, and times, and half a time, from the face of the serpent." (Revelation 12:6, 14)

"The two witnesses" are eventually killed by the beast [the Antichrist] and ascend up to heaven after *"they shall have finished their testimony" (Revelation 11:7)*. However, they also will continue on earth after the rapture to fulfill God's designated purpose during their supernatural 3-1/2 year ministry as mighty instruments of the judgment of God (Revelation 11:3-14).

The Lord rejoices in showing His mercy, and these 144 Thousand *"servants of our God"* will be His instruments of mercy during the end times as foretold in Daniel 11:32-35, 12:3, 10. They are seen as those who have insight and understanding instructing the many, being purged and purified during their Redemption Ministry.

This notable time of the end group of saints in Daniel 11 also appear after the mid-point of Daniel's 70th Week after the abomination of desolation is set up:
"And arms [forces] shall stand on his [the Antichrist] part, and they shall pollute the sanctuary of strength, and shall take away the daily sacrifice, and they shall place the abomination that makes desolate. And such as do wickedly against the covenant shall he corrupt by flatteries; but the people that do know their God shall be strong and do exploits. And they that understand among the people [Jews] shall instruct many: yet they shall fall by the sword, and by flame, by captivity, and by spoil, many days. And some of them understanding shall fall, to try them, and to purge, and to make them white, even to the time of the end: because it is yet for a time appointed."
(Daniel 11:31-33, 35)

At the beginning of the 70th Week *"[the] many"* Jews (Daniel 9:27) will *"confirm the covenant"* with the Antichrist. These Jews will be thoroughly deceived, not knowing they are in fact consenting to *"a covenant with death" (Isaiah 28:15)* which will eventually bring about their destruction.

There will be those who are instructed by the 144 Thousand, those *"that understand among the people" (Daniel 11:33)* and they will *"turn many to righteousness"* receiving the Messiah, the Lord Jesus Christ:
"And they that be wise shall shine as the brightness of the firmament; and they that turn many to righteousness as the stars for ever and ever." (Daniel 12:3)

Those Jews who continue on in darkness will eventually *"forsake the holy covenant" (Daniel 11:30)* taking *"the mark... of the beast" (Revelation 13:17)* during the time of Satan's *"great wrath"* (Revelation 12:12), which is also referred to as *"great tribulation"* (Matthew 24:21). They will subsequently die during the Day of the Lord's wrath:
"And it shall come to pass, that in all the land, saith the Lord, two parts therein shall be cut off and die." (Zechariah 13:8a).

The prophet continues:
"But the third part shall be left therein. And I will bring the third part through the fire, and will refine them as silver is refined, and will try them as gold is tried: they shall call on My name, and I will hear them: I will say, It is My people: and they shall say, The LORD is My God." (Zechariah 13:8b, 9)

These of Zechariah's *"third part"* are those of Daniel's *"many"* who will be instructed by the 144 Thousand:
*"The people that do know their God...they that understand among the people...they that be wise...they that turn **many** to righteousness...the wise shall understand." (Daniel 11:32, 33; 12:3, 10)*

After the abomination of desolation, at the mid-point of Daniel's 70th Week, God has not yet sealed the 144 Thousand but they are among those in Israel referred to in the above Daniel passages and will successfully minister to the many unsaved.

This same group of Jews is evident continuing in the land after *"the woman"* fleas into the wilderness:
"And the dragon [Satan] was wroth with the woman, and went to

153

make war with the remnant [rest] of her seed, which keep the commandments of God, and have the testimony of Jesus Christ." (Revelation 12:17b

The *"remnant of her seed"* indicated here refers to the rest of her physical seed, those Jews who remain in the land after the faithful (most likely: women, children, and men too old to go to war) flee into the wilderness. Their spiritual credentials are given in the last part of the verse: *"which keep the commandments of God, and have the testimony of Jesus Christ".*

These Jews who remain in the land, *"the rest of her seed"*, will be these chosen men:
"Thy people shall be willing in the day of Thy power [Day of the Lord], in the beauties of holiness from the womb of the morning: Thou hast the dew of Thy youth [young men]/" (Psalm 110:3)

These are those priest/warriors of the Messiah, who will be part of the physical army of Israel who defend the land against the Antichrist when he first enters Israel. He makes war with the Jews as described in Micah 5:4-9 where those who remain are called *"the remnant of Jacob" (Micah 5:7, 8).*

Some of them will be martyred or taken captive by the Antichrist: *"many days...even to the time of the end" (Daniel 11:35).* This refers to the duration of the great tribulation being cut short when Christ comes to resurrect/rapture/rescue/receive the saints (Matthew 24:21-31; I Thessalonians 4:13-18; Revelation 7:9-17).

The 144 Thousand will continue into the Day of the Lord being *"purged and purified"* eventually being *"made white and tried." (Daniel 11:35, 12:10)* It is at this point in time that the most prophesied event in the whole of Scripture begins, *"the great and dreadful day of the Lord' (Malachi 4:5).*

This event in God's program is also referred to as *"the end"* by the Lord (Matthew 24:6, 14) and *"the time of the end...end of days"* by Daniel (Daniel 11:35, 40, 12:4, 9, 13) both indicating the same point in time.

It is on this very day that God's prophetic *"time of the end"* program takes a major turn from the Antichrist's vicious persecution of God's people during the great tribulation to the Lord's Second Coming in glory:

"And then shall that wicked [Antichrist] be revealed whom the Lord will consume with the spirit of His mouth, and shall destroy [render powerless] with the brightness of His coming." (II Thessalonians 2:8)

It is on this same day, the sign of the Second Coming/Day of the Lord is given, (Revelation 6:12-17), the 144 Thousand are sealed (Revelation 7:1-8) and the Lord returns to rescue/receive (John 14:3) His saints by rapture (I Thessalonians 4:13-18), receiving them in heaven (Revelation 7:9-17).

The Lord will first seal and secure His servants, the 144 Thousand, before He rescues the saints with the sign of the Day of the Lord being given as a marvelous heavenly prelude to it all. These events will all occur the same day just as the Lord Jesus Christ taught when He emphasized *"**the same day**"* rescue before the retribution of God's judgment:

*"For as the lightning, that lightens out of the one part under heaven, shines unto the other part under heaven; so shall also the Son of man be in His day. But first He must suffer many things, and be rejected of this generation. And as it was in the days of Noah, so shall it be also in the days of the Son of man. They did eat, they drank, they married wives, they were given in marriage, until **the day** that Noah entered into the ark, and the flood came, and destroyed them all. Likewise also as it was in the days of Lot; they did eat, they drank, they bought, they sold, they planted, they builded; But **the same day** that Lot went out of Sodom it rained fire and brimstone from heaven, and destroyed them all. Even thus shall it be in **the day** when the Son of man is revealed." (Luke 17:24-30)*

Paul describes this same time just prior to the Day of the Lord:
"But of the times and seasons, brethren, ye have no need that I write unto you. For yourselves know perfectly that the day of the Lord so comes as a thief in the night. For when they [unsaved] shall say peace and safety; then sudden destruction comes upon them and they shall not escape." (I Thessalonians 5:1, 2)

155

Although the Antichrist will come on his *"white horse"* as the end times world ruler *"conquering, and to conquer...taking peace from the earth...having a pair of balances"* and in the process will implement worldwide economic control (Revelation 6:1-6), there will be a time of *"peace and safety"* just prior to the Day of the Lord when a "business as usual" attitude will prevail among the lost.

At this same time, persecution of the saints will reach the maximum level ever recorded in history (Matthew 24:15-28; Revelation 6:7-11). Then God will send His Son, the Lord Jesus Christ, to rescue/rapture the saints who have been *"sealed with that Holy Spirit of promise...unto the day of redemption" (Ephesians 1:13, 4:30)*. Those whom He chooses to remain on earth will also be protected from His wrath just as He promised (Revelation 3:10, 9:4).

The 144 Thousand will be protected by having the name of the Father and the Lamb on their foreheads (Revelation 14:1), while the faithful of Israel [the woman] will be safe in *"a place prepared by God" (Revelation 12:6)* during the last 3-1/2 years of the 70th Week of Daniel.

She will *"fly into the wilderness" (Revelation 12:14)* and remain there until the end of the 70th Week. Eventually this will become the core group, along with the 144 Thousand and those of Israel who will be saved at the end of the 70th Week, who will populate the Promised Land during Christ's earthly 1000-year rule, called the Millennium. (Revelation 20:1-10)

This protection during judgment by God is similar to the time when He brought the plagues upon Egypt and the Israelites were given safety in the land of Goshen while Moses and Aaron were actively confronting Pharaoh as the instruments of God's judgment.

Like Moses and Aaron, the two witnesses will serve as God's instruments of judgment during this unparalleled period of destruction which God brings upon the earth and its inhabitants, the cataclysmic Day of the Lord described in Revelation 8-11, 15-19.

While Moses and Aaron were the instruments of God's judgment to the lost and also the instruments of God's mercy to His people, the time of the end will see these same actions performed by *"the two witnesses' (Revelation 11:3-14)* and the 144 Thousand Sons of Israel.

God will continue to extend His eternal mercy to mankind through His 144 Thousand human servants just as He has done throughout the ages past. His primary purpose for the Day of the Lord is to purge and purify His people Israel; those referred to in Daniel 9:27, 11:33, 35, 12:3, 10. This time of the end purpose of God has also been foretold and underlined in other Old Testament prophecies:
(Isaiah 1:24-28, 27:9; Jeremiah 30:7; Ezekiel 7:16-27; Zechariah 13:8, 9; Malachi 3:1-3).

His second purpose is the rightful judgment of planet earth and its unbelieving inhabitants who throughout all of the supernatural devastation, death and wholesale destruction repeatedly refuse to repent:
"And the rest of the men which were not killed by these plagues yet repented not of the works of their hands, that they should not worship devils, and idols of gold, and silver, and brass, and stone, and of wood; which neither can see, nor hear nor walk: Neither repented they of their murders, nor of their sorceries, nor of their fornication, nor of their thefts." (Revelation 9:20, 21)

"And the fourth angel poured out his vial upon the sun; and power was given unto him to scorch men with fire. And men were scorched with great heat, and blasphemed the name of God, which hath power over these plagues: and they repented not to give Him glory. And the fifth angel poured out his vial upon the seat of the beast; and his kingdom was full of darkness; and they gnawed their tongues for pain. And blasphemed the God of heaven because of their pains and their sores, and repented not of their deeds." (Revelation 16:8-11)

Many Jews will turn to the Lord during this time, for the Lord will surely fulfill His promise:
*"And it shall come to pass, that in all the land, saith the Lord, two parts therein shall be cut off and die; but the third shall be left therein. And I will bring the third part through the fire, and will refine them as silver is refined, and will try them as gold is tried: they shall **call** on My name, and I will hear them: I will say, It is My people: and they shall say, The Lord is my God." (Zechariah 13:8, 9)*

*"For whosoever shall **call** on the name of the Lord shall be saved. How then shall they **call** on Him in whom they have not **believed**? And how shall they **believe** on Him of whom they have not heard? And how shall they hear without a preacher? And how shall they preach, except they be sent? As it is written how beautiful are the feet of them that preach the Gospel of peace, and bring glad tidings of good things."* (Romans 10:13-15)

*"And I will show wonders in the heavens and in the earth, blood, and fire, and pillars of smoke. The sun shall be turned into darkness, and moon into blood, before the great and the terrible day of the Lord come. And it shall come to pass, that whosoever shall **call** upon the name of the LORD shall be delivered: for in mount Zion and in Jerusalem shall be deliverance, as the Lord hath said, and in the remnant whom the Lord shall call."* (Joel 2:30-32)

*"And the Redeemer shall come to Zion, and unto them that **turn** from transgression in Jacob, saith the Lord."* (Isaiah 59:20)

"And so all Israel shall be saved: as it is written, There shall come out of Zion the Deliverer, and shall turn away ungodliness from Jacob: For this is My covenant unto them, when I shall take away their sins." (Romans 11:26, 27)

These Scriptures clearly show God's plan of salvation in the future deliverance of His people continues to operate just as it has in the past and present. Those whom He calls respond by believing, turning and calling upon Him in order to be saved from their sin. The entire work of salvation is of the Lord as He alone has the ability to *"turn away ungodliness from Jacob…when I shall take away their sins."* (Romans 11:26)

God will send His end times preachers, the 144 Thousand sealed *"servants of our God"*, to His people so that those whom He calls will be able to hear, believe, turn and call on His name. They will be redeemed when they see their Redeemer, the Lord Jesus Christ, come to Zion at the end of the 70th Week of Daniel.

This is when He victoriously appears with the 144 Thousand (Revelation 14:1), who are also identified by Obadiah:

"And saviors [deliverers] shall come up on Mount Zion to judge the mount of Esau; and the kingdom shall be the Lords."
(Obadiah 21; Revelation 11:15)

These obedient servants of God will *"follow the Lamb wherever He goes" (Revelation14: 4)* both physically and spiritually. They as the merciful saviors/deliverers will in fact be the compassionate instruments of the one and only compassionate Savior, the Lamb, the Lord Jesus Christ, unto Jew and Gentile alike, during the Day of the Lord's wrath. These Day of the Lord soldiers of the Lamb are also indicated to be *"with Him"* at the battle of Armageddon:
*"These [the ten horns/kings] shall make war with the Lamb, and the Lamb shall overcome them: for He is Lord of lords, and King of kings: and they that are **with Him** are called, and chosen, and faithful." (Revelation 17:14)*

The 144 Thousand, as the earthly members of *"His army" (Revelation 19:19)* along with *"the armies which were in heaven" (Revelation 19:14)* indicating the angelic host of heaven (Daniel 4:35), will defeat *"the kings of the earth, and their armies" (Revelation 19:19)* when the Lord Jesus Christ comes as *"KING OF KINGS, AND LORD OF LORDS" (Revelation19: 16)* to also defeat *"the beast...and...the false prophet...These both were cast alive into a lake of fire burning with brimstone. And the remnant [rest] were slain with the sword of Him that sat upon the horse which sword proceeded out of His mouth." (Revelation 19:20, 21)*

These events describe, in brief, the final and culminating battle of the great and dreadful Day of the Lord, *"the battle of that great day of God Almighty' (Revelation 16:14)*, which is the renowned battle of Armageddon.

After the Day of the Lord judgment ends at Armageddon, the 144 Thousand will continue to *"follow Him wherever He goes" (Revelation 14:4)* becoming a part of that great gathering of God's people (Genesis 49:10; Psalm 102:21, 22; Hosea 1:11, 3:5; Micah 5:4) who enter and populate the promised land during the literal 1,000 year earthly reign of Christ (Revelation 20:1-10).

15.b

The 144 Thousand-Their Source: The Twelve Tribes of Israel

The twelve tribes of Israel as a group are listed in Genesis 49:1-28 when the dying patriarch Jacob prophesies to his twelve sons:
"And Jacob called unto his sons, and said, Gather yourselves together, that I may tell you that which shall befall you in the last days." (Genesis 49:1)

The significance of this list of the twelve sons of Jacob is that it appears to provide the basic structure for the list of the twelve tribes found in Revelation 7:4-8. The tribes are listed in Revelation 7, the last time in Scripture, as the 144 Thousand are sealed for protection (Revelation 9:4) for their future Day of the Lord ministry.

Although there are changes in the order and the specific sons listed, the list in Revelation 7:4-8 has within it definite identifying features showing that this prophesy of Jacob found in Genesis 49:1-28 has the same basic structure as the list in Revelation 7:4-8. The sons of Leah are first, then the sons of the two handmaids who are followed by the sons of Rachel, which is the general outline for both lists.

In verse one of Genesis 49 Jacob indicates that what he is going to say will have its effect *"in the last days"* which points to the time of the end as the period when these prophesies will take place. This prophetic section of the Word of God provides definite insight for those who will be sealed during Daniel's 70th Week, the last remaining week of the seventy weeks which were determined upon Daniel's people and their holy city Jerusalem:
"Seventy weeks are determined upon thy people and upon thy holy city." (Daniel 9:24)

*"And Jacob called unto his sons, and said, Gather yourselves together, that I may tell you that which shall befall you **in the last days**. Gather yourselves together, and hear, ye sons of Jacob, and*

160

hearken unto Israel your father." (Genesis 49:1, 2)

Then Jacob addresses his firstborn son Reuben:
"Reuben, thou art my firstborn, my might and the beginning of my strength, the excellency of dignity, and the excellency of power Unstable as water, thou shalt not excel, because thou went up to thy father's bed; then defiled thou it: he went up to my couch."
(Genesis 49:3, 4)

Jacob is referring to the sex sin Reuben committed with Bilhah, Rachel's handmaid, with whom Jacob fathered two sons, Dan and Naphtali. Reuben's heinous sin cancelled his birthright, making him unstable, not having the ability to excel due to this defiling conduct which also removed the possibility of God's blessing.

Simeon and Levi, who are the next two sons born of Leah to Jacob were involved in the cruel sin of mass murder when they slaughtered the defenseless people in the town of Shechem (Genesis 34).

They also do not receive a blessing, instead Jacob pronounces a curse upon them:
"Simeon and Levi are brethren; instruments of cruelty are in their habitations. O my soul come not thou into their secret; unto their assembly, mine honor, be not thou united: for in their anger they slew a man, and in their self will they digged down a wall. Cursed be their anger, for it was fierce, and their wrath, for it was cruel. I will divide them in Jacob, and scatter them in Israel." (Genesis 49:7-9)

The most significant section of Jacob's prophecy comes in (v.8-12) when he speaks to his fourth son Judah:
"Judah, thou art he whom thy brethren shall praise: thy hand shall be in the neck of thine enemies, thy father's children shall bow down before thee. Judah is a lion's whelp, from the prey, my son, thou art gone up, he stooped down, he couched as a lion, and as an old lion, who shall rouse him up? The scepter shall not depart from Judah, not a lawgiver from between his feet, until Shiloh come, and unto Him shall the gathering of the people be. Binding his foal unto the vine, and his ass's colt unto the choice vine; he washed his garments in wine, and his clothes in the blood of grapes: His eyes shall be red with wine, and his teeth white with milk." (Genesis 49:8-12)

The first two verses indicate the supremacy of Judah over his eleven brothers, his future military prowess and the position Judah would and will take in the order of the twelve tribes of Israel, for out of the loins of Judah kings would come forth (Genesis 49:10).

The focus here is upon the King of kings and Lord of lords the Savior of mankind, the Son of God and Jewish Messiah, the Lord Jesus Christ, God Incarnate, for the Lord Jesus Christ descended from the tribe of Judah (Hebrews 7:14). This is the reason Judah is mentioned first in the order of the last days tribal list in Revelation 7:4-8.

Judah, being placed in the first position of the sons of Jacob, began in the book of Numbers where he is listed as the first of the standard bearers *"toward the rising of the sun" (Numbers 2:3)*. Judah is the first tribe to give an offering (Numbers 7:12) and the first place went the standard of the camp of Judah according to their armies.

The Lord Jesus Christ is called *"Shiloh"* in Genesis 49:10 meaning *"The Peaceful Ruler"* showing the promise of the Ruler Who would come *"in the last days"* when *"unto Him shall the gathering of the people be"*. This refers to that future time when the twelve tribes will gather to Him, which is fulfilled in Revelation 14:1 when the 144 Thousand are seen with *"the Lamb"* on *"mount Zion"*.

The 144 Thousand will gather unto the Lord Jesus along with those Israelites who will be redeemed at the end of the 70th Week of Daniel (Isaiah 59:20; Romans 11:25, 26). *"The woman"* of Revelation 12, who represents the 70th Week faithful of Israel, will also be present at this great gathering of God's earthly people as indicated by the prophet Micah:
"Therefore will He [Messiah] give them [Israel] up until the time [End of the 70th Week/End of The Time of Jacob's Trouble] that she [Israel] which travails has brought forth [all Israel saved]: then the remnant [remainder/rest] of His brethren [the woman/faithful of Israel] shall return unto the children [sons] of Israel [the 144 Thousand]." (Micah 5:3)

These three distinct groups of Jews will gather to their Messiah (Genesis 49:10; Psalm 102:21, 22; Hosea 1:11, 3:5), the Lord Jesus

Christ, at the end of the 70th Week of Daniel. They will populate the land of Israel during the Millennium (Revelation 20:1-6) when the Lord Jesus will physically rule on earth with a *"rod of iron"* *(Psalm 2:9; Revelation 19:15) "upon the throne of His father David" (Isaiah 9:7; Luke 1:32).*

Zebulun, the tenth son born to Jacob, is listed next in order that all the sons of Leah, Jacob's lawful wife, would come first for she bore six of his sons: Reuben, Simeon, Levi, Judah, Issachar and Zebulun. Jacob, who is now on his deathbed, shows his recognition of God's sovereign plan in selecting the Godly Leah who gave him half of his twelve sons.

Leah also was buried in the cave of Machpelah with Jacob, in the family burial place where the patriarchs Abraham, Isaac and their wives were laid to rest (Genesis 49:31).

Zebulun's blessing would come through him being *"a haven of ships"* as *"his border shall be unto Zidon"* which is located on the northern coasts of the Promised Land on the Mediterranean Sea.

Issachar, is the last of Leah's sons:
"Issachar is a strong ass couching down between two burdens: And he saw that rest was good, and the land that it was pleasant; and bowed his shoulder to bear, and became a servant unto tribute." *(Genesis 49:14, 15)*

Issachar is a bearer of burdens who acknowledged the value of rest and the pleasantness of the promised land in that future day which is now taking place as prophesied here. It is evident that Israel has been transformed from a literal desert to a fruitful and productive land during this last half century [1948-2007] following the Jews return to their homeland.

After the sons of Leah are complete, Jacob speaks to his son Dan:
"Dan shall judge his people, as one of the tribes of Israel. Dan shall be a serpent by the way, an adder in the path, that bites the horse heels, so that his rider shall fall backward. I have waited for Thy salvation O Lord." *(Genesis 49:16-18)*

Dan, whose name literally means "He judged", is the firstborn of Bilhah, Rachel's handmaid. Although Dan is not one of the tribes sealed in the end times list of Revelation 7:4-8 he will be present then to perform the act of judging his people. This may include pleading their cause or contending for his brethren as this word *"Shall judge"* also means: To avenge, plead the cause, or contend.

Dan's serpent-like description vividly illustrates the characteristics of a small subtle entity having the physical ability to bring down the high and mighty warrior mounted upon a horse alluding to the likely defeat of a military foe.

These actions along with contending for his brethren during the last days fits with prophecies of wars being frequent in the land of Israel during that time (Joel 2; Ezekiel 38, 39). Dan will wait for the Lord to provide salvation/deliverance from these, his enemies, in that day.

Gad, a troop shall overcome him: but he shall overcome at the last."
(Genesis 49:19)
The next son of Jacob is Gad, Leah's handmaid Zilpah's firstborn. He replaces Levi in the tribal lists found in the book of Numbers for Levi, the priestly tribe, is God's portion and was no longer included in most of the lists of the sons of Jacob.

Gad's future in the last days is also framed with a military tone as he is overcome at the first by a troop. However, in the end he is victorious, which could point to the possibility of an early defeat at the hands of the Antichrist when he initially invades the land after the mid-point of the 70th Week of Daniel when he:
"Shall devour the whole earth, and shall tread it down, and break it in pieces...when the Assyrian shall come into our land: and when he shall tread in our palaces" (Daniel 7:23; Micah 5:5a).

This mighty crusade of the Antichrist is further described:
"And his power shall be mighty, but not by his own power: and he shall destroy wonderfully, and shall prosper, and practice, and shall destroy the mighty and the holy people [Israelites]." (Daniel 8:24)

"And he shall enter also into the glorious land [Israel] ...And he shall

plant the tabernacles of his palace between the seas in the glorious holy mountain [Mount Zion]." (Daniel 11:41, 45)

In the end, Gad and his brethren of the other tribes of Israel will come forth as gold when they go to battle along *"with the Lamb" (Revelation 17:14)* the Lord Jesus Christ at *"the battle of that great day of God" (Revelation 16:14)* the battle of Armageddon which is described in Revelation 19:11-21.

"Out of Asher his bread shall be fat, and he shall yield royal dainties." (Genesis 49:20)

Asher, who is the last son born of Zilpah, will receive the blessings of richness by experiencing bountiful plenty during the latter days in the Promised Land. So rich in fact that it is here described as delicacies of royal quality. This supply of food will likely be brought forth and shared with all of the other tribes by the people of the tribe of Asher whose name literally means "happy".

"Naphtali is a hind let loose: he gives goodly words." (Genesis 49:20)

The last son born of Bilhah is described as a female deer that is set free or sent forth. This newfound liberty of Naphtali produces good and pleasant speech or communication during the last days.

The tribe of Naphtali occupied the land of southern Galilee where the Lord Jesus ministered and spoke most of His parables and performed the majority of His miracles.

"Joseph is a fruitful bough, even a fruitful bough by a well; whose branches run over the wall: The archers have sorely grieved him, and shot at him, and hated him: But his bow abode in strength, and the arms of his hands were made strong by the hands of the mighty God of Jacob; (from thence is the Shepherd, the Stone of Israel:) Even by the God of thy father, who shall help thee; and by the Almighty, Who shall bless thee with blessings of heaven above, blessings of the deep that lie under, blessings of the breasts, and of the womb: The blessings of thy father have prevailed above the blessings of my progenitors unto the utmost bound of the everlasting hills: they shall be on the head of Joseph, and on the crown of the head of him that was separate from his brethren." (Genesis 49:22-26)

Joseph, Rachel's firstborn, receives the longest and most extensive blessing from the lips of his father Jacob. Although the royal tribe of Judah has the Messianic pre-eminence, inheriting the position of firstborn of Jacob, Joseph's rich blessing reveals his great love for the firstborn son of his beloved Rachel.

He bestows upon him the blessing of overflowing fruitfulness having overcome the afflictions of the archer's bow and the separation from his brethren. Jacob details Joseph's present (v.22) his past (v.23, 24) and his future blessings (v.25, 26) laying full emphasis upon the help and supernatural power of God Almighty.

He utilizes the following five titles for God emphasizing the actual reality of exactly Who is responsible for these miraculous future blessings which Jacob pronounced upon his eleventh son Joseph:
1. The Mighty God of Jacob (v.24)
2. The Shepherd (v.24)
3. The Stone [Rock] of Israel (v.24)
4. The God of thy father (v.25)
5. The Almighty (v.25)

Joseph will of a certainty receive the bountiful blessings of heaven, the unfathomable blessings of the deep, and the fruitful multiplication of his tribe through the matriarchal blessings of breast and womb. Jacob summarizes this magnificent bounty of God's goodness in (v.26) by revealing that his blessing will prevail even above the blessings of Abraham and Isaac the patriarchs who came before him. These blessings bestowed upon Joseph and his last days descendants will reach unto the farthest known boundary of the everlasting hills.

The tribes of Ephraim and Manasseh are represented under the name of their father Joseph as Manasseh's name appears in the Revelation 7:4-8 list and Ephraim's descendants are those sealed under the name of Joseph for Ephraim and Manasseh were Joseph's only sons.

"Benjamin shall ravin as a wolf: in the morning he shall devour the prey, and at night he shall divide the spoil." (Genesis 49:27)

The last, the least, and the littlest, is the much-loved tribe of

Benjamin whose name means *"son of my old age"*. He was specifically given this name by his father Jacob (Genesis 35:18). He is the twelfth son of Jacob and the last son born of Rachel who died during his birth.

Benjamin is described as eating voraciously like a wolf in the wild when it devours and consumes its prey. This brings to mind the picture of the might and strength of a warrior who has the power to fully overcome the enemy in the heat of battle and later divides the spoils of his overwhelming victory among his fellow soldiers.

Matthew Henry, commenting on this verse, said that the tribe of Benjamin shall be "Warlike, strong and daring, enriching themselves with the spoils of their enemies." Some of the most notable Bible characters from the tribe of Benjamin are:
1. King Saul
2. Jonathan, son of Saul
3. Jeremiah the prophet
4. Mordecai
5. Esther
6. Saul of Tarsus/Apostle Paul

The common characteristics this group manifests in Scripture portray a clear picture of those future Benjamites clearly prophesied by Jacob and pointed out by Matthew Henry. This small but significant tribe will continue to display these most descriptive warlike attributes during *"the last days"* as foretold by Jacob. Then, there shall be "w*ars and rumors of wars" (Matthew 24:6)* during which time the twelve tribes including this last little tribe of Benjamin will take a most significant and victorious role.

While Jacob's first three sons, Reuben, Simeon and Levi, receive a negative prophecy, of the remaining nine, five will have success against their foes:
1. Judah's hand shall be in the neck of his enemies. (v.8)
2. Dan shall be a serpent that causes the rider to fall. (v.17)
3. Gad shall overcome a troop. (v.19)
4. Joseph's bow abode in strength. (v.24)
5. Benjamin shall devour his prey and divide the spoil. (v.27)

This military might has been evident down through Israel's history and will continue to be prevalent during the time of the end when the twelve tribes will band together once again to defeat their enemies under the leadership of their Messiah, the Lord Jesus Christ (Micah 5:4-8; Revelation 17:14, 19:11-21). Since the 144 Thousand will definitely come from *"the twelve tribes of Israel' (Revelation 7:3-8)* it is necessary to briefly review the history of these tribes.

When Jacob took his family down into Egypt they numbered *"threescore and ten" (Genesis 46:27)*, but when Moses brought Jacob's family out of Egypt a little over four centuries later it is estimated that they had grown to over 1.5 million. After 40 years of wilderness wandering the division of the land by Joshua took place and the tribes took up permanent residence in the land of Canaan living together as a unit until the kingdom was divided after the death of King Solomon.

These ten tribes made up the northern kingdom:
(1) Reuben, (2) Simeon, (3) Issachar,, (4) Zebulon,, (5) Dan,
(6) Gad, (7) Asher, (8) Naphtali, (9) Manasseh, (10) Ephraim

Judah and Benjamin are the two tribes of the southern kingdom. They controlled Jerusalem where the tribe of Levi continued to serve the Lord in the temple built by Solomon although many Levites also lived among the ten tribes of the northern kingdom.

In 722 B.C. the ten northern tribes were defeated and taken into captivity and dispersed abroad by Sennacherib the Assyrian king. He made an attempt to do the same to the two southern tribes but was unsuccessful due to the miraculous intervention of God (II Kings 19:15-37).

In 586 B.C. the two southern tribes, Judah and Benjamin, along with the remaining Levites, were defeated by Nebuchadnezzar who destroyed the city of Jerusalem and Solomon's temple. The two southern tribes were taken captive and moved to Babylon. After 70 years approximately 50,000, a small minority of the Babylonian captives from the tribes of Judah, Benjamin and Levi returned to the land of Israel to rebuild the temple (Ezra 1:5, 2:2) under Zerubbabel.

Approximately 80 years later Ezra the priest/scribe returned to Jerusalem from Babylon to bring revival to those already in the land of Israel (Ezra 7-10). The Levites, Nethinims [Temple servants] and people of Israel from the tribes of Judah and Benjamin who came with Ezra totaled about 1800.

Then, Nehemiah returned to the Promised Land from Babylon about 14 years after Ezra and rebuilt the wall around the city of Jerusalem (Nehemiah 1-6) along with members of the tribes of Levi, Judah, and Benjamin who were already in the land.

While there were only three tribes involved in these returns from Babylon, after the temple and wall were rebuilt and Jerusalem was once again inhabited, many Jews from the other tribes made the pilgrimage to their holy city. This is evidenced by the gathering recorded four centuries later on the day of Pentecost in A.D.33:

*"And there were dwelling at Jerusalem, Jews, devout men, out of **every nation** under heaven. And they were all amazed and marveled, saying one to another, Behold are not all these which speak Galileans? And how hear we every man in our own tongue, wherein we were born? Parthians, and Medes, and Elamites, and the dwellers in Mesopotamia, and in Judea, and Cappodocia, in Pontus, and Asia, Phrygia, and Pamphylia, in Egypt, and in the parts of Libya about Cyrene, and strangers of Rome, Jews and proselytes, Cretes and Arabians, we do hear them speak in our tongues the wonderful works of God." (Acts 2:5, 7-10)*

This multi-national gathering of Jews from all parts of the Roman Empire likely has in its makeup members from the northern ten tribes for these Jews came from as far as the city of Rome. This passage reveals that in the centuries since their captivity the Jews had migrated to the farthest reaches of the Roman Empire.

While the ten tribes are called "The ten lost tribes" by some in the present day indicating that it is not known where or whether they still exist, they are definitely not lost in the eyes and heart of almighty God.

About 40 years after this day of Pentecost, in 70 A.D., the Roman armies of Titus completely destroyed Jerusalem and the rebuilt temple which was prophesied by the Lord Jesus Christ (Matthew 24:2). Most of the Israelites were either killed or scattered at that time although there was an uprising of some Jews in the land called the Bar-Kochba rebellion a little over six decades later [A.D.130-135].

This last attempt by the Jews to free themselves was summarily and brutally crushed by the army of the Roman emperor Hadrian. During the centuries that have passed since this final purge of the Jews the Promised Land has been controlled by various kings and rulers.

The Lord in His plan for the end times has brought His earthly people back into the holy land once again and they now occupy their holy city Jerusalem which are definite pre-requisites for the 70th Week of Daniel (Daniel 9:24).

The twelve tribes listed in Revelation 7:4-8 may already be represented in the land of Israel. But, the great number [144 Thousand] of young men that will be sealed in that future day indicates the likely possibility that many of these young men will still be scattered throughout the world.

They definitely will all be in the land at the end of the 70th Week of Daniel (Revelation 14:1) when they appear in Jerusalem with the Lord on Mt. Zion. However, it is not necessary for them to be in the land of Israel when they are sealed just prior to the beginning of the Day of the Lord.

Until recently the United States of America was the home of the largest Jewish population. Now [2007], the land of Israel (Approx. 7 Million) is the largest with the U.S.A. (Approx. 6 Million) in second place and Europe (Approx. 1.5 Million) in third.

The region formerly called the U.S.S.R., although rapidly dwindling in Jewish population due to the Jews return to the land of Israel, still has approximately 435 Thousand professing Jews making it the fourth largest area.

The focus of evangelism for the church in these last days should be centered upon the Jew with emphasis upon these areas of the world where the majority of the twelve tribes of Israel now reside.

Even though Paul was unmercifully persecuted and soundly rejected by the great majority of the Jews during his ministry, he continued to go to their synagogues in each city attempting to win them to Christ as revealed in these texts (Acts 9:20, 13:5, 14:1, 17:1, 10, 17, 18:4, 19).

He was simply following his heart (Romans 1:15, 16, 10:1) and the method that His Lord used during His ministry. For, at the end of the Lord Jesus Christ's First Coming, He gave this brief description of His public ministry:
"I spoke openly to the world; I ever taught in the synagogue, and in the temple, whither the Jews always resort; and in secret have I said nothing." (John 18:20)

In God's purpose there is coming a day, during the 70th Week of Daniel, when *"The veil shall be taken away" (II Corinthians 3:16b)* from the spiritual eyes of His earthly people the Jews. Then, their *"Redeemer shall come to Zion, and unto them that turn from transgression in Jacob, saith the Lord." (Isaiah 59:20)*
"And so all Israel shall be saved: as it is written, There shall come out of Zion the Deliverer, and shall turn away ungodliness from Jacob." (Romans 11:26)

But at the present hour *"the veil is upon their heart"*
(II Corinthians 3:15) and the age old methods used by the Lord Jesus Christ and the Apostle Paul are still the best ways to reach the Jews. They utilized Old Testament Messianic preaching (Luke 4:15-21; Acts 13:16-39, 17:1-3, 18:28) and Holy Spirit-led confrontational one on one evangelism (John 3:1-21, 4:1-26; Acts 16:31, 18:4, 19:8).

In the purpose of God, it is the duty of the Church of Jesus Christ to pray for the Lord to send forth laborers into His harvest. They must focus their Holy Spirit filled soul-winning expertise upon the earthly people of God, the Jews, wherever they may be found as we close in on the Second Coming of the Lord Jesus Christ.

The time is drawing near when these young men (Psalm 110:3), the 144 Thousand, will be called, prepared and later sealed for their

Day of the Lord service to God. This great conversion of the earthly people of God may well take place during the powerful restoration ministry of the Elijah-like prophet whom God will send to His people.

He will of necessity follow the pattern of his two predecessors, Elijah and John the Baptist, by preaching repentance and revival, *"Turning hearts...Restoring all things" (Malachi 4:5, 6; Matthew 17:11)* in the process.

It is likely that the Lord will use this mighty prophet to bring revival to the Church of Jesus Christ and spearhead the mass evangelization of His earthly people, the Jews, including the 144 Thousand. The 144 Thousand are given a unique title that points to this very possibility:
*"These were redeemed from among men, being the **firstfruits unto God and to the Lamb**." (Revelation 14:4c)*

These young men will be the first Jews to be redeemed during the 70th Week of Daniel, which is the last week of the *"Seventy weeks are determined upon thy people and thy holy city" (Daniel 9:24)*.

There will be many more Jews redeemed later during this restored *"holy covenant" (Daniel 11:28-32)* Jewish dispensation when God will surely bring to pass His great and precious promises to His earthly people (Isaiah 59:20; Zechariah 13:8, 9; Romans 11:25, 26) the Jews.

15.c

The 144 Thousand:
Their Supernatural Calling

The spiritual condition of these young Hebrew men at the time of their sealing (Revelation 7:3-8) with the signature of God (Revelation 14:1) is established by the Biblical record based upon the following truths:

1. Their descriptive title: *"The servants [bondslaves] of our God"* *(Revelation 7:3)* **before** they are sealed
2. Three Bible examples of other redeemed men marked by God
   a. Old Testament example: (Ezekiel 9:4-7)
   b. New Testament example #1: (Revelation 3:12)
   c. New Testament example #2: (Revelation 22:4)
3. The Lord would never place His holy name (Revelation 7:3, 14:1) upon unredeemed men.

These truths establish the fact of their redemption prior to their sealing. Therefore, it is necessary to consider the impact that their redemption and subsequent preparation has upon the Church of Jesus Christ for the Church will be the source or seedbed for these young Jewish disciples of the Lord Jesus Christ (Revelation 14:4).

The Church must now focus its evangelistic efforts upon *"the Jew first"* as was the priority of the Lord Jesus Christ and the Apostle Paul (Matthew 15:24; Romans 1:15, 16) for these 144 Thousand young Jewish servants of God must be redeemed and prepared for their end times Redemption Ministry.

It is possible that many present-day Jews are unaware of their lineage as demonstrated by the following brief but illustrative true account. Two brothers were recently made aware of their real estate ownership in Austria. A multi-million dollar structure belonged to their family prior to World War II and was seized by the Nazis in the late 1930's. A recent investigation of the rightful ownership took place and they were told of their good fortune.

Through the unfolding of these events they found out that their mother, now deceased, who had brought them to the U.S.A. before full-scale war had broken out, was a Jewess and kept her background secret when they fled the Nazis and found refuge in the U.S.A.

It was not until they, the two brothers, as the surviving property owners, were sought out that they were made aware of their Jewish lineage which had been lost and unknown to them in merely one generation. This scenario most likely has been repeated down through the ages, as the Jews have been the targets of various purges and persecutions from the beginning of their existence.

This type of event has likely caused many others whose bloodline descends from the twelve sons of Jacob to be lost through the ages…lost, that is, to man, but definitely not lost in the eyes and heart of Almighty God.

Moses was a man who descended from the tribe of Levi, but was raised from an infant in the palace of the Pharaoh of Egypt. How long was it until he realized his lineage and God called him to deliver his people from bondage? He may have remained unaware of his bloodline well into adulthood.

Many generations have come and gone since A.D.70 when the Jews were scattered after the destruction of the temple and the city of Jerusalem which destruction also eliminated any and all written ancestry records of the twelve tribes of Israel

The ascertaining of exactly who is a Jew and the tribe of Israel from whence they came can only be determined by Almighty God. Just as in the past Biblical record, the Lord will continue His practice of choosing out from among His people those whom He calls and prepares as His servants.

Like Moses, the servant of God (Exodus 14:31), the 144 Thousand may be initially unaware that their bloodline comes directly from one of the twelve sons of Israel who are listed in Revelation 7:3-8.

However, when God calls, He will also make them aware of His plan for their lives in much the same manner that He has done with His servants of old that He has called, prepared and mightily used for His service down through the centuries.

The Lord definitely has spoken to His past servants through supernatural communication:
1. Abraham: (Genesis 12:1-3, 7, 13:14-17, 15:1-21, 17:1-22, 18:1-33, 21:12, 13, 22:1-18)
2. Isaac: (Genesis 26:24, 25)
3. Jacob: (Genesis 28:10-22, 32:1, 2, 24-32, 35:1)
4. Moses: (Exodus 3:1-4:26)
5. Samuel: (I Samuel 3:1-21)
6. Isaiah: (Isaiah 6:1-13)
7. Jeremiah: (Jeremiah 1:1-19)
8. Ezekiel: (Ezekiel 1:1-28, 2:1-3:27)
9. Daniel: (Daniel 7:1-28, 8:1-27, 9:20-27, 10:1-12:13)
10. John the Baptist: (John 1:23-34)
11. Paul the Apostle: (Acts 9:3-16, 16:6-10)
12. John the Apostle: (Revelation 1:1, 10-20)

When these supernatural communications are surveyed a number of common practices of God unfold:
1. He gives promises and blessings to His servants.
2. He foretells the ministry of His servants.
3. He gives explicit personal details to His servants.

Three economies are covered in this list of God's servants, promise, law and grace with John the Baptist the transitional prophet (Matthew 11:13) between law and grace who knew exactly who he was (Isaiah 40:3; John 1:23) and exactly what he came to accomplish (John 1:23-34).

These future servants of God, the 144 Thousand, are also entitled: *"the firstfruits unto God and to the Lamb" (Revelation 14:4)* indicating that they are the first Jews to be redeemed during the restored *"holy covenant" (Daniel 11:28-32)* period, which is the 70th Week of Daniel.

They are the first of a great company of Jews who will follow

(Isaiah 59:20; Romans 11:25, 26) when they are redeemed at the end of these seven years when the Lord will *"bring in everlasting righteousness" (Daniel 9:24).*

This period of time has been called by some "The last Jewish dispensation" when God will once again deal with His earthly people, the Jews by reverting to the Old Covenant. This Old Covenant period will bring with it similar circumstances and practices as were prevalent during the first 483 years of this 490 year period as evidenced by a number of Old and New Testament prophetic texts:

1. The Jews will be a *"people"*/nation (Daniel 9:24)
2. The Jews will be in their Promised Land
   (Deuteronomy 30:5-9; Daniel 9:24; Matthew 24:16)
3. The Jews will occupy their "*holy city*" Jerusalem
   (Daniel 9:24)
4. The Lord will send "*Elijah*" to revive/restore (Malachi 4:5, 6; Matthew 17:11; Mark 9:12)
5. "*The holy covenant*" will be restored (Daniel 11:28-32)
6. "*The temple of God*" will be rebuilt
   (Daniel 11:31; II Thessalonians 2:1- 4; Revelation 11:1, 2)
7. "*The holy place*" included (Matthew 24:15)
8. "*The regular sacrifices*" will be instituted
   (Daniel 8:11, 12, 9:27, 11:31, 12:11)
9. The Jews will "*worship*" in "*the temple of God*"
   (Revelation 11:1.2)
10. "*The Sabbath*" will be reinstated (Matthew 24:20)
11. The Lord will send His "*prophet[s]*" to His people
    (Malachi 4:5, 6; Revelation 11:3-17)
12. "*The tribes of Israel*" will be recognized (Revelation 7:3-8)

During this last seven year period, the 70th Week of Daniel, the 144 Thousand are redeemed, called, trained and serve the Lord. They too will receive supernatural communication from the Lord just as His servants of old who were told of their calling and future ministry as faithful *"servants of our God" (Revelation 7:3).* They will provide their vital Redemption Ministry to those people whom God will call.

15.d

The 144 Thousand
The Passing of the Torch - [Part I]

From the beginning of Biblical history God has always prepared the next generation to represent Him and His Word on earth before the proceeding generation passed on into eternity. Moses trained Joshua and Paul trained Timothy and the Lord trained His disciples before they "Passed the Torch" to the next generation. This illustrates just a few instances of God's practice of working in the lives of successive generations of His servants.

So it will be at the end of the age when the saints are removed from the earth by rapture. God will prepare the next generation to carry His Word to those who will be redeemed during the Day of the Lord. Then, He will judge Jew and Gentile alike, and in the process purge the nation of Israel so that at the end of the 70th Week of Daniel *"all Israel shall be saved." (Romans 11:25, 26)*

Revelation chapter seven is the key section of Scripture showing "The Passing of the Torch" as the saints are raptured bringing an innumerable multitude to heaven (Revelation 7:9-17) after the 144 Thousand are sealed (Revelation 7:1-8) for protection (Revelation 9:4) during their coming Day of the Lord ministry.

The saints will be "Raptured from Wrath", rescued from the persecution of the Antichrist just before the Lord brings His wrath upon those that remain on the earth, just as He promised,
(I Thessalonians 1:10, 5:1-10) but He will not leave the earth without a human witness.

This great company of Jews, the 144 Thousand, will *"follow the Lamb wherever He goes" (Revelation 14:4)* indicating their full surrender and total commitment to the Lord Jesus Christ. They will be model disciples, witnessing of the Lord's redemption to those that do not know Him during those days of devastating fiery judgment of the

Day of the Lord's wrath.

How will this great company of the sons of Israel be chosen? Will they be saved before or after the rapture of the saints? Are they merely physical descendants of the twelve tribes of Israel who are sealed, or are they already believing sons of God before the sealing takes place?

If the Lord continues to operate the way He has throughout the ages, these who are sealed will already be mightily prepared *"servants of our God" (Revelation 7:3)* whom He has chosen and who will already have fully surrendered their lives to the service of the Lamb their King. The Scripture clearly indicates that they are:
"Sealed...servants of God...children (sons) of Israel...having His (the Lamb's) Father's name written in their foreheads...could learn that song...were redeemed from the earth...not defiled with women for they are virgins...follow the Lamb wherever He goes...were redeemed from among men, being the firstfruits unto God and the Lamb...in their mouth was found no guile: for they are without fault before the Throne of God." (Revelation 7:3-8, 14:1-5)

This impeccable group of God's faithful servants are duly called and qualified to be the Lord's faithful representatives during the most trying of circumstances ever experienced by a child of God. A choice group of God's bond-servants indeed, who fully know their position and calling and willingly give themselves to their precious Lord for His service whatever it might be.

These are not just a generic group of Jews mystically selected to be protected during the Day of the Lord in order that the physical seed of Israel survives the judgment of God. No, this is a prime group of men, chosen saints of God who have been called out of the twelve tribes for *"such a time as this" (Esther 4:14.)* The Lord will bring upon all of mankind His fiery judgment of planet earth and all its inhabitants which is called *"the great and dreadful Day of the Lord"*
(Malachi 4:5) also described as the wrath of God (Isaiah 13:6-10; Zephaniah 1:14, 15).

This group, because of the complete description given them in Revelation 7:3-8, 14:1-5, is clearly identified as first of all *"sealed'*. This indicates the protection of God **in the midst of** (Revelation 9:4)

His Day of the Lord wrath. The Lord in the past has removed His own people prior to His judgment as shown during the worldwide cataclysmic flood when He rescued the family of Noah in the ark.

He also *"delivered just Lot"* and his family before the fiery judgment fell upon Sodom and Gomorrah. But, in this instance, the Lord gives the 144 Thousand His signature (Revelation 14:1) upon their foreheads to protect them **in the midst of** His judgment.

In Ezekiel chapter nine a number of parallels are recorded which are similar to what is going to happen just prior to the Day of the Lord's wrath as described in Revelation chapter seven. First of all it must be emphasized that it is the Lord, the sovereign Ruler of the universe, the God of heaven and earth, Who is bringing this Day of the Lord's wrath upon the earth and its inhabitants. The end of Revelation chapter six confirms this to be the case:

"For the great day of His wrath is come; and who shall be able to stand?" (Revelation 6:17)

This statement supplies us with the fact of Who is responsible for the impending judgment which will begin when the first trumpet is blown in chapter eight. Ezekiel chapter eight also verifies that the Lord is responsible for what occurs in chapter nine:

"He cried also in mine ears with a loud voice, saying, Cause them that have charge over the city to draw near, even every man with his destroying weapon in his hand. And, behold six men came from the way of the higher gate, which lies toward the north, and every man a slaughter weapon in his hand; and one man among them was clothed with linen, with a writer's inkhorn by his side: and they went in, and stood by the brazen altar. And the glory of God was gone up from the cherub, whereupon he was, to the threshold of the house of God. And He called to the man clothed with linen, which had the writer's inkhorn by his side; And the Lord said unto him, Go through the midst of the city, through the midst of Jerusalem, and set a mark (signature) upon the foreheads of the men that sigh and that cry for all the abominations that be done in the midst thereof. And to the others he said in mine hearing, Go ye after him through the city, and smite: let not your eye spare, neither have ye pity: Slay utterly old and young both maids, and little children: but come not near any man upon whom is the mark (signature); and begin at My sanctuary."

(Ezekiel 9:1-6)

Here, in Ezekiel's vision, the Lord commands His representatives to bring His judgment upon the inhabitants of Jerusalem. But, before the judgment falls, He supernaturally protects His own and sets His mark or signature upon their foreheads. **In the midst of** His judgment He protects His own.

In the book of the Revelation a similar event occurs:
"And after these things I saw four angels standing on the four corners of the earth, holding the four winds of the earth, that the wind should not blow on the earth, nor on the sea, not on any tree. And I saw another angel ascending from the east, having the seal of the living God: and he cried with a loud voice to the four angels, to whom it was given to hurt the earth and the sea, Saying hurt not the earth, neither the sea, nor the trees, till we have sealed the servants of our God in their foreheads. And I heard the number of them which were sealed: and there were sealed and hundred and forty and four thousand of all the tribes of the children (sons) of Israel."
(Revelation 7:1-4)

God sends His representatives to place His protective signature or mark upon those He is going to protect. In Revelation 7:3 *"The seal of the living God"* applied by His angel is later identified as *"His...name written in their foreheads" (Revelation 14:1).*

In Ezekiel the word for *"mark"* could also be translated *"signature"* and therefore is identical with what will take place in Revelation chapter seven just prior to God's judgment, the Day of the Lord's wrath. Here again, the Lord supernaturally protects His own **in the midst of** His Day of the Lord judgment. Another parallel is recorded in Ezekiel 9:3:
"And the glory of the God of Israel was gone up from the cherub, whereupon he was, to the threshold of the house."

This action taken by God before the protection of His own and the judgment of those in Jerusalem is illustrated by the promise of the Lord to the saints found in I Thessalonians 4:17:
"Then we which are alive and remain shall be caught up together with them in the clouds to meet the Lord in the air: and so shall we

ever be with the Lord."

The rapture of the saints, the blessed hope and glorious appearing of the great God and our Savior to take His own to heaven illustrates a similar event. It took place in the vision of Ezekiel as God removes His glory from its place, which is similar to the saints departing earth by rapture, when His glory is then removed.

The timing of this great event is just before His wrath begins in Revelation 8:1. He promised the saints they would be delivered from the wrath to come (I Thessalonians 1:10, 5:1-10), and so He will rapture the saints just before it begins. Just before He seals the 144 Thousand with His signature, the saints will "Pass the Torch" to the 144 Thousand.

Five parallels or similarities to the Revelation are seen in Ezekiel's vision:
1. The Lord is responsible for the judgment (Ezekiel 9:1-6 Revelation 6:17)
2. The Lord's representatives bring the judgment (Ezekiel 9:1-6; Revelation 8-11, 15-18)
3. The Lord's glory is removed before the judgment (Ezekiel 9:3; Revelation 7:9-17)
4. The Lord marks His own before the judgment (Ezekiel 9:4, 11; Revelation 7:1-8)
5. The Lord protects His own in the midst of judgment (Ezekiel 9:4-6; Revelation 3:10, 7:1-8, 9:4)

In addition, there are two other groups who have the Lord's name written upon them. The overcomers of the church of Philadelphia (Revelation 3:12) and the *"servants"* of the Lamb in heaven (Revelation 22:3, 4). Both of these groups are proven to be saints before they have the name of the Lord written upon them.

These two groups of saints receive these blessings as eternal rewards for their overcoming lives and service to the Lord. Right after the sealing of the 144 Thousand (Revelation 7:3-8), the raptured saints are seen in heaven:
*"**After this** I beheld, and, lo, a great multitude, which no man could* number, of all nations, and kindreds, and people, and tongues, stood

before the throne, and before the Lamb, clothed with white robes, and palms in their hands; And cried with a loud voice, saying, Salvation to our God which sits upon the throne, and unto the Lamb."
(Revelation 7:9, 10)

This great multitude comes *"out of great tribulation"* which indicates not the actual geographic location but the time period from whence they came. This just happens to be the right time period at this point in the chronology of the book of the Revelation for the saints to be raptured because we have come to the end of the great tribulation according to Revelation 6:12-17 and the Lord's chronology in Matthew 24:29-31.

We are right on schedule as the Lord indicated:
*"Immediately **after** the tribulation of those days shall the sun be darkened, and the moon shall not give her light, and the stars shall fall from heaven, and the powers of the heavens shall be shaken."*
(Matthew 24:29)

This is exactly where we are in the sequence of events in the book of the Revelation, for this is the sign which occurs **before** the Day of the Lord (Joel 2:30, 31), which is the wrath of God. It is about to occur with the removing of the seventh seal thereby opening the scroll which contains the wrath of God beginning with the first trumpet judgment.

The saints have been promised to be *"delivered from wrath"*
(I Thessalonians 1:10, 5:9) by the God of heaven and the timing is perfectly exact. However, before we can move from Revelation 6 which ends with the sixth seal and the announcement of *"the great day of His wrath"* (Revelation 6:17), "The Passing of the Torch" must take place.

The 144 Thousand are sealed (Revelation 7:3-8) with the signature of God on their foreheads. Then the glory of God departs (Revelation 7:9ff). The saints are raptured just before the wrath of God begins. Now…1/2 hour of silence in heaven (Revelation 8:1)…all praise to the Lord of glory is silenced…for the first time in the history of heaven…all is quiet and still…the calm before the storm. The most prophesied event in the Scripture, the Day of the Lord, is about to begin…and then the Lord initiates His fiery judgment of planet earth and its inhabitants with the sounding of the first trumpet (Revelation 8:1-7).

And so, "The Passing of the Torch" takes place. The saints are home in heaven (Revelation 7:9-17). The 144 Thousand are sealed, protected and ready to serve the Lord during the coming Day of the Lord's Wrath when they will: *"follow the Lamb wherever He goes" (Revelation 14:4)* showing their complete dedication to His will and leading as they serve Him during the fiery and tumultuous days ahead.

15.e

The 144 Thousand
The Passing of the Torch - [Part II]

As we have seen in Part I, Revelation chapter seven focuses on two significant groups of God's children. The first is the 144 Thousand and the second is the great multitude in heaven, which are the raptured saints of the ages. The 144 Thousand are now God's representatives on earth during the Day of the Lord's wrath and the resurrected and raptured saints are home in heaven.

If this chosen group of men, the 144 Thousand, are truly children of God, then why were they not raptured when the saints were caught up into heaven? How could they be God's children and not be raptured with the great multitude now in heaven? In order to answer these questions we must recognize just where we are in God's program.

At this point in time we are well into what is known as Daniel's 70th Week. The period known as the Day of the Lord is about to begin. God will be dealing with His chosen earthly people, the Jews, in these last seven years of Daniel's prophesied time period which is 490 years in duration (Daniel 9:24).

The 70th Week of Daniel is almost over, there may be but a few years left before these seven years are finished. We must recognize that the Lord always brings those whom He has chosen into His family the same way and that is *"by grace...through faith" (Ephesians 2:8).*

In the Old Testament era that ran its course until John the Baptist, the Holy Spirit of God did not indwell all those who believed. This blessing of the indwelling Holy Spirit, was and now is *"the promise of the Father" (Luke 24:49; Acts 1:4, 2:33, 39)* which was given after Jesus ascended to heaven and was glorified on the day of Pentecost (Acts 2) as taught in the New Testament.

It is theoretically possible that the 144 Thousand will be redeemed under the Old Covenant that appears to be in effect during these last seven years, which is the 70th Week of Daniel, and may not receive the indwelling Holy Spirit of God.

Then, when the rapture occurs, they will remain to serve the Lord as they do not have *"the earnest of the Spirit" (II Corinthians 1:22)* in their hearts. The earnest or down payment which is the indwelling Holy Spirit *"is the earnest of our inheritance until the redemption (rapture) of the purchased possession" (Ephesians 1:14)* which in short means that those with the indwelling Holy Spirit will be raptured and those without will not.

Those who believe God, just as Abraham: *"And he (Abraham) believed in the Lord, and He counted it to him for righteousness" (Genesis 15:6)*, will be bona-fide children of God. But, they might not possess the indwelling Spirit Who supplies the believer with the means whereby they are raptured into heaven.

The graves will open:
"The dead in Christ shall rise first, then we which are alive and remain (those with the indwelling Spirit) shall be caught up together with them in the clouds to meet the Lord in the air: and so shall we ever be with the Lord." (I Thessalonians 4:16, 17)

There are other believing Jews who will also remain on earth after the rapture. The *"two witnesses"* will prophesy *for "a thousand two hundred and three score days"* [3-1/2 years]. The rapture occurs during this 3-1/2 year time period. *"The woman"* [faithful nation of Israel] too, will remain on earth during this same time period (Revelation 12:6)

During the 70th Week, God's plan of redemption may revert to the restored (Malachi 4:5, 6; Matthew 17:11) *"holy covenant"* [Old Covenant] *(Daniel 11:28-31)* as He once again deals with the nation of Israel just as He did during the previous 483 years or 69 weeks of Daniel's 70 weeks.

If that is the case, there will those believers in the Church who enter the 70th week of Daniel, but, when those last seven years begin

(Daniel 9:24-27), God will once again deal with the Jew under the Old Covenant.

And so, "The Passing of the Torch" will be accomplished. The Church saints will "pass the torch" to the 144 Thousand and they in turn will be the Lord's representatives providing their Redemption Ministry during the Day of the Lord judgment.

This chosen group of men will remain on the earth as they *"follow the Lamb whithersoever He goes" (Revelation 14:4)* indicating their full and complete dedication to His will. This mighty group of disciples will witness of their redemption and their glorious Lord and Savior Jesus Christ to those who will remain, Jew and Gentile alike, during the great and dreadful Day of the Lord.

They will be supernaturally protected from the cataclysmic judgment of God as indicated:
*"And it was commanded them that they should not hurt the grass of the earth, neither any green thing, neither any tree: but only those men which have **not** the seal (signature) of God in their foreheads." (Revelation 9:4)*

Here is the confirmation for the purpose of the signature of God in the foreheads of the 144 Thousand. These choice young men, the 144 Thousand, who have been supernaturally sealed at the beginning of the Day of the Lord's wrath, will be protected from the tormenting judgment of the fifth trumpet.

We must recognize that what has been written above is merely a theory of how things may unfold during the time of the end concerning these two major groups of God's children. However, it is based upon Biblical truth and could well be the way the Lord brings about His plan for the end times.

If we examine the Scripture that describes these two groups it will be obvious as to whom they are and where they fit into God's plan. The 144 Thousand have at least twelve descriptive attributes that provide the Bible student with the information necessary to determine their specific role during the Day of the Lord. The first of these twelve is found in Revelation 7:3:

"Hurt not the earth, neither the sea, nor the trees, till we have sealed the servants of our God in their foreheads."

We have already covered the sealing or signature of God in their foreheads, which provides their supernatural protection during the Day of the Lord. The second attribute tells of their duty to God. They are called *"servants"* which literally means "slave or bondservant". This title is reserved for those who have surrendered their lives to the Lord for His service and glory.

Paul, James, John, Peter, Moses and the prophets are just a few of the men that are described by this word in the New Testament. These are not just nominal or newly saved children of God, no, these are the "cream of the crop", the best there is on the planet, chosen and choice bond-servants of the Living God.

The third attribute mentioned is found in Revelation 7:4:
"And I heard the number of them which were sealed: and there were sealed and hundred and forty and four thousand of all the tribes of the children (sons) of Israel."

Here we learn that they are *"sons"* which is the meaning of this Greek word translated *"children"*, so, they are men. The Lord also makes it clear that their heritage or bloodline is from His earthly chosen people, the twelve tribes of the nation of Israel.

The tribe of Dan is omitted and the tribe of Ephraim, although missing in name, is sealed under Joseph as he had only two sons, Manasseh and Ephraim. This brings up another question, "Who is a Jew?" Is a Jew a self-proclaimed proselyte of Judaism? Is a Jew one who wears the orthodox garb and is seen on the news at the Wailing Wall? No, a Jew is one who is of the bloodline of the original twelve sons of Jacob as listed in Genesis 49.

Their fourth attribute is found in Revelation 14:1:
"And I looked, and, lo, a Lamb stood on the mount Zion, and with Him and hundred forty and four thousand."

These select servants of God are seen *"with the Lamb"*. It appears that they are inseparable as the Lord's presence on mount Zion at the

187

end of the 70th week of Daniel is recorded. The next thing we are told concerns their ability:
"And no man could learn that song but the hundred and forty and four thousand." (Revelation 14:3)

They will be the only men that can learn *"the new song"* which will be played by the heavenly *"harpers"*. Their extraordinary musical ability is demonstrated here as they sing unto the Lord with the scene taking on a holy heavenly aura *"before the throne"* with both heaven and earth harmonizing in instrument and song.

Also, in verse three we are told of their redemption: *"which were redeemed from the earth."* The focal point of all Scripture is the word redemption. Here the word emphasizes the Price that was paid for the redemption or buying back of something, which in fact is already owned by God because He created all that exists.

Now He gives the life of His own Son to buy back, out of the slave market of sin, the souls of men, which He already owned. Underline the Price that was paid, the precious life Blood of Christ! This prize group of men stand upon Mount Zion with the Lamb…one of the first and the last title given to the Lord Jesus Christ in the New Testament: *"Behold, the Lamb of God that takes away the sin of the world!" (John 1:29)*

"And there shall be no more curse, but, the throne of God and of the Lamb shall be in it." (Revelation 22:3)

This is a book of redemption. No less than twenty-eight times the Lord takes the Old Testament redemption title of *"the Lamb"* in this the final book of Scripture, which has as its emphasis throughout its entirety the glorious topic of redemption.

Then, Revelation 7:4 tells of their undefiled physical purity: *"These are they which were not defiled with women; for they are virgins."* They have given themselves fully to the Lord. They have kept themselves pure physically, thereby lessening one of the great temptations that in the last days of this age will be at the highest level ever, drawing men into sin.

"These are they which follow the Lamb whithersoever He goes."
(Revelation14:4b).
This brief but fully descriptive statement indicates their total dedication to the Lord Jesus Christ. "Follow, follow, I will follow Jesus, anywhere, everywhere, I will follow Him" should be the heart-song of all who have been redeemed by the precious Blood of the Lamb.

"These were redeemed from among men, being the first fruits unto God, and to the Lamb." (Revelation 14:4c)
Here, the same word is used describing their redemption, once again emphasizing the Price paid for their eternal souls. An additional statement reveals their unique position of being *"the firstfruits"* or first to be redeemed under the Old Covenant of that future harvest of Israelites (Romans 11:25, 26) during the 70th Week of Daniel.

Their moral purity is also indicated:
"And in their mouth was found no guile for they are without fault before the throne of God." (Revelation 14:5)

The word *"guile"* lays emphasis on lies or falsehoods. *"Without fault"* indicates their blameless conduct. These men, as part of the believing remnant of Israel *"shall not do iniquity, nor speak lies; neither shall a deceitful tongue be found in their mouth"*
(Zephaniah 3:13) thereby providing them with continual abiding access before the throne of God.

This mighty group of end times Disciples of Christ is clearly identified as:
1. Sealed by the Signature of God (7:3)
2. Servants of God (7:3)
3. Sons of Israel (7:4)
4. Standing with the Lamb of God (14:1)
5. Singing a New Song (14:3a)
6. Saved from the Earth (14:3b)
7. Sanctified Physically (14:4a)
8. Surrendered Saints (14:4b)
9. Saved from among Men (14:4c)
10. Saved as the First fruits unto God and The Lamb (14:4d)
11. Sanctified Morally (14:5a)

13. Serving before the Throne of God (14:5b)

In order to fully realize the potential of this magnificent group of disciples of Christ, consider their number, 144 Thousand, revealing that they will be a mighty dynamic force for Christ during the end times when they *"follow Him wherever He goes"*. Remember that they are 12,000 times His original group of twelve disciples *"who turned the world upside down"* during the beginning of this age.

While the known world has exponentially grown since those days, their impact will be tremendously effective indeed for the Gospel of Jesus Christ, during the great tribulation (Daniel 11:32-35; 12:3, 10) when they are being prepared for their Day of the Lord Redemption Ministry.

They will be the instruments of God's mercy to those Jews and Gentiles who will be saved during the closing days of this age and the following time period called *"The great and dreadful Day of the Lord" (Malachi 4:5, 6)*. They will be ready and willing to serve the King of kings, and Lord of lords Who is:
"The Lamb of God Who takes away the sin of the world" (John 1:29)!

15.f

The 144 Thousand
The Passing of the Torch - [Part III]

The Lord has given prototypes in the persons of Daniel the prophet and his three companions, Mishael, Azariah, and Hananiah in order to understand more clearly the circumstances and characteristics of the 144 Thousand. These four young men were brought under the authority of a ruthless king when they were taken to Babylon as captives of King Nebuchadnezzar in 606 B.C.

Nebuchadnezzar is a type of the Antichrist as similarities and parallels to the end times can be seen within the historical section (Daniel 1-6) of the book of Daniel. His making of an image and demanding that all of the peoples of the known world fall down and worship it (Daniel 3) is one of the most striking parallels Nebuchadnezzar demonstrates.

This action by Nebuchadnezzar parallels the Antichrist's prophesied end time demand for universal worship, when he also will rule the world and seek to force all to worship his image as recorded in Revelation 13:1-18.

Daniel and his three companions, according to Daniel chapter one where the word eunuch is used to describe the man who was over them *"the prince of the eunuchs"*, were made eunuchs in order to serve in the palace of the king. Their duties included dealing with and being in the presence of the king's wives/women.

It was the prevailing custom for these men to be emasculated in order for them to effectively serve royalty, a custom which continued through New Testament times (Acts 8:27ff). The resulting effect on them is similar to the 144 Thousand who will be called out of every tribe as is indicated in Revelation 14:4 to serve the King of kings: *"These are they which were not defiled with women; for they are virgins."*

These men who will be protected by the Lord during the end times will also be similar to eunuchs. Although not physically emasculated, they will keep themselves physically pure giving their full devotion to the King of kings, the Lord Jesus Christ. The Lord taught a three-fold source of becoming a eunuch in Matthew 19:12:

"For there are some eunuchs, which were so born from their mother's womb: and there are some eunuchs, which were made eunuchs of men; and there be eunuchs, which have made themselves eunuchs for the kingdom of heaven's sake. He that is able to receive it, let him receive it."

Therefore, according to the Lord's teaching a man can become a eunuch:
1. Naturally
2. Man-made
3. Self-made

The 144 thousand are described as men who *"were not defiled with women"* indicating their physical purity belying their choice to fully *"follow the Lamb whithersoever He goes." (Revelation 14:4)* This personal choice amply demonstrates their complete surrender in all things in order to give every area of their lives for the maximum service and glory of their Lord. This is also a fitting description of Daniel, Hananiah, Mishael, and Azariah. These young men may well have recognized early on the call of God on their lives.

The prophecy, which Isaiah pronounced to their great-great-grandfather Hezekiah, king of Judah, could have been known by them for they themselves were *"of the king's seed" (Daniel 1:3)*. Isaiah's words spoken to Hezekiah over a century and a half earlier are clear and unmistakable:

"Behold the days come, that all that is in thine house, and that which thy fathers have laid up in store unto this day, shall be carried into Babylon: nothing shall be left, saith the Lord. And of thy sons (Daniel and his four companions) that shall issue from thee, which thou shalt beget, shall they take away; **and they shall be eunuchs in the palace of the king of Babylon.** *" (II Kings 20:17, 18)*

These four young men of royalty, who likely had access to the Scriptures, may have known ahead of time some of what God was going to do with them as the king of Babylon closed in on the city of Jerusalem. He eventually took them captive and enlisted them in his own service as recorded in the book of Daniel 1:1-7.

Their lives and impeccable service to God recorded in the book of Daniel certainly have infinite value for those who follow their pattern of service to their God. There are at least eight similarities or parallels between Daniel and his three companions and the 144 Thousand:
1. They are *"sons of Israel"*
   (Revelation 7:3; Daniel 2:25)
2. They are called *"servants of God"*
   (Revelation 7:3; Daniel 3:26)
3. They refuse to be defiled (Revelation 14:4a; Daniel 1:8)
4. They choose to follow God
   (Revelation 14:4b; Daniel 3:16-18, 28)
5. They refuse to worship an idolatrous image under the threat of death (Revelation 13; Daniel 3)
6. They are without fault (Revelation 14:5; Daniel 6:4)
7. They are seen with the Lord
   (Revelation 14:1, 17:14; Daniel 3:26, 6:22)
8. They are supernaturally protected by the Lord
   (Revelation 7:3, 9:4; Daniel 3:23-28, 7:21, 22)

The Lord, being the unchangeable and faithful God that He is, will accomplish these same things in the lives of those He will choose to represent Him during the time of the end. He will prepare this great company of *"servants of our God" (Revelation 7:3)* who will faithfully serve Him during those tumultuous but exciting days ahead.

Regardless of what theory is held concerning the timing of the events of the end times, one thing we can rely upon and that is the unchanging faithfulness of our God. He will most certainly call out and prepare that great company of 144 Thousand servants from the twelve tribes of Israel who will:
1. Be the firstfruits of the Jews to be redeemed during the 70th Week of Daniel (Revelation 14:5)
2. Serve the Lord during the Great Tribulation
   (Daniel 11:32-35, 12:3; Revelation 12:17b)
3. Serve the Lord during the Day of the Lord's wrath
   (Revelation 9:4, 14:1-5, 17:14)

15.g.1

<u>The 144 Thousand</u>
<u>The Servants of Our God – As Priests</u>

As indicated by their appearance on Mt. Zion with the Lord Jesus Christ, the Lamb, in Revelation 14:1, this group of men provide the fulfillment of a number of important Old Testament prophecies (Genesis 49:10; Psalm 110:3; Obadiah 21).

Their first and most significant role of fulfillment is tied to their origin as Hebrew *"servants of our God"* chosen from the twelve tribes of Israel named in Revelation 7:4-8. The list begins with the leader of the tribes, the most heralded son of Jacob, Judah, the one from which God in human flesh, the Messiah, the Lord Jesus Christ would descend (Hebrews 7:14).

Judah, the fourth born son of Leah, Jacob's lawful wife, inherited the position of firstborn. His three older brothers forfeited their right due to their sinful conduct as evidenced by firstborn Reuben's wicked sexual sin (Genesis 35:22) and Simeon and Levi, the second and third born, who brutally slaughtered all the men of Shechem (Genesis 34).

This list of Jacob's sons in Revelation 7:3-8 is similar in structure to the prophecy of Jacob in Genesis 49:1-28 as he first mentions the sons of Leah, then the sons of the two maids, Bilhah and Zilpah, with Rachel's two sons listed last.

Dan, who is replaced by Manasseh, Joseph's oldest son, is the only tribe not seen in the Revelation 7:3-8 list. Ephraim, whose name is absent, is silently represented because his seed are accounted for in the 12,000 sealed under his father Joseph's name as Joseph had only two sons, Manasseh and Ephraim. Those sealed under Joseph's name are also the descendants of Ephraim.

The 144 Thousand are singled out by their unique position as the only group called the *"first fruits unto God and unto the Lamb"* *(Revelation 14:4).* These young men who have been chosen, prepared and physically sealed by God for His divine protection (Revelation 9:4), are the first to be saved, during the restored (Malachi 4:5, 6; Matthew 17:11) *"holy covenant"* *(Daniel 11:28-31)* dispensation, the 70th Week of Daniel, which is the last week of the seventy weeks that God has determined upon Daniel's *"people"* *(Daniel 9:24).*

They are the first of that great company of Israelites who will later be saved when *"the Redeemer [Lord Jesus Christ] comes to Zion"* *(Isaiah 59:20)* and *"all Israel shall be saved"* *(Romans 11:26).* The 144 Thousand are not just a random group of Israelites chosen to guarantee a remnant to inherit the physical promises given to the Jews under the Old Covenant. No, these men are selected, saved, sealed and serve the King of kings as they *"follow Him wherever He goes"* *(Revelation 14:4)* showing their full and complete surrender to His will.

One of their likely duties as God's end of the age *"holy nation"* *(Exodus 19:5, 6; Psalm 110:3; I Peter 2:9; Revelation 14:1-5),* may be to fulfill the conditional covenant made by God with the nation of Israel in Exodus 19:1-6. when He physically met with the people of Israel as a nation for the first time.

The statement made in Exodus 19:5, 6 shows His intent for the nation and each individual Israelite:
*'Now, therefore, **if** ye will obey My voice indeed, and **keep My covenant**, then ye shall be a peculiar treasure unto Me above all people: for all the earth is Mine. And ye shall be unto me a kingdom **of priests and an holy nation.**"*

This conditional covenant made at Mt. Sinai was ultimately broken and left unfulfilled by the disobedience, rebellion, and idolatry of the people of Israel (Exodus 32). The Lord Jesus Christ in His full and complete obedience fulfilled the Old Covenant. His sacrificial death on the Cross paid the penalty for all sin and in reality paid the sin debt for all mankind (I John 2:2). Therefore this broken covenant in fact was atoned for by His once for all sacrifice (Hebrews 10:10, 14).

The importance of this conditional covenant remains intact. God's desire to have this great company of priests ministering to Him continues, (Psalm 110:3; I Peter 2:5, 9; Revelation 1:5; 5:10; 20:6) as the Scripture affirms that there have been *"priests unto God"* ministering to Him and for Him throughout the ages in every dispensation.

He has given each and every new covenant believer the privilege and opportunity to enter into the holiest (Hebrews 10:19) and fulfill this covenant. This was God's original intention and primary calling for each and every person in the nation of Israel just as it now is for each and every born-again believer.

When the Church saints are raptured removing God's priests from the earth and the Day of the Lord judgments begin, the 144 Thousand will remain to perform this most vital ministry.

That this great company of 144 Thousand will be holy priests unto God during the Day of the Lord is indicated by this prophetic description:
"Thy people [troops/warrior/priests] shall be willing in the day of Thy power [Day of the Lord] in the beauties of holiness [priestly vestments/garments], from the womb of the morning, Thou hast the dew [multitude] of Thy youth [young men]." (Psalm 110:3)

Based on the position and character of the 144 Thousand as they enter into this unique time of service to God during the Day of the Lord, they will likely fulfill this broken covenant as they will be serving during a time when this kingdom of priests will be protected during the Day of the Lord (Revelation 9:4) *"following the Lamb wherever He goes" (Revelation14:1-5).* They will be ministering to and for the Lord, thereby orchestrating the plan of God on earth through powerful praise and intercessory prayer during the most intense spiritual battle of the ages.

Psalm 110 is regarded as the crown jewel of the book of Psalms. This short but powerful revelation by King David provides the believer with marvelous insight concerning David's Lord, the Messiah, the King of kings, our Great High Priest the Lord Jesus Christ.

While it is one of the most quoted Psalms in the New Testament, the important fact here is the One Who quoted its truth as He dealt with the Pharisees concerning His identity as the Messiah, David's Lord and the Son of Jehovah God.

The Lord Jesus referred to this Psalm a number of times during His earthly ministry (Matthew 22:44, 26:64; Mark 12:64, 14:62; 16:19; Luke 20:42, 22:69). It is also utilized over a dozen other times in the New Testament demonstrating its vital importance in the overall scheme of God's unfolding revelation.

The focus in this brief look at Psalm 110 is prophetic, for the majority of the subject matter covered in this Psalm has yet to take place in the course of history. This Messianic Jewel of the Psalms, revealing past and present truth concerning the Lord Jesus Christ, also provides the believer with vital truth in understanding the end times and "The People of the Apocalypse" as indicated in the Revelation of Jesus Christ in concert with this Psalm.

The coronation of the King of kings, the Lord Jesus Christ is indicated in the opening verse of Psalm 110:
"The LORD said unto my Lord, sit Thou at My right hand until I make Thy enemies Thy footstool."

This clearly underlines Jehovah God's certain intent to give the Lord Jesus Christ eventual physical dominion over the entire earth (Psalm 2:6-9). This first verse also pinpoints the timing of the Psalm as the Lord Jesus Christ has just ascended to heaven (Acts 1:9-11) and is invited by His Father to sit at His right hand.

He sat down at the Father's right hand and was exalted (Acts 2:33) and subsequently sent *"the promise of the Father"*, the Holy Spirit, to His people (Acts 2:1-4) which He promised (Luke 24:49; John 14:16, 17, 26, 15:26, 16:7, 13, 14; Acts 1:4).

The second verse begins the progressive unfolding of end times events which God the Father will bring to pass as He brings Christ's enemies into submission:
"The LORD shall send the rod [tribe] of Thy strength out of Zion, rule Thou in the midst of Thine enemies." (Psalm 110:2)

The phrase *"rod of Thy strength"* some apply to the Church or the Holy Spirit for He was and is now the Person Who empowers and strengthens believers thereby glorifying and exalting the Lord Jesus Christ. He is the Holy Instrument by which Jesus now rules as Lord.

The Church and the Holy Spirit both came *"out of Zion"*, which is the city of Jerusalem, and loosely "fit" the requirements of the passage. However, bringing the Lord Jesus Christ's enemies into submission is not His primary purpose for the Church.

The Church's primary purpose is to be a *"witness"* unto Christ as indicated by the Lord in all five of His commissions: (Matthew 28: 18-20; Mark 16:15; Luke 24:46-48; John 15:16; Acts 1:8) which He gave His disciples and now apply to His Body the Church.

Although it is through the Holy Spirit that God's work and will are now accomplished by the Church, the focus of this Psalm is in the future day when Jehovah God brings into submission the enemies of His Son, not the present-day witnessing of the Church of Jesus Christ.

God will ultimately bring the enemies of the Lord Jesus Christ into submission during His day, the eschatological Day of the Lord. This future end times event is clearly defined in Scripture as it is the most prophesied time in the Word of God.

The Hebrew word "matteh" translated *"rod"* in Psalm 110:2 is found in the Old Testament (251) times with (182) of those occurrences translated *"tribe"*, (52) occurrences translated *"rod"* and (15) times it is translated *"staff"*.

The Theological Wordbook of the Old Testament supplies the following information concerning this word: "Although the term properly means "staff" or "rod," it is usually rendered (some 180 times) "tribe". The reference is usually to one of the twelve tribes by name. At first, apparently, each tribal ruler led his group with a staff. This suggests that the ruler's staff may have originally been a symbol of the tribe (cf. Num 17:2-10 [H 17-25] and eventually betokened leadership and authority (cf. Ps 110:2; Jer 48:17)." p.574 Vol.1

Also, the Hebrew word "shebet" a synonym of "matteh" is the

word translated "rod" or "scepter" in all of the other Old Testament Messianic passages which speak of the Messiah's rod/scepter (Genesis 49:10; Numbers 24:17; Psalm 2:9, 45:6; Isaiah 11:4).

This is the word the Bible utilizes to define the ruling or smiting of the nations by the Messiah, which will occur during the Day of the Lord. The "shebet" passages above refer to the future rule and the accompanying discipline of the Messiah, the Lord Jesus Christ, when He comes as *"King of kings and Lord of Lords" (Revelation 19:15).*

The phrase *"rod of Thy strength"* might be better translated *"tribe of Thy strength"* indicating the tribe of Judah from which the Lord Jesus Christ descended (Hebrews 7:14).

To the tribe of Judah, *"a lion's whelp" (Genesis 49:9)* a prolonged dominion is promised [ISBE p.1738 Vol.3] through the Messiah, so it is listed first in Revelation 7:5 as the leader of the twelve tribes.

Judah will likely lead the assault upon *"the Assyrian" [Antichrist] (Micah 5:5)* not unlike the days during Antiochus Epiphanes [type of Antichrist] similar invasion of Israel in the past (168 B.C.). Then Judas Maccabeus "The Hammer" of the tribe of Judah led his warriors to an incredible and most miraculous victory over Antiochus Epiphanes, the ruthless ruler of that day (I Maccabees).

The Lord Jesus Christ as *"The Lion of the Tribe of Judah" (Revelation 5:5),* will lead His forces in that day. This is indicated in Micah's *"last days" (Micah 4:1)* passage recorded in the second message (Micah 3:1-5:15) of his book, which focuses on the Coming King, the Lord Jesus Christ:
"And this Man [The Lord Jesus Christ/Messiah] shall be the Peace when the Assyrian shall come into our land: and when he shall tread in our palaces, then shall we raise against him seven shepherds and eight principal men." (Micah 5:5)

"Thy people shall be willing in the day of Thy power, in the beauties of holiness, from the womb of the morning, Thou hast the dew of Thy youth." (Psalm 110:3)

The next period of time immediately following the present age of grace is *"the day of Thy power'* also known as the Day of the Lord, when Christ returns *"in power and great glory" (Matthew 24:30)*. During the Day of the Lord, the Lord Jesus Christ will have *"with Him" (Revelation 14:1, 17:14)* a group of obedient followers (Revelation 14:4) known as these 144 Thousand servants of God.

Psalm 110:3 describes them, providing some distinct qualities and duties of this group of God's servants who *"shall be willing in the day of Thy [Lord Jesus Christ] power"*.

The word *"people" (Psalm 110:3)* appears in the Old Testament over 1800 times and is variously translated. On occasion, as recorded in I Samuel 11 where it is found six times, it has the emphasis of *"troops"* specifically in (v.11) when *"Saul put the people [troops] in three companies"* which is recorded in the Theological Wordbook of the Old Testament p.676 Vol.2 ". There are also a number of passages where the word [people] means 'troops'.

In keeping with the dominating militant theme of this Psalm the NIV gives this interpretation of (Psalm 110:3):
"Your troops shall be willing on your day of battle. Arrayed in holy majesty, from the womb of the dawn you will receive the dew of your youth."

The NASV translates this same verse:
"Thy people will volunteer freely in the day of Thy power; In holy array, from the womb of the dawn, Thy youth are to Thee as the dew."

The same willing obedience of the 144 Thousand is recorded in Revelation 14:4 where they *"follow the Lamb wherever He goes"*, having already surrendered themselves to His Lordship long before when they decided to follow Jesus, giving themselves as literal bond-servants of the King of kings (Revelation 7:3).

Their personal holiness before God *"In the beauties of holiness" (Psalm 110:3)* also is confirmed in Revelation 14:4, 5:
"These are they which were not defiled with women...And in their mouth was found no guile: for they are without fault before the throne of God."

Their physical purity and spiritual holiness affords them the ability to continually *"follow the Lamb"* giving them unbroken access to the throne of God where they fulfill their ministry priority as priests unto God.

The last phrase of Psalm 110:3 *"Thou hast the dew of Thy youth"* provides additional information concerning the 144 Thousand. The word *"dew"* most likely indicates their great number, and, as the dew provides refreshment and blessing to the earth, they too, will give these same benefits to those to whom they minister:

*"And the remnant of Jacob shall be in the midst of many people as a **dew** from the Lord, as the showers upon the grass, that tarries not for man, nor waits for the sons of men." (Micah 5:7)*

As priests unto God they will be a blessing direct from God, not dependent on men. The word "*youth*" of Psalm 110:3 is only found in the Old Testament three times with the other two occurrences in Ecclesiastes 11:9, 10:

*"Rejoice, O **young man**, in thy youth; and let thy heart cheer thee in the days of thy youth, and walk in the ways of thine heart, and in the sight of thine eyes; but know thou, that for all these things God will bring thee into judgment. Therefore remove sorrow from they heart, and put away evil from thy flesh: for **childhood** and youth are vanity."*

This word in Psalm 110:3 indicates a designated group of young men, who will be active during the end times, willing to follow the Lord which accurately describes the 144 Thousand.

This approximates their age and agrees with the tenor of Revelation 14:4 where their virginity is recorded requiring a decision which must be made by these young men early in manhood. The age of twenty was specified in the book of Numbers when the first census was taken for those men who were able and old enough to go to war:

"Take ye the sum of all the congregation of the sons of Israel, after their families, by the house of their fathers, with the number of their names every male by their polls: From twenty years old and upward, all that are able to go forth to war in Israel." (Numbers 1:2, 3

This indicates the age that may likely determine the lower limit for these young soldiers of Christ. They will in fact see spiritual and physical combat as war against the saints occurs during the end times which is clearly indicated in Scripture (Daniel 7:21; Revelation 12:17, 13:7, 17:14, 19:19).

These young men will remain in the land when *"the woman"* [Faithful Israel] of Revelation 12 flees into the wilderness for every young man in present-day Israel is required to serve in the armed forces.

There will be two major assaults against Israel prior to Armageddon with the first beginning at the mid-point of the 70th Week of Daniel which centers upon Judea and the city of Jerusalem (Ezekiel 38:8-16; Daniel 12:1; Matthew 24:15-21).

The second battle will take place in the *"valley of Jehosophat" (Joel 3:1-8; Zechariah 14:1, 2)* with these young men taking part as *"the remnant of Jacob"* when:
"The Assyrian [Antichrist] shall come into our land: and when he shall tread in our palaces" (Micah 5:5-8).

Bible commentator W. Graham Scroggie, D.D. speaks on Psalm 110:3 in his commentary on the Psalms, p.87: "The beauties of holiness..." the reference is to holy attire, holy garments, priestly vestments. The soldiers are priests. The consecrated are warriors. These two sides of Christian calling and character are vitally related. Because we are *"Priests unto God"* we are to *"put on the whole armour of God" (Revelation.1: 6; Ephesians 6:11).* "Thou hast the dew of thy youth" Maclaren translates as "From the womb of the dawn (comes) to Thee the dew of Thy youth (s)"; and he says, 'the principal point of comparison of the army with the dew is probably its multitude.'

From:
Spurgeon's Treasury of David
Ver. 3. —The subjects of the Priest King are willing soldiers. In accordance with the warlike tone of the whole Psalm, our text describes the subjects as an army. That military metaphor comes out more closely when we attach the true meaning of the words, "in the day of thy power". The word rendered, and rightly rendered, "power",

has the same ambiguity which that word has in the English of the date of our translation, and for a century later, as you may find in Shakespeare and Milton, who both used it in the sense of "army". Singularly enough we do not employ "powers" in that meaning, but we do another word which means the same thing—and talk of "forces", meaning thereby "troops"..."The day of thy power" is not a mere synonym for "the time of thy might", but means specifically "the day of thine army", that is, "the day when thou dost muster thy forces and set them in array for the war". The King is going forth to conquest. But he goes not alone. Behind him come his faithful followers, all pressing on with willing hearts and high courage. — Alexander McLaren, 1871.

Ver. 3. —Thy people, etc. In homage, they shall be like a company of priests in sacred vestments, for they shall appear "in the beauties of holiness". In number, they shall be like the countless dewdrops "from the womb of the morning", sparkling in the rays of the rising sun, and reflecting his radiance. In glory they shall bear the likeness of Christ's resurrection in all its vernal freshness: "Thou hast the dew of thy youth". —Benjamin Wildon Cart.

Ver. 3. —In the beauties of holiness. In holy vestments as priests. They are at once warriors and priests; meet for the service of Him who was King and Priest. Neander (Mem. of Chr. Life, ch. 4) remarks on the connection between these two sides of the Christian character. God's soldiers can only maintain their war by priestly self-consecration. Conversely: God's priests can only preserve their purity by unintermitted conflict. —William Kay.

Ver. 3. —In the beauties of holiness. This expression is usually read as if it belonged either to the words immediately proceeding, or to those immediately following. In either case the connection is somewhat difficult and obscure. It seems better regarded as a distinct and separate clause, adding a fresh trait to the description of the army. And what that is we need not find any difficulty in ascertaining. "The beauties of holiness" is a frequent phrase for the sacerdotal garments, the holy festal attire of the priests of the Lord. So considered, how beautifully it comes in here. The conquering King whom the psalm hymns is a Priest forever; and an army of priests follows him. The soldiers are gathered in the day of the muster, with high courage and willing devotion, ready to fling away their lives; but they are clad not in mail, but in priestly robes; like those who wait before the altar rather than like those who plunge into the fight, like those who compassed Jericho with the ark for their standard and the trumpets for all their weapons. We can scarcely fail to remember the words, which echo these and interpret them. "The armies which were in heaven followed him on white horses, clothed in fine linen, white and clean" —a strange armor against sword cut and spear thrust. —Alexander McLaren.

Ver. 3. —Thou hast the dew of thy youth. These words are often misunderstood, and taken to be a description of the fresh, youthful energy attributed by the Psalm to the Priest King of this nation of soldier priests. The misunderstanding, I suppose, has led to the common phrase, "the dew of one's youth". The reference of the expression is to the army, not to its leader. "Youth" here is a collective noun, equivalent to "young men". The host of his soldier subjects is described as a band of young warriors, whom he leads, in their fresh strength and countless numbers and gleaming beauty like the dew of the morning... It is as a symbol of the refreshing which a weary world will receive from the conquests and presence of the King and his host, that they are likened to the glittering morning dew. Another prophetic Scripture gives us the same emblem when it speaks of Israel being "in the midst of many people as a dew from the Lord". Such ought to be the effect of our presence. We are meant to gladden, to adorn, to refresh this parched, prosaic world, with freshness brought from the chambers of the sunrise. —Alexander McLaren.

Matthew Henry writes-p.660 'That they should be a willing people, a people of willingness, alluding to servants that choose their service and are not coerced to it...to soldiers that are volunteers and not pressed men...That they should be so in the day of His power, in the day of Thy muster (so some) when Thou art enlisting soldiers thou shalt find a multitude of volunteers...Or when Thou art drawing them out to battle they shall be willing to *"follow the Lamb whithersoever He goes" (Revelation 14:4).*

W. Graham Scroggie, William Kay, Alexander McLaren, and Matthew Henry all see the *"people"* here in Psalm 110:3 as soldiers of the Lord's army with most of these commentators also giving them the duty of priests. Matthew Henry also indicates they are the 144 Thousand as he refers to them following *"the Lamb whithersoever*

He goes."
    (Revelation 14:4)

   This future army of the King of Kings will be completely submissive to the will of God during the Day of the Lord. These young soldiers of Christ will be involved in the intense spiritual warfare at the end of the age as priests unto God. They will be arrayed in holiness doing the Lord's service *"before the throne of God"* (Revelation 14:1, 4).

   These *"priests unto God"* are involved in this future holy warfare when the battle is at its most heightened level, when Satan *"knows that he has but a short time" (Revelation 12:12).*

   Scroggie, in his commentary on the Psalms, adds "Messiah's soldiers are declared to be priests (Psalm 110:3) before His own priesthood is announced." p.88.

   In Psalm 110:4 David continues to address the Lord Jesus Christ telling Him of His eternal priesthood which is pronounced by Jehovah:
"The LORD hath sworn and will not repent, Thou art a priest forever after the order of Melchizedek."

   The LORD Jehovah, told Jesus of His future actions in Psalm 110:2, 3 before He declared the Lord Jesus Christ's present High Priestly office in Psalm 110:4, remembering that the Psalm (Psalm 110:2-4) is addressing the Lord Jesus after He ascended to heaven.

   Jehovah in Psalm 110:4 takes an oath and tells of Jesus' present ministry to the Father and the saints as:
"He ever lives to make intercession for those who come unto God by Him." (Hebrews 7:25)

   The consecration of our Great High Priest King is accomplished in this the key verse of Psalm 110 being thoroughly explained in the book of Hebrews chapters 5-9. However, our focus here is on the 144 Thousand and in (v.5-7) they are directly addressed:
"The Lord at thy right hand shall strike through kings in the day of His wrath."(Psalm 110:5)

Here, the people [troops/priests/144 Thousand] (Psalm 110:3) are given the promise of the Lord's presence *"at thy right hand"* when He pours out His devastating wrath upon the earth dwellers during the Day of the Lord.

This agrees with Revelation 6:16, 17:
"From the wrath of the Lamb: For the great day of His wrath is come; and who is able to stand?"

Although the Day of the Lord is described as the wrath of God (Isaiah 13:9; Zephaniah 1:15), in the first reference to wrath in the book of the Revelation it is also designated *"the wrath of the Lamb"*.

The overriding tone of Psalm 110 is one of dominion, troops, warfare and human carnage which is brought on by the Lord's judgment of earth through the outpouring of His eschatological Day of the Lord/ *"day of His wrath" (Psalm 110:5)*. This couples accurately with the warfare and judgment thoroughly detailed in the Revelation of Jesus Christ (Revelation 8, 9, 15-19).

Notice, the word *"Lord"* [Adonai] *(Psalm 110:5)* continues to refer to the Lord Jesus Christ, as in Psalm 110:1. This promise of the Lord's presence with His people as indicated by His *"right hand"* is found in the Psalms twenty one times and refers to the power, authority and blessing of the Lord to His people in nineteen of these occurrences.

Here, the promise of the blessed presence of the Lord Jesus Christ is given when *"this Man [Messiah] will be the peace" (Micah 5:5)* for those who will be *"with Him" (Revelation 14:1, 17:14)* during *"the day of His wrath" (Psalm 110:5)*.

Psalm 110:6 vividly portrays the Divine Judge's wrath as it is poured out upon earth:
"He shall judge among the heathen, He shall fill the places with the dead bodies, He shall wound the heads [kings of the earth] over many countries."

His Day of the Lord judgment includes the death of over one third of the world population (Revelation 9:15, 16:3) and the final event of the Day of the Lord, the battle of Armageddon, will execute deadly judgment upon the *"kings of the earth" (Revelation 19:19-21).*

The closing verse pictures the Lord Jesus Christ's actions and attitude of complete victory after the Day of the Lord's wrath is ended:
"He shall drink from the brook in the way, therefore shall He lift up the head." (Psalm 110:7)

The Lord is physically refreshed and assumes the well-deserved appearance and expression of His triumphant victory after His work of judgment is over, after the climactic battle of Armageddon (Revelation 19:11-21) has ended.

This brief Psalm comes to a quiet close after covering the time from the Lord's ascension to the Father's right hand, moving over the present Church age in order to focus completely on the great and dreadful Day of the Lord when God the Father will make the Lord Jesus Christ's enemies His footstool.

While the emphasis is upon the Messiah, the Lord Jesus Christ and His eternal position of King/Great High Priest, much additional information is given concerning *"Thy people...thy youth"*, those who will be His loyal subjects during those coming days at the time of the end:
1. They are willing servants.
   (Psalm 110:3; Revelation 7:3, 14:4, 5)
2. They minister during *"The day of Thy power"*/Day of the Lord.
   (Psalm 110:3; Revelation 9:4, 14:1, 17:14)
3. They are holy priests/warriors.
   (Psalm 110:3; Revelation 14:4, 5)
4. They will be refreshing *"as dew"* to Israel/God's people.
   (Psalm 110:3; Micah 5:7; Revelation 14:4, 5)
5. They will be destructive *"as lions"* to Gentiles/earth dwellers.
   (Psalm 110:3; Micah 5:8; Revelation 17:14)
6. They will be a great multitude *"as dew"*.
   (Psalm 110:3; Revelation 7:3-8)
7. They will be young Hebrew men.
   (Psalm 110:3; Revelation 7:3, 14:4)

These young men will play a key role during the days leading up to the time of their sealing which includes the time of the Great Tribulation. Daniel chapter seven tells of the saints being *"given into the hand" (Daniel 7:25)* of the Antichrist. He makes *"war with the saints"* and *"prevails against them" (Daniel7: 21)* wearing out the saints (Daniel 7:25) for a period of three and one half years which is also indicated in Revelation 13:7.

This intense time of persecution will be unparalleled and the Redemption Ministry of this great kingdom of priests, the 144 Thousand, during that time will be the Lord's line of protection for the saints on earth in an hour when Satan's wrath will be at its maximum strength. (Revelation 12:12)

This theory is based upon the 144 Thousand being Old Covenant believers having full knowledge of the New Testament, *"redeemed from the earth...and from among men" (Revelation 14:3, 4)*. Their first priority is to fulfill the primary purpose and calling of every New Testament believer, which is to be a priest unto God (I Peter 2:5, 9; Revelation 1:5, 5: 10, and 20:6).

This is the focus of the believer's service and is listed in conjunction with redemption on two occasions (Revelation 1:5, 5:10) indicating that the primary purpose for redemption itself is to create this great company of priests unto God, for ministry to Him and men on His behalf.

They also represent the nation of Israel. As the Lord begins to again deal with Israel during the 70th Week of Daniel the restored (Matthew 17:11) *"holy covenant" (Daniel 11:28-32)* economy will once again prevail, just as it was in effect during the first 69 Weeks of this period of 70 Weeks that God has determined upon His people and upon His holy city. (Daniel 9:24)

This single theory based on Bible truth provides the answer to the questions: Why did not the 144 Thousand, and *"the woman"* [Faithful Israel] of Revelation 12, and the *"two witnesses"* of Revelation 11 get caught up together with the other saints when the Lord Jesus Christ came in the clouds?

One possibility is that they were saved under the Old Covenant and were not sealed by the Holy Spirit as New Covenant believers but were physically sealed with the name of God and the Lamb in their foreheads. Therefore they may not have the *"earnest of their inheritance" (Ephesians 1:13, 14),* the indwelling Holy Spirit.

Another possibility is that the Lord has simply chosen to select certain of His earthly people, the Jews, to remain and accomplish His purposes during His Day of the Lord wrath. Then He will execute *"the time of Jacob's trouble" (Jeremiah 30:7)* which is specifically designed to purge and purify those Jews (Zechariah 13:9) who will be saved when their Redeemer comes to Zion (Isaiah 59:20; Romans 11:25, 26) at the end of the 70th Week (Revelation 11:15, 14:1).

"The woman" [Faithful Israel] of Revelation 12 will be fed and nourished in the wilderness during the last half of Daniel's 70th Week. The *"two witnesses"* of Revelation 11:3-14 will minister during the last half of Daniel's 70th Week and the 144 Thousand will perform their Redemption Ministry during those same 3-1/2 years (Revelation 9:4, 14:1).

All of these faithful Jews will remain on earth after the resurrection of the dead in Christ and the rapture of the living saints (I Thessalonians 4:16, 17). This end times timeline is based upon the chronological order of events (Matthew 24:3-31) the Lord Jesus Christ clearly gave to *"Peter and James and John and Andrew" (Mark 13:3),* His inner circle of disciples.

This also answers the question concerning the saints who are given into the hand of the Antichrist (Daniel 7:25) for 3-1/2 years which is the last half of Daniel's 70th Week. These Jews will be saved under the Old Covenant and might not be sealed with the Holy Spirit. They will be purposely left behind to serve the Lord during the *"time of Jacob's trouble"* which occurs during the seven trumpet judgments (Revelation 8:1-11:19) at the very beginning of the *"great and dreadful Day of the Lord" (Malachi 4:5, 6).*

The 70th Week of Daniel will, just as the other dispensations, transition or merge into effect with the confirming of the covenant by the many of Israel and the Antichrist (Daniel 9:27) as the actual starting point, just as the Day of Pentecost in Acts 2 became the actual starting point of the dispensation of grace.

But, there was a merging of economies as John the Baptist preached and the Lord's earthly ministry unfolded and then the Old Covenant continuing to operate after Pentecost in practice by the Jews while the New Covenant was in fact fully effective and functioning on the Day of Pentecost.

This merging of economies has been the Lord's pattern throughout the ages as the economy of Conscience, Human Government, Promise and Law also transitioned into effect with all of them continuing to run in the background still having effect in principle even now as the ages roll.

We also must keep in mind that when the majority of the New Testament was written the required elements were in place in order for the Lord to return. The Jews were in the land, as a people/nation, they occupied Jerusalem, the temple was on Mount Zion, and the Old Covenant with the sacrificial system was operating.

These conditions definitely influenced the anticipation for the Lord's Second Coming by the Early Church, and caused an intense urgency in the believers to expect the Lord's coming post-haste. They correctly viewed the prophetic Scriptures and understood the possibility for the Lord to return in that day as the above prerequisites were in place.

When all five of these prerequisites were brought to their end in A.D. 70 by the Roman army's decimation of the Jews as a people, the complete destruction of the temple and the city of Jerusalem, Israel as a nation and the Old Covenant practices with its sacrificial system were also brought to their conclusion.

However, the Apostle John's epistles (I, II, III John) were all written **after** the destruction of Jerusalem in 70 A.D. and the dispersion of the Jews. These books of the Bible authored by John between A.D. 80-95 do not echo the same urgency as the epistles of Paul and Peter concerning the Lord's Coming for John knew that the above prerequisites were necessary in order for the Lord to return in that day.

At this present time [2007] three of those five elements are now back in place. We must ever be aware of exactly where we stand in this day as the merging of this last "Jewish" economy has begun for the Jews are a people, in the land, and occupy the city of Jerusalem.

These prophesied events are the first three prerequisites in order for the 70th Week of Daniel to begin and the Lord Jesus to return (Deuteronomy 30:3-5; Daniel 9:24). The following list shows those prerequisites mentioned above and includes a number of other events required for the *"time of the end/70th Week of Daniel"* to unfold:
1. The Jews will be a *"people"*/nation (Daniel 9:24)
2. The Jews will be in their promised *"land"* (Deuteronomy 30:5; Matthew 24:16)
3. The Jews will occupy their *"holy city"* Jerusalem (Daniel 9:24)
4. The prophet Elijah will be sent to *"restore all things"* (Malachi 4:5, 6; Matthew 17:11)
5. The *"holy covenant"* will be restored (Daniel 11:28-32)
6. *"The temple of God"* will be rebuilt (Daniel 11:31; II Thessalonians 2:1-4; Revelation 11:1, 2)
7. The *"holy place"* will be included (Matthew 24:15)
8. The *"regular/daily sacrifices"* will be instituted (Daniel 8:11, 12, 9:27, 11:31, 12:11)
9. The Jews will *"worship"* in the temple (Revelation 11:1.2)
10. *"The Sabbath"* will be honored (Matthew 24:20)
11. The sending of prophets to the people of God will occur (Malachi 4:5, 6; Matthew 17:11; Revelation 11:3-14)
12. *"The twelve tribes of Israel"* will be recognized (Revelation 7:4-8)

Also, the Lord's prophecy concerning the *"beginning of sorrows"* *(Matthew 24:8)* has already begun to take place as the 19th century witnessed the most massive influx of *"false Christs"* with the birth and rise of the major 'Christian' cults:
1. The Jehovah 'false' Witnesses
2. The Mormons/Latter Day 'false' Saints
3. The Seventh Day Adventist
4. The Christian Science 'false' Church

211

Then, the last half of the 19th century, along with the first half of the 20th· saw USA's Civil War, World War I, World War II and numerous other major conflicts which defines the period of *"wars and rumors of war" (Matthew 24:6).*

The last part of the 20th century, and now, the beginning of the 21st reveal that we are nearing the very end of the *"the beginning of sorrows"* as increasing *"famines and pestilences [AIDS, Ebola, Avian Flu] and earthquakes"* are evident and continue to rise in magnitude, intensity and number. (Matthew 24:5-8)

Lest this may sound as though anticipation for the soon Coming of the Lord is waning, it is a certain and indisputable fact that God is able to bring about the necessary conditions and events rapidly, in His perfect timing, just as He wills.

The expectation for the return of the Lord Jesus Christ, during this very *"generation"* when *"all these things" (Matthew 24:33, 34)* are surely coming to pass, will continue to be on high alert, until we see Him ***"in the clouds"****! (Daniel 7:13; Matthew 24:30; Acts 1:9-11; I Thessalonians 4:17; Revelation 1:7)*

15.g.2

The 144 Thousand
The Servants of Our God – As Warriors

Revelation 17:14 tells of the Lord's end of the age victory:
*"These [10 horns/kings] shall make war with the Lamb, and the Lamb shall overcome them: for He is Lord of lords, and King of kings: and **they that are with Him** [144 Thousand] (Revelation 14:1, 4) are called, and chosen, and faithful."*

This brief description of the 144 Thousand warriors shows them as those who are chosen from the twelve tribes and are:
*"**with the Lamb...**following Him wherever He goes"* (Revelation 14:1, 4)...*"for many are called, but few are chosen." (Matthew 22:14)*

This verse in Matthew's gospel underlines the meaning of what is said about these choice saints for they are not only called to be the end times warriors but they are also chosen and faithful. While some identify those who are *"called"* to be with the Lord in this verse (Revelation 17:14) as the raptured saints in heaven, the only ones in time of the end Scripture who are clearly shown to be *"with Him"* and *"follow Him wherever He goes"* are the 144 Thousand Jewish soldiers of Christ *(Revelation 14:1-5).*

The word *"faithful"* in Revelation 17:14 really eliminates the glorified saints for faith is no longer necessary when face to face with the Lord in heaven for to be unfaithful is not a possibility for one who is no longer able to sin.

The faithfulness of the 144 Thousand gives them the desire and ability to *"follow the Lamb whithersoever He goes"* putting them in the midst of the intense warfare which will be waged during the end times. They will become the primary targets of Satan after *"the woman" [faithful Israel]* flees to safety to her place in the wilderness which is prepared by God (Revelation 12:6, 14):
"And the dragon [Satan] was wroth with the woman, and went to

make war with the remnant [rest] of her seed [144 Thousand], which keep the commandments of God, and have the testimony of Jesus Christ." (Revelation 12:17)

It appears that the 144 Thousand are the physical warriors who go with the Lord Jesus Christ to battle against the army of the ten horns/kings (Revelation 17:12-14), the *"kings of the east" (Revelation 16:12),* and *"the kings...of the whole world" (Revelation 16:14).* These kings are collectively known as *"the kings of the earth" (Revelation 19:19)* who go to *"the battle of the great day of God Almighty" (Revelation 16:14)* which is the battle of Armageddon.

They may also be active as physical soldiers in Israel during the Antichrist's initial assault upon Jerusalem:
"And this Man [Messiah] shall be the peace, when the Assyrian [Antichrist] shall come into our land: and when he shall tread in our palaces, then shall we raise against him seven shepherds, and eight principal men. And they shall waste the land of Assyria with the sword." (Micah 5:5, 6)

But this is not where their ministry begins. They are present (Revelation 12:17b) during the persecution which intensifies at the mid-point of the 70th Week of Daniel. Then, the Antichrist stops the daily sacrifice and the abomination of desolation [Antichrist's image] is set up in the holy place (Daniel 8:11, 9:27, 11:31, 12:11; Matthew 24:15; II Thessalonians 2:3, 4).

Revelation 12, which focuses on Israel and the Hebrew people, closes with a statement telling of *"the dragon" [Satan]* as he makes *"war with the remnant [rest] of her [The woman/faithful Israel] seed, [the ones which are keeping] the commandments of God and [the ones having] the testimony of Jesus Christ." (Revelation 12:17b)*

The phrase *"of her seed"* indicates the physical seed of the woman and the rest of the verse *"which keep the commandments of God, and have the testimony of Jesus Christ"* shows them as faithful obedient brethren. There will also be those Jews in the land who do not keep the commandments of God nor will they have the testimony of Jesus Christ (Daniel 11:30).

This verse points out their physical relationship to *"the woman"*. They are Jews, and their faithful obedience to the Lord during the second half of the 70th Week of Daniel is also indicated.

That Satan's persecution will be focused upon these saved Jews indicates that there will also be unsaved Jews who will not be Satan's target. This is clearly indicated in Daniel 11:28-31 where the unsaved Jews collaborate with the Antichrist and *"forsake the holy covenant"* along with still another group of Jews:

"They that understand [the rest of her seed (Revelation 12:17b)] among the people shall instruct many" indicating there will be three different groups of Jews in the land after the abomination of desolation (Daniel 11:31).

This records the continuing assault of Satan on those saved Jews whom God chooses to continue bearing His testimony after *"the woman"*, who represents the faithful of the nation of Israel, flees: *"into the wilderness, into her place, where she is nourished for a time, and times, and half a time [Last 3-1/2 years of Daniel's 70th Week], from the face of the serpent." (Revelation 12:14)*

These young soldiers of Christ will continue to serve Him and their country as every young man in present-day Israel is required to serve in the military, They will remain in the land *when "the woman...flees into her place"*.

Then, Satan's personal attention will be focused upon the earthly people of God, those saved Jews [*they that understand/the rest of her seed*], who are in the line of fire during the last half of the 70th Week of Daniel. This is when Satan's wrath is at its peak, for *"he knows that he has but a short time" (Revelation 12:12)*.

Daniel 7:21, 25 refers to the same time period assault by the Antichrist upon the Church:
"I beheld, and the same horn [Antichrist] made war with the saints and prevailed against them...And he shall speak great words against the most High, and shall wear out the saints of the most High, and think to change times and laws: and they [the saints] shall be given into his hand until a time and times and the dividing of time

[Last 3-1/2 years of Daniel's 70ᵗʰ Week]."

These references are definite indications of the Antichrist's worldwide war upon the saints of the Church for the global scope of his efforts are clearly indicated:
"The fourth beast...shall be diverse from all kingdoms and shall devour the whole earth, and shall tread it down, and break it in pieces." (Daniel 7:23)

This parallel passage underscores this future global assault upon the Church saints: *"And it was given unto him [Antichrist] to make war with the saints, and to overcome them: and power was given him over all kindreds, and tongues, and nations." (Revelation 13:7)*

Satan, the dragon of Revelation 12, will zero in on the faithful Jews, *"The rest of her seed"*, primarily in the land of Israel. His henchmen, the Antichrist and the false prophet, will conduct a worldwide assault upon the Church saints.

Another passage describing physical warfare at the end of the age is Micah 5:1-9. Through the ages, this powerful Messianic Scripture has been looked to as the renowned passage that predicts the Lord Jesus Christ's birthplace of Bethlehem.

However, there is more prophetic truth here yet to be fulfilled involving the Messiah during the end times:
"Now muster yourselves in troops (Psalm 110:3), daughter of troops; he [the Antichrist] has laid siege against us; with a rod they will smite the judge of Israel on the cheek. But as for you, Bethlehem, Ephratah, though thou be little among the thousands [clans/military divisions] of Judah, yet out of thee shall He [Messiah] come forth unto Me [Jehovah] to be Ruler in Israel; whose [Messiah] goings forth have been from of old, from everlasting. Therefore, He [Lord] will give them [Israel] up until the time [end of the age] that she [Israel] which travails [time of Jacob's trouble] hath brought forth [all Israel saved]. Then the remnant [rest] of His [Messiah] brethren [the woman/faithful Israel] shall return unto the children [sons] of Israel [144 Thousand]. And He [Messiah] shall stand and feed His flock [All Israel Saved/The Woman/144 Thousand] in the strength of the LORD, in the majesty of the name of the LORD His God. And they

216

[His flock] shall abide, for now [Millennium] shall He [Messiah] be great unto the ends of the earth. And, this Man [Messiah] shall be the peace, when the Assyrian [Antichrist] shall come into [invades] our land: and when he shall tread [tramples] in our palaces, then we will raise against him seven shepherds and eight principal men. And they shall waste [tend/rule] the land of Assyria with the sword, the land of Nimrod in the entrances thereof; thus shall He [Messiah] deliver us from the Assyrian [Antichrist] when he comes into [attacks] our land and when he treads [tramples] within our borders. And the remnant [144 Thousand] of Jacob shall be in the midst of many people as a dew (Psalm 110:3) from the LORD, as the showers upon the grass, that tarries not for man, nor waits for the sons of men. And the remnant [144 Thousand] of Jacob will be among the Gentiles in the midst of many people as a lion among the beasts of the forest as a young lion among the flocks of sheep: who, if he go through, both treads down and tears in pieces, and none can deliver. Thine hand shall be lifted up upon thine adversaries, and all thine enemies shall be cut off." (Micah 5:1-9)

These nine verses begin with a call for battle preparation: *"Now muster yourselves in troops...He has laid siege against us..." (Micah 5:1)* because the Antichrist has come against Jerusalem.

In verse two Bethlehem is described as *"too little"* to be counted among the *"clans"* or military divisions even though it is the birthplace of the Messiah, the Lord Jesus Christ. *"He [the Lord] will give them up"* referring to the setting aside of Israel (Romans 11:8, 25, 26) *"until the time" (Micah 5:3)* when He will thoroughly purge, purify (Jeremiah 30:7; Zechariah 13:9) and redeem Israel at the end of the 70th Week of Daniel (Isaiah 59:20, 21).

There is a *"return to the sons of Israel" (Micah 5:3)* by *"the remainder of His brethren"* showing that there will be an eventual gathering of Jews:
1. The Woman (Revelation 12)
2. The 144 Thousand (Revelation 14:1)
3. The Nation Saved @ End of 70th Week of Daniel (Genesis 49:10, Psalm 102:22; Isaiah 59:20; Daniel 9:24; Hosea 1:11, 3:5; Zechariah 13:8, 9; Romans 11:26; Revelation 11:15, 14:1-5)

These redeemed Jews will gather and eventually populate their promised land during the glorious 1000 year earthly reign of Christ (Revelation 20:1-6) also known as the Millennium.

This passage continues describing the Messiah's actions (Micah 5:4, 5a) when the Antichrist enters the land of Israel with his armies after the abomination of desolation and attacks Jerusalem as described in Ezekiel 38, 39; Zechariah 12:1-14, 14:2.

There will be *"seven shepherds and eight principal men"*
(Micah 5:5b, 6a) raised against the aggression of the king of Assyria [Antichrist] having great military success as they rule *"the land of Assyria with the sword"*.

The Septuagint [Greek Old Testament] translates *"principal men"* as *"attacks of men"* possibly indicating the number of assaults upon the enemy by the seven shepherds. The Hebrew word translated *"principal men"* can also mean *"poured out or libation"* per Strong's lexicon indicating the possibility of the shepherds or rulers seven-fold giving of themselves to the Lord.

The Messiah's deliverance is then recorded:
"Thus shall He deliver us from the Assyrian" (Micah 5:6b) referring to the ultimate victory of the Lord Jesus Christ when He comes as *"King of kings and Lord of lords" (Revelation 19:16)*.

Then *"the remnant of Jacob"* [144 Thousand] are once again focused upon in Micah 5:7 where they are a blessing *"in the midst of many people as a dew from the LORD"*. This is similar to Psalm 110:3 where they are also referred to as *"dew"* indicating this great multitude of young servants of God.

They will truly be a blessing as they are the instruments of God's divine mercy during the end times when their Redemption Ministry is provided to those who do not know the Lord Jesus Christ as Savior and Messiah. Their ministry is also described in Daniel 11:32-35, 12:3, 10.

The next few verses in Micah 5 illustrate their ferocious prowess as warriors thereby becoming a curse to their enemies:

"And the remnant of Jacob shall be among the Gentiles in the midst of many people as a lion among beasts of the forest, as a young lion among the flocks of sheep: who, if he go through, both treads down and tears in pieces, and none can deliver. Thine hand shall be lifted up upon thine adversaries, and all thine enemies shall be cut off."
(Micah 5:8, 9)

In Micah 5:9 God ends this section with His promise of complete victory to these marvelous soldiers of Christ as they go to battle against the ultimate end times enemy of God. The Antichrist and all the forces he can muster are crushed in his futile attempt to defeat the great and mighty King of Glory.
"Thy people [troops] shall be willing in the day of Thy power [forces/army/battle] in the beauties of holiness from the womb of the morning, Thou hast the dew of Thy youth [young men]."
(Psalm 110:3)

Here the 144 Thousand are described as the Lord's warrior/priests during the Day of His power indicating the Day of the Lord which immediately follows His Second Coming to resurrect, rescue, rapture and receive the saints (Revelation 7:9-17). The theme of Psalm 110 is given in Psalm 110:1:
"Sit thou at My right hand until I make Thy enemies Thy footstool."

The rest of the Psalm shows the LORD Jehovah progressively bringing the Lord Jesus Christ's enemies into submission. This begins with the sending of *"the rod [tribe] of Thy strength"* which refers to the tribe of Judah as the Lord Jesus Christ, *"the Lion of the tribe of Judah" (Revelation 5:5)* will lead His tribe/people in the warfare.

It is during *"the day of His wrath" (Psalm 110:5)* the Day of the Lord, which is described in Psalm 110:5-7, that God supernaturally intervenes with His judgment upon earth and its rebellious inhabitants. Satan unleashes his greatest assault upon the people of God during the last half of Daniel's 70th Week.

Even though Satan will battle with all his might inflicting many casualties among God's people *"All things work together for good to them that love God to those who are called according to His purpose." (Romans 8:28)*

The Lord will use the wickedness of men during the Great Tribulation to purge and purify His Church saints in order:
"That He might present it to Himself a glorious church not having spot or wrinkle, nor any such thing but that it might be holy and without blemish." (Ephesians 5:27)

These soldiers of the Cross, the 144 Thousand, will continue on earth during the Day of the Lord when God purges and purifies His people (Zechariah 13:9). They will provide their Redemption Ministry to those Jews who will be saved at the end of the 70th Week when *"their Redeemer will come to Zion" (Isaiah 59:20) and "all Israel shall be saved." (Romans 11:25, 26)*

The 144 Thousand will remain *"with"* and continue to *"follow the Lamb wherever He goes" (Revelation 14:1, 4, 17:14)* taking part in the army of the Lord Jesus Christ. He will come on His white horse to execute the victory over the kings of the earth, the beast [Antichrist] and the false prophet at the climax of the Day of the Lord, *"the battle of that great day of God Almighty" (Revelation 16:14)*, the battle of Armageddon (Revelation 19:15-21).

15.g.3

The 144 Thousand
The Servants of Our God
As Saviors/Mediators/Deliverers

During every situation when the Lord delivered His earthly people, the Jews, He used a human mediator, deliverer or savior. Noah brought deliverance for his family before God destroyed the earth (Genesis 6-8) with a universal flood. Abraham provided the necessary mediation to bring about the deliverance of Lot and his family before God destroyed Sodom and Gomorrah (Genesis 18:23-33).

When Israel was in bondage in Egypt, Moses was called by God to be their deliverer, and he went on to minister mightily and was without question Israel's human savior/mediator. He cried out to God on the people's behalf throughout his lengthy forty-year sojourn with the Israelites.

So, too, during the following time of Joshua, the subsequent series of Judges and Queen Esther the Lord continued this pattern of utilizing a human mediator for the deliverance of His people.

Daniel, although not physically involved in Israel's deliverance from Babylon, nevertheless was their spiritual mediator and could even be termed their spiritual deliverer/savior. He prayed mightily to God in chapter nine of his prophecy confessing *"we have sinned"* on four occasions, crying out to God on behalf of his people and himself for forgiveness:
"O Lord, hear, O Lord, forgive; O Lord; hearken and do; defer not for Thine own sake, O my God: for Thy city and Thy people are called by Thy name." (Daniel 9:19)

In like manner, at the time of the end, when God's people are once again in desperate need of deliverance during *"the time of Jacob's trouble" (Jeremiah 30:7),* God will call out and send, not just one

human savior, but, a great company of saviors:
*"And saviors shall come up on mount Zion to judge the mount of Esau; and **the kingdoms shall be the Lords**." (Obadiah 21)*

The time [End of the 70th Week of Daniel] of the fulfillment of this prophecy is indicated in the Revelation: *"And the seventh angel sounded; and **the kingdoms of this world are become the kingdoms of our Lord**, and of His Christ; and He shall reign for ever and ever." (Revelation 11:15)*

"And I looked and lo a Lamb stood on mount Zion, and with Him an hundred forty and four thousand, having His Fathers name written in their foreheads." (Revelation 14:1)
These 144 Thousand priests unto God will provide their Redemption Ministry which the Lord will use to bring about the spiritual deliverance of their brethren, the nation of Israel *"when all Israel shall be saved" (Romans 11:26).*

The prophet David initially describes them:
"Thy people [troops/prayer warriors] shall be willing in the day of Thy power [army/battle], in the beauties of holiness [priestly garments] from the womb of the morning, Thou hast the dew [multitude] of thy youth [young men]." (Psalm 110:3)

These *"people"* described here are young men adorned with holy character who are the saviors/soldiers in the Lord's army, His priests unto God, the 144 Thousand of the Revelation. This holy company of prayer warriors, who willingly enlist in the Lord's army, are the human instruments God will use to bring into His kingdom that future company of Jews who will be redeemed by The Lamb, The Redeemer, The Messiah, The Lord Jesus Christ, at the end of the 70th Week of Daniel (Isaiah 59:20; Zechariah 13:9; Romans 11:25, 26).

Their position on Mount Zion with the Lamb, the Lord Jesus Christ, worshipping before the throne of God along with the four beasts, the twenty-four elders and the heavenly harpers places them in the presence of God Himself with His Son. This attests to their undefiled, holy condition as indicated in these Scriptures:
(Psalm 110:3; Revelation 14:4, 5).

These 144 Thousand *"servants of our God" (Revelation 7:3)* will be responsible during their end times ministry to pray mightily and witness fervently to those whom God will call in that day as the Lord Jesus Christ redeems this great harvest of souls at the end of the 70th Week of Daniel.

The continuation of this most necessary ministry to the lost, which is carried out by the Church saints until they are raptured, will be one of the responsibilities of the 144 Thousand.

The rapture will occur right after they are sealed guaranteeing the Lord's priesthood and continuing testimony on earth in order for His program of redemption to be carried on during the Day of the Lord which begins the same day the saints are raptured (Luke 17:22-37; Revelation 6:12-8:2).

There will be an increasingly intensive spiritual battle for the souls of men (Revelation 12:12) which will be the primary charge of the 144 Thousand fulfilling their calling as soul winners and priests unto God being obedient followers of the Lord Jesus Christ (Revelation 14:4).

As the Lord's mediators, His end times kingdom of priests, they will also have the privilege of fulfilling an important conditional covenant of old:
"Now therefore if ye will obey My voice indeed, and keep My covenant, then ye shall be a peculiar treasure unto Me above all people: for all the earth is Mine. And ye shall be unto Me a kingdom of priests, and an holy nation." (Exodus 19:5, 6).

Although this conditional covenant was never fulfilled due to the disobedience and rebellion of the people of Israel, the end times Israel of God, the 144 Thousand, will indeed bring it to pass. This powerful group of God's servants will in fact minister to the Lord and thereby bring about His will on earth during the Day of the Lord.

It is through powerful prayer and timely witnessing (Daniel 11:33-35, 12:3, 10) that the salvation of the lost will be effected at the end of the age just as it is today. The Lord will continue to be the same *"yesterday, today and forever" (Hebrews 13:8)* as He calls to Himself those who are written in the Lamb's book of life from the foundation of the world.

He will have His *"saviors" (Obadiah 21),* the end times *"servants of our God" (Revelation 7:3)* who provide their Redemption Ministry being protected (Revelation 3:10, 9:4) and ultimately victorious (Revelation 14:1-5) during those horrendous days of deadly Day of the Lord judgment (Revelation 9:18, 16:3).

16

<u>The Great Multitude in Heaven</u>

In Revelation 7:9-17 the Scripture records the arrival of a certain multi-national throng:
"After this, I beheld, and, lo, a great multitude, which no man could number, of all nations, and kindreds, and people, and tongues, stood before the throne, and before the Lamb, clothed with white robes, and palms in their hands." (Revelation 7:9)

This innumerable host is made up of every different people group on earth, having on *"white robes"* like those given to the fifth seal martyrs of Revelation 9:9-11. They are the focal point of this, The Glorious Reception, as they celebrate utilizing *"palms in their hands"* similar to the day the Lord Jesus triumphantly entered Jerusalem (John 12:12-15).

However, in this situation, the ones making their triumphant entrance into heaven itself are this *"great multitude"*, and they are not doing it quietly:
"And cried with a loud voice, saying: SALVATION TO OUR GOD WHICH SITS UPON THE THRONE, AND UNTO THE LAMB." (Revelation 7:10)

What is occurring here in Revelation 7:9-17 is The Glorious Reception that is promised by the Lord Jesus Christ:
*"Let not your heart be troubled, ye believe in God, believe also in Me. In My Father's house are many mansions: if it were not so I would have told you. I go to prepare a place for you and if I go and prepare a place for you, I will come again, and **RECEIVE** you unto Myself; that where I am, there ye may be also." (John 14:1-3)*

The Lord is definitely coming again to RECEIVE all those who have been redeemed through His precious Blood that He shed for the sins of mankind. Those redeemed are seen here, en masse, with Him, the Lamb slain from the foundation of the world.

They are ascribing to the Father and to the Lamb, the Lord Jesus Christ, their great work of salvation, for the very presence of this *"great multitude"* in heaven indicates the final step of this marvelous salvation which the Lord gives to every saint:

"For whom He did foreknow, He also did predestinate to be conformed to the image of His Son, that He might be the firstborn among many brethren. Moreover, whom He did predestinate, them He also called: and whom He called, them He also justified: and whom He justified, them He also glorified." (Romans 8:29, 30)

This grand glorified company stands in the presence of their matchless Savior. With all their being, they give great praise and glory to Him, for He has brought this marvelous event to pass. They are standing in heaven, *"Before the throne, and before the Lamb"* in the very presence of God Himself.

These saints have fully experienced God's great plan of salvation, having been delivered from the penalty and power of sin through God's justification by their faith, and now, being glorified, they are experiencing firsthand their eternal deliverance from the very presence of sin.

What a magnificent and most glorious salvation! And, they are evidently not alone in this heavenly celebration:

"And all the angels stood round about the throne, and about the elders and the four beasts, and fell before the throne of God on their faces, and worshipped God, Saying, Amen: Blessing, and glory, and wisdom, and thanksgiving, and honor, and power, and might, be unto our God for ever and ever. Amen." (Revelation 7:11, 12)

All of the heavenly throne room attendants are present for this, The Glorious Reception, as the redeemed of the ages are in glory with every living creation of God in heaven. They are giving Him and His Son, the Savior, the Lamb, whose blood was given to redeem such a company as this, all of the glorious exaltation.

"And one of the elders answered, saying unto me, What are these which are arrayed in white robes? And whence came they? And I said unto him, Sir, thou knowest. And he said to me, These are they which come out of [the] great tribulation, and have washed their robes, and

made them white in the blood of the Lamb." (Revelation 7:13, 14)

The great multitude's specific identification is now made clear, according to the chronology the Lord Jesus Christ gave in Matthew 24:3-31 where He too mentions this very time called the Great Tribulation. This great multitude are those elect, who are gathered from *"the four winds" (Matthew 24:31)*, the resurrected saints [dead in Christ] and the raptured saints [living in Christ] who have endured the Great Tribulation.

*"For this we say unto you by the word of the Lord, that we which are alive and remain unto the **coming** of the Lord shall not prevent [precede] them which are asleep. For the Lord Himself shall descend from heaven with a shout, with the voice of the **archangel**, and with **the trump of God**: and the dead in Christ shall rise first: Then we which are alive and remain shall be caught up [raptured] together with them in **the clouds** to meet the Lord in the air: and so shall we ever be with the Lord. Wherefore, comfort one another with these words." (I Thessalonians 4:15-18)*

Notice the parallels in the I Thessalonians 4 rapture passage and the following Matthew 24 rapture passage:
1. **Coming** is the subject
2. **Clouds** are the place
3. **Angels** are involved
4. **Trumpet** of God sounds

*"For as the lightning comes out of the east and shines even unto the west; so shall also the coming of the Son of man be. For wheresover the carcass is, there will the eagles [vultures] be gathered. Immediately after that tribulation shall the sun be darkened and the moon shall not give her light, and the stars shall fall from heaven and the powers of heaven shall be shaken. And then shall appear the sign of the Son of man in heaven, and then shall all the tribes of the earth mourn, and they shall see the Son of man **coming** in **the clouds** of heaven with power and great glory. And He shall send His **angels** with a great sound of a **trumpet**, and they shall gather together the elect from the four winds, from one end of heaven to the other.' (Matthew 24:27-31)*

This is the end of the chronological sequence the Lord gave to His disciples answering their two questions, *"What shall be the sign of Thy coming and the end of the world?" (Matthew 24:3)*

His step by step sequence ending with this series of events details these facts concerning His Coming:

1. His Second Coming will not be secret but openly evident and universally seen [as lightning] (v.27)
2. His Second Coming will not be uncertain but definite [as vultures on corpses] (v.28)
3. His Second Coming will shorten the Great Tribulation (v.28, 21, 22)
4. His Second Coming will occur the same day the sign of the Day of the Lord/sign of the Son of man are given (v.29, 30)
5. His Second Coming will occur in the clouds (v.30)
6. His Second Coming will be with power and great glory (v.30)
7. His Second Coming will be accompanied by the sound of a trumpet (v.31)
8. His Second Coming will gather the elect [rapture the saints] by His angels (v.31)

By utilizing the Lord's Matthew 24 sequence, the answer given to John by the elder concerning the identity of this great multitude is clear. These are those saints who have just been resurrected and raptured, the elect who have been gathered by the Lord Jesus Christ's angels, when He rescues/raptures the elect by shortening the Great Tribulation.

The Lord's Matthew 24 sequence is the same as the order of events in Revelation. The fifth seal martyrs (Revelation 6:9-11) are martyred during the Great Tribulation, the sixth seal reveals the sign of the Day of the Lord as the heavenly wonders are described (Revelation 6:11-17) for the Lord's wrath is about to begin.

Next is an event not mentioned in Matthew 24, but, the sealing of the 144 Thousand (Revelation 7:1-8) is a necessary event, in order to give them protection (Revelation 9:4) during their Day of the Lord ministry. This happens the same day [just before] the Lord comes to resurrect the dead in Christ and rescue the saints by rapture (Revelation 7:9-17).

Some theorize that the rapture has occurred at the beginning or the middle of the 70th Week of Daniel. If that is the case, a few questions must be asked: If the saints of the ages have already been resurrected and raptured into heaven as claimed by those who hold the theory of a pre-tribulation or mid-tribulation rapture, then, where are they during this The Glorious Reception in heaven?

All of heaven has gathered to celebrate this magnificent event, God the Father, the Lamb, all of the angels, the twenty-four elders, the four beasts...but, that's it! There are no glorified saints...other than this great multitude who, as the Scripture confirms, have just arrived. Surely the glorified saints of the ages would be part of heaven's welcome if they had arrived earlier.

Secondly, if this great multitude is made up of only those who have been saved during the Great Tribulation, how did world evangelism take place in just a few short years producing saints from every corner of the globe? The *"great multitude"* is made up of every type of known people group as (Revelation 7:9) indicates:

"Of all nations, and kindreds, and people, and tongues":
1. Nations is the Greek word "ethnos" meaning ethnic group.
2. Kindreds is the Greek word "phulay" meaning those of the same tribe or race.
3. People is the Greek word "laos" meaning all those of the same stock and language.
4. Tongues is the Greek word "glossa" meaning all those who speak any language or dialect.

These four words are all inclusive starting with the largest group of people, a nation or ethnic group, and ending with the smallest group having only a language in common. The purpose of using these multiple terms is to show that the Lord has brought His so great salvation to all the different peoples from every corner of the globe.

Number three; the saints of the ages are previously described using these same four terms:
"And when He [the Lamb/Lord Jesus Christ] had taken the book, the four beasts and four and twenty elders fell down before the Lamb, having every one of them harps, and golden vials full of odors, which

229

are the prayers of the saints. And they sung a new song, saying, Thou art worthy to take the book, and to open the seals thereof: for Thou was slain, and has redeemed men to God by Thy blood out of every kindred, and tongue, and people and nation." (Revelation 5:8, 9)

Here, after the Lord Jesus Christ takes the book [containing the Day of the Lord judgments] from the Father and just before He opens the seals, the worship leaders in heaven sing a new song to Him. They indicate His worthiness to open the book because He was slain, bringing about this great work of redemption among all of the different people groups of earth **before** the start of the 70th Week and the Great Tribulation.

These four words are used a number of other times in the Revelation (10:11, 11:9, 14:6). In these texts they continue to indicate all the different types of inhabitants on the planet. However, they refer to those who are not children of God, who are living on earth during the end times. But, the same purpose applies in both situations, as these four words continue to comprehensively describe all peoples.

The only way that this great multitude could be standing here from every known people group is that the dead in Christ are included. The saints who have died have now been resurrected just prior to those whom the Lord rescues from the Great Tribulation by rapture according to Paul's doctrine in I Thessalonians 4:13-18.

In addition, the questions and answer posed by the elder back in Revelation 7:13 provide another key. The questions: *"What are these which are arrayed in white robes? and whence came they?"* are asking for their identity, and location.

The response he gives does not answer either of these questions. Instead, the elder reveals **the time** when they arrived, which when analyzed in view of the Lord's Matthew 24 passage, it becomes clear why he chose this reply.

His reply draws the focus upon **the time** they arrived and perfectly agrees with the Lord's timing when He step-by-step chronologically unfolded His Coming and the end of the age. The Lord shortens/cuts off (Matthew 24:21, 22) the Great Tribulation in order that His elect would be spared. He shortens it by rescuing/rapturing the saints out of the Antichrist's deadly persecution.

His angels will *"**gather the elect**" (Matthew 24:29-31)* and, just prior, He resurrects all those who have been saved throughout the ages according to Paul's rapture passage (I Thessalonians 4:13-18).

The reason for the great diversity of those standing in the throne room of God is that all of the redeemed from the beginning of time are here, just as they are described earlier in Revelation 5:8, 9 using these same four all encompassing words.

All the saints of the ages, including Adam and Eve, will be there. And, if you have been redeemed by the Blood of the Lamb, you will be there too. It's that simple! The remainder of this passage supports this conclusion:

"Therefore are they [great multitude/saints of the ages] before the throne of God, and serve day and night in His temple: and He that sits on the throne shall dwell among them. They shall hunger no more, neither thirst any more; neither shall the sun light on them, nor any heat. For the Lamb which is in the midst of the throne shall feed them, and shall lead them unto living fountains of water: and God shall wipe away all tears form their eyes." (Revelation 7:15-17)

The brief but precise description given here of the saints continually serving God, in His presence, without having concern for physical sustenance, or experiencing any affliction, being fed and led by the Lamb of God, the Lord Jesus Christ, with all sorrow completely eliminated, eloquently describes the eternal environment of the blessedness in heaven.

God has promised these eternal blessings to every person who has ever been redeemed by the Blood of the Lamb...namely to these glorified saints of the ages who are now standing in His presence as this passage clearly reveals.

17

The Saints

Understanding the language structure of the book of Daniel provides key insights into just who is being spoken of in the Scripture text. Chapters 1:1-2:4, the introduction of the book, are written in Hebrew.

Chapter 2:4 through 7:28, including 2:4-6:28 the historic section and Daniel's first prophetic vision 7:1-28, are written in Aramaic/Chaldee and focus upon Gentile/world history with chapter 8-12, the Hebrew/Jewish section, emphasizing the Jews, Jerusalem and the nation of Israel.

"The saints" who are mentioned in the Chaldee/Gentile section, which includes Daniel's vision of chapter seven, indicates the worldwide end times Church of Jesus Christ, made up mainly of Gentiles, but also containing Jews as has been the case throughout the Church's existence.

While the Aramaic/Chaldee language of chapter seven is an indicator of the continuing Gentile worldwide application, the text itself also provides the key to this important fact as the word *"saints"* appears six times:

1. *"But the **saints** of the most High shall take the kingdom, and possess the kingdom for ever, even for ever and ever (Daniel 7:18)*
2. *I beheld, and the same horn made war with the **saints**, and prevailed against them (Daniel 7:21)*
3. *Until the Ancient of days came, and judgment was given to the **saints** of the most high (Daniel 7:22)*
4. *And the time came that the **saints** possessed the kingdom (Daniel 7:22)*
5. *And he shall speak great words against the most High, and shall wear out the **saints** of the most High (Daniel 7:25)*
6. *And the kingdom and dominion, and the greatness of the kingdom under the whole heaven, shall be given to the people of the **saints***

of the most High" (Daniel 7:27)

In these six occurrences three important facts concerning all end times saints are recorded which are repeated in the Revelation:
1. The *"little horn"* [Antichrist] leads a global war with the saints (Revelation 13:7)
2. The *"little horn"* [Antichrist] prevails against the saints worldwide (Revelation 13:7)
3. The saints are given judgment, dominion, and the kingdom which they possess eternally (Revelation 20:4, 22:5)

In the book of the Revelation the word *"**saints**"* is found (13) times referring once again to faithful Jews and Gentiles with a direct parallel to Daniel 7:21 found in Revelation 13:7:
*"And it was given to him [The beast/Antichrist] to make war with the **saints**, and to overcome them: and power was given him over all kindreds, and tongues and nations."*

The global scope of the Antichrist's actions during the end times against the saints, both Jew and Gentile, is seen in both of these references. The six occurrences of the word *"**saints**"* in Daniel chapter seven do not differentiate between Jew or Gentile saints.

These saints, both in Daniel chapter seven and Revelation chapter thirteen, comprise the worldwide Church of Jesus Christ and not just specifically Jews, for the kingdom will eventually belong to all children of God, Jews and Gentiles alike.

So, the saints mentioned in Daniel chapter seven and Revelation chapter thirteen make up the end times Church, which is the source for the majority of the other believers who are called:
"The People of the Apocalypse".

The Church will be the source group from which Elijah (Malachi 4:5, 6), The Woman (Revelation 12), The Remnant [rest] of Her [The Woman] Seed (Revelation 12:17), and Those that understand and have insight who instruct many in the land of Israel (Daniel 11:32,35,12:3,10), The Martyrs (Revelation 6:11ff), and the 144 Thousand (Revelation 7:3-8) will all come forth.

233

These saints will experience Satan's *"great wrath" (Revelation 12:12)* which is the *"great tribulation" (Matthew 24:21; Revelation 7:14)* when the Antichrist makes war with them and overcomes them during the most intensive time of persecution ever inflicted upon the people of God.

Those that endure and remain will be rescued (Matthew 24:14) when the Lord Jesus Christ comes to rapture the saints as He shortens the great tribulation in order to preserve His elect (Matthew 24:21, 22; Revelation 7:9-17).

These are those saints who will experience first hand the Lord's merging of economies, the Old and the New, the Church and the Jew, as His earthly people first of all, return to the Promised Land, become a nation, and occupy their beloved Jerusalem. In the process the Jews will fulfill the necessary 70th Week Bible prophecy with each progressive step (Daniel 9:24).

These saints are that privileged generation who will be:
"Looking for that blessed hope and glorious appearing of the great God and Savior Jesus Christ; Who gave Himself for us, that He might redeem us from all iniquity, and purify unto Himself a peculiar people, zealous of good works." (Titus 2:13, 14)

"That He might present it to Himself a glorious church not having spot or wrinkle or any such thing, but that it might be holy and without blemish." (Ephesians 5:26)

"The prayers of the saints" are mentioned three times in the Revelation:
(1) *"And when He [the Lamb] had taken the book, the four beasts and four and twenty elders fell down before the Lamb, having every one of them harps, and golden vials full of odors, which are **the prayers of the saints." (Revelation 5:8)***

This event occurs just prior to the beginning of the 70th Week of Daniel when the Lord Jesus opens the seven seals at the beginning of the 70th Week of Daniel. The first four seals reveal the four horsemen of the apocalypse who symbolize the Antichrist's actions upon earth.

(2 & 3) *"And when He had opened the seventh seal, there was silence in heaven about the space of half an hour. And I saw the seven angels which stood before God; and to them were given seven trumpets. And another angel came and stood at the altar, having a golden censer; and there was given unto him much incense, that he should offer it with **the prayers of all saints** upon the golden altar which was before the throne. And the smoke of the incense, which come with **the prayers of the saints**, ascended up before God out of the angel's hand."* *(Revelation 8:1-4)*

The prayers of the saints are mentioned before Revelation 5:8 and after Revelation 8:1-4 the rapture of the saints (Revelation 7:9-17) indicating that prayer to God will continue to be offered when the saints of the ages are in heaven.

There will also be a continuing presence of saints upon earth after the rapture, as these three categories of saints will be on earth for the entire 70th Week of Daniel:
1. The 144 Thousand (Revelation 7:3, 4, 9:4, 14:1, 17:14)
2. The Woman/Faithful Israel (Revelation 12:1-17)
3. The Two Witnesses (Revelation 11:3-14)

(4) *"And the nations were angry, and Thy wrath is come, and the time of the dead, that they should be judged, and that Thou should give reward unto Thy servants the prophets, and to the **saints** and them that fear Thy name, small and great; and should destroy them which destroy the earth."* *(Revelation 11:18)*

The saints of the ages are included here, as it is the time God gives eternal rewards to His own at the bema seat of Christ. Notice, from the prophets, His servants who are mentioned first, to the saints, all are given rewards regardless of calling. This event occurs at the end of the 70th Week of Daniel after the sounding of the seventh trumpet (Revelation 11:15).

The saints are also mentioned during the Great Tribulation, the time dominated by the Antichrist:
(5 & 6) *"And it was given unto him to make war with the **saints**, and to overcome them: and power was given him over all kindreds, and tongues and nations...He that leads into captivity shall go into*

235

captivity: he that kills with the sword must be killed with the sword. Here is the patience and the faith of the __saints__." (Revelation 13:7, 10)

Although many of God's people will go into captivity or be killed during the time the Antichrist dominates the world, the saints must exercise great patience *"For in your patience possess ye your souls" (Luke 21:19)* which patience has its source in overcoming faith:
"Therefore being justified by faith, we have peace with God through our Lord Jesus Christ: By whom also we have access by faith into this grace wherein we stand, and rejoice in hope of the glory of God. And not only so, but we glory in tribulations also; knowing that tribulation works patience, And patience, experience; and experience hope: And hope makes not ashamed; because the love of God is shed abroad in our hearts by the Holy Ghost which is given unto us." (Romans 5:1-5)

The *"patience of the __saints__"* is also focused upon in the next passage:
(7) *"And the smoke of their torment ascends up for ever and ever: and they have no rest day nor night, who worship the beast and his image, and whosoever receives the mark of his name. Here is the patience of the __saints__: here are they that keep the commandments of God, and the faith of Jesus." (Revelation 14:11, 12)*

The patience of the saints is once again linked to their faith, *"The just shall [always] live by faith"*. Here during the end times when persecution is at its maximum level and martyrdom is the rule not the exception, patient endurance that can only be exercised by faith is the most necessary ingredient for the overcomer.

Faith stands before the beheading sword and the crackling flame of the stake with strong confidence that the Lord Himself has gone before and has allowed the consequences being faced as He supplies the grace in abundance which produces love for Him, which energizes faith (Galatians 5:6). This is the source of overcoming patience.

(8) *"And I saw another sign in heaven, great and marvelous, seven angels having the seven last plagues; for in them is filled up [finished] the wrath of God. And I saw as it were a sea of glass mingled with fire: and them that had gotten the victory over the beast, and over his image, and over his mark, And over the number of his*

236

name, stand on the sea of glass, having the harps of God. And they sing the song of Moses the servant of God, and the song of the Lamb, saying, GREAT AND MARVELOUS ARE THY WORKS, LORD GOD ALMIGHTY; JUST AND TRUE ARE THY WAYS, THOU KING OF **SAINTS**. *WHO SHALL NOT FEAR THEE, O LORD, AND GLORIFY THY NAME? FOR THOU ONLY ART HOLY: FOR ALL NATIONS SHALL COME AND WORSHIP BEFORE THEE; for Thy judgments are made manifest." (Revelation 15:1-4)*

The Lord is here called *"KING OF* **SAINTS**" during this *"Song of the Lamb"* which underscores exactly who His subjects will be during the Millennium when *"ALL NATIONS SHALL COME AND WORSHIP BEFORE THEE"*. Although He will *"Rule with a rod of iron" (Revelation 19:15)*, only the saints will rightly submit and become His subjects during that time.

(9) *"And the third angel poured out his vial upon the rivers and fountains of waters; and they became blood. And I heard the angel of the waters say, Thou art righteous, O Lord, which are, and was, and shall be, because Thou has judged thus. For they [the men which had the mark of the beast] have shed the blood of* **saints** *and prophets, and Thou has given them blood to drink; for they are worthy." (Revelation 16:6)*

The angel, after pouring out his vial upon the fresh waters of earth, affirms that the Lord is right for having judged the followers of the beast because they are the ones responsible for putting to death those innocent saints and prophets of God.

(10&11) *"And I saw the woman [Mystery Babylon the Great] drunken with the blood of the* **saints**, *and with the blood of the martyrs of Jesus: and when I saw her, I wondered with great admiration....And in her was found the blood of prophets, and of* **saints**, *and of all that were slain upon the earth." (Revelation 17:6, 18:24)*

While those who take the mark of the beast are responsible for the martyrdom of God's people, the false religious system Romanism is the great whore who through the centuries of the Church age has been the major source of martyrdom upon God's people.

(12) *"Let us be glad and rejoice, and give honor to Him: for the marriage of the Lamb is come, and His wife has made herself ready. And to her was granted that she should be arrayed in fine linen, clean and white: for the fine linen is the righteousness of __saints__. And he said unto me, Write, Blessed are they which are called unto the marriage supper of the Lamb. And he said unto me, These are the true sayings of God." (Revelation 19:7-9)*

This passage gives all of God's saints the blessed promise of attending this great celebration in heaven. The wedding garment is described as *"Fine linen clean and white...the righteousness of the __saints__".*

This garment is given to every saint when they are justified by faith, thereby receiving *the "robe of [imputed] righteousness [of Christ]"* as described by Isaiah:
"I will greatly rejoice in the LORD, my soul shall be joyful in my God; for He has clothed me with the garments of salvation, He has covered me with the robe of righteousness, as a bridegroom decks himself with ornaments, and as a bride adorns herself with her jewels." (Isaiah 61:10)

The end of the age martyrs also are given these same white robes of righteousness:
"And white robes were given unto every one of them [martyrs]; and it was said unto them, that they should rest yet for a little season, until their fellow servants also and their brethren that should be killed as they were, should be fulfilled." (Revelation 6:11)

The raptured saints of the Great Tribulation and the resurrected saints of the ages will also be clothed with these same *"garments of salvation...robes of righteousness"*:
"After this I beheld, and, lo, a great multitude, which no man could number, of all nations, and kindreds, and people, and tongues, stood before the throne, and before the Lamb, clothed with white robes, and palms in their hands." (Revelation 7:9)

The last mention of the word saints in the Scripture occurs at the end of the Millennium:

238

(13) *"And they [Satan, Gog, Magog and the nations] went up on the breadth of the earth, and compassed the camp of the __saints__ about, and the beloved city: and fire came down from God out of heaven, and devoured them." (Revelation 20:9)*

Satan is loosed at the end of the 1,000-year reign of the Lord Jesus Christ. Even though conditions will be ideal upon earth, with sin and wickedness suppressed, many will not receive the Lord Jesus by grace through faith but instead will openly rebel against God.

This rebellion will come to its peak when the Lord allows Satan to be loosed for a season in order for him to gather those rebellious nations under the leadership of Gog and Magog. This final attempt to overthrow the Lord's kingdom on earth, as they surround *"The camp of the __saints__"* and gather to attack Jerusalem, will be in vain as the God of heaven brings Satan's plan to its well deserved end.

Although theories abound concerning the removal of all saints from the earth at different points during the end times, the Scripture records throughout its prophecies the continuing presence of the saints, the people of God, upon earth as this brief study indicates.

The Lord has never nor will He ever leave the earth void of His human witnesses...as the saints are the only ones who have this *"treasure in earthen vessels" (II Corinthians 4:7)* carrying within them the grand and glorious redemption message of the Gospel of the grace of God.

18

The Two Witnesses

The two-man team described in Revelation 11:3-14 could accurately be called the two mightiest prophets ever sent to the people of God. The first text describing them reveals their simple and most compelling title:

"And, I will give power unto My two witnesses, and they shall prophesy a thousand two hundred and threescore days clothed in sackcloth." (Revelation 11:3)

The word translated *"witnesses"* is used in the New Testament over seventy times with the Apostle John's writings containing more than half of these occurrences. It is the same word the Lord Jesus Christ used in His farewell commission to those gathered at His ascension:

"But ye shall receive power after the Holy Ghost is, come upon you: and ye shall be witnesses unto Me both in Jerusalem, and in all Judea, and in Samaria, and unto the uttermost part of the earth." (Acts 1:8)

These two witnesses will in fact witness of the Lord Jesus *Christ "unto the uttermost part of the earth"* as this passage eventually reveals. This first title indicates that any faithful witness can be used of God to perform the mightiest of deeds as evidenced in the two witnesses' ministry.

This verse tells us who they are, what they will be doing, when they will accomplish their ministry, and what type of ministry they will have:

1. They are "*My two witnesses*" or God's personal witnesses.
2. They will prophesy.
3. They will prophesy for 1260 days or 3-1/2 years which is the last half of Daniel's 70th Week.
4. They will prophesy of judgment indicated by their attire and the description of their activities.

That they are God's personal witnesses is also indicated in the next verse:

"These are the two olive trees, and the two candlesticks standing before the God of the earth." (Revelation 11:4

But, before their personal position before God is given, their next title as *"the two olive trees"* reveals that these two witnesses also are spoken of previously in the book of Zechariah:

"And the angel that talked with me came again, and waked me, as a man that is wakened out of his sleep, And said unto me, What seest thou? And I said, I have looked, and behold a candlestick all of gold, with a bowl upon the top of it, and his seven lamps thereon, and seven pipes to the seven lamps, which are upon the top thereof: And two olive trees by it, one upon the right side of the bowl, and the other upon the left side thereof." (Zechariah 4:1-3)

This vision given to the prophet Zechariah was intended to supply him with encouragement concerning his work of rebuilding the temple after the Jews returned from captivity in Babylon. The vision reveals that God's Spirit would provide the necessary power to accomplish this immense task as the angel explained utilizing the now oft quoted verse:

"Not by might nor by power but by My Spirit says the Lord of hosts." (Zechariah 4:6)

However, Zechariah wanted to know exactly what *"the two olive trees"* were as he repeatedly asked the angel:

"What are these, my lord? (Zechariah 4:4)...What are these two olive trees upon the right side of the candlestick and upon the left side thereof? (Zechariah 4:11)...What be these two olive branches [clusters: NASB] which through the two golden pipes empty the golden oil out of themselves?" (Zechariah 4:12)

His repeated and expanding inquiries end up providing more descriptive information identifying them as God's *"two olive trees...the two witnesses"* of Revelation 11. It appears that Zechariah understood what the candlestick with its bowl, seven lamps and seven pipes was, but, he did not immediately comprehend the meaning of the *"two olive trees"* causing him to continue looking, seeing every single detail.

Then, after remaining silent until Zechariah completes his thorough examination, the angel responds: *"And he answered me and said, Knowest thou not what these be? And I said, No, my lord. Then said he, These are the two anointed ones, that stand by the Lord of the whole earth." (Zechariah 4:13, 14)*

Three parallels emerge in Zechariah 4 and Revelation 11:
1. They are called "*the two olive trees*".
   (Zechariah 4:3, 11, 12; Revelation 11:4)
2. They are given the power of the Holy Spirit.
   (Zechariah 4.14, Revelation 11:3)
3. They are standing in the presence of God.
   (Zechariah 4:14; Revelation 11:4)

In all these two men are given five different titles:
1. The Two Olive Trees (Zechariah 4:3, 11, 12; Romans 11:11-27; Revelation 11:4) [Israel Connection]
2. The Two Anointed Ones (Zechariah 4:14)
   [Instruments of the Holy Spirit]
3. The Two Witnesses (Revelation 11:3) [Instruments of Testimony]
4. The Two Candlesticks (Revelation 11:3) [Illuminators of Truth]
5. The Two Prophets (Revelation 11:10) [Instruments of Judgment]

Although much of the information given in Zechariah's vision is symbolic in nature, there is enough there to tie the Revelation 11 account of *"the two witnesses"* to Zechariah 4 by examining and discerning the intent of the symbolic language without destroying the unity of the passage.

Paul also uses this symbolic term *"olive tree"* to describe the Israelites when discussing their fall and how it was through their fall that the Gentiles *"the wild olive tree"* was grafted into *"the olive tree"* receiving the salvation blessing of Israel as a direct result. (Romans 11:11-27)

This title used repeatedly in Zechariah and again in Revelation is the Israel Connection indicating that these *"two witnesses"* will definitely be in the same mold as the Hebrew prophets of old.

It is evident that the focus here is *"the two olive trees"* for the angel deliberately omitted giving any information about them to Zechariah in his initial answer.

He only covered the candlestick and its features at the first, causing Zechariah's persistent questions concerning *"the two olive trees"* to eventually provide more detail. The third time his question includes three more facts concerning them:
1. They are called two olive branches of clusters showing their productivity
2. They are beside the golden pipes
3. They empty the golden oil from themselves through the golden pipes

They are emptying themselves of *"the golden oil"* which symbolizes their *"spending and being spent" (II Corinthians 12:15)* by the Holy Spirit for the kingdom of God, becoming the source and supply for the illumination of the candlestick which is a symbol for the illuminating Word of God:
"Thy word is a lamp [candle] unto my feet, and a light unto my path." (Psalm 119:105)

The two witnesses, after giving themselves totally to their Lord during their 3-1/2 year ministry, will eventually empty themselves completely becoming the most heralded martyrs of the time of the end as the remainder of this passage reveals (Revelation 11:7-14).

In Revelation 11:3 the Lord *"gives power"* to these two with the word *"power"* supplied by the translators, not appearing in the original text. In essence, the Lord gives to these two an immeasurable amount of His Holy Spirit that they pour out of themselves for His glory:
"How much more shall your heavenly Father give the Holy Spirit to them that ask Him?" (Luke 11:13)

They are accurately identified as *"the two anointed [by the Holy Spirit] ones"* literally meaning *"The sons of fresh oil"* or as the Septuagint has in the margin *"The sons of fatness"*.
These *"two anointed ones"* also *"stand by the Lord of the whole earth" (Zechariah 4: 14)* corresponding to the *"two*

witnesses...standing before the God of the earth." (Revelation 11:3, 4

This last designation, *"the two anointed ones"* meaning *"The sons of fresh oil/fatness"* gives rise to an additional possibility concerning these two men. The Apostle John and his brother James were called *"The sons of thunder" (Mark 3:17)* by the Lord Jesus Christ and worked together as a two-brother team.

It has been the practice of the Lord to call out and use two-brother teams in the past including Moses and Aaron, Peter and Andrew and James and John.

James and Jude who were the Lord Jesus' own half-brothers, while not necessarily seen together as a team, were used mightily during the same time period, in the Early Church at Jerusalem with both eventually writing inspired letters in the New Testament.

It could be that the Lord may once again call two brothers ("For blood is thicker than water") to fulfill these most intense and trying end times positions. His two inseparable prophets of judgment will minister during a time when the world as a whole will be fully set against them for its inhabitants will be suffering under the mighty judgments of God.

The following patterns support this theory showing that other events connected to the Day of the Lord plagues/judgments have similarities and parallels to the time God sent plagues/judgments upon Pharaoh and the land of Egypt:
1. Then, God called His first two-brother team, Moses and Aaron, as His prophets of judgment, similar to these two end times prophets of judgment
2. Then, He provided safe haven for His people in the land of Goshen and He will also provide a similar haven to "*the woman*" which represents faithful Israel of Revelation 12
3. The judgments/plagues themselves also have definite similarities as the actions of these two witnesses have power to bring judgments similar to those which occurred during the plagues in Egypt.

"These have power to shut heaven, that it rain not in the days of their prophecy: and have power over waters to turn them to blood, and to

smite the earth with all plagues as often as they will."
(Revelation 11:6)

The water was turned to blood, (Exodus 7:14-25) and Moses and Aaron were used to bring other plagues upon Egypt during their mighty ministry of judgment (Exodus 7-11). The *"two witnesses"* in the Revelation eventually are brought to a seemingly gruesome end:
"And when they shall have finished their testimony, the beast that ascends out of the bottomless pit shall make war against them, and shall overcome them, and kill them. And their dead bodies shall lie in the street of the great city, which spiritually is called Sodom and Egypt, where also our Lord was crucified. And they of the people and kindreds and tongues and nations shall see their dead bodies three days and an half, and shall not suffer their dead bodies to be put in graves. And they that dwell upon the earth shall rejoice over them, and make merry, and shall send gifts one to another; because these two prophets tormented them that dwelt on the earth."
(Revelation 11:7-10)

Notice, when their work on earth is complete, the Antichrist personally makes war against them, and overcomes them. This implies that it was necessary for the Antichrist to personally formulate a military plan and focus his own efforts upon eliminating these two prophets for they were definitely not brought to their end easily.

Although they do suffer their deaths at his hand, in the process they receive great reward from the Lord for they will be the most heralded end of the age martyrs, putting themselves in the place of enduring violent persecution throughout their 3-1/2 ministry. Their deaths as martyrs for the Lord Jesus Christ is the eternally shining capstone of their selfless and sacrificial ministry for their Lord.

After their martyrdom a worldwide party atmosphere breaks out including the almost unthinkable *"sending of gifts"* as though the most celebrated event of that time has taken place. (Revelation 11:10) But, as the Scripture records, God always has the last word and He is definitely not finished with His two witnesses just yet.

"And after three days and an half the Spirit of life from God entered into them, and they stood upon their feet; and great fear fell upon

them which saw them. And they heard a great voice from heaven saying unto them, Come up hither, And they ascended up to heaven in a cloud; and their enemies beheld them." (Revelation 11:11, 12)

The Lord miraculously resurrects His servants: *"Great fear fell upon them which saw them"* indicating the world will also witness the climactic ending of this supernatural event. Their natural response is great fear, for they, in essence, have taken part by showing their approval of the deaths of these two servants of God demonstrated by their grandiose worldwide celebration during the previous 3-1/2 days:

"And the same hour there was a great earthquake, and the tenth part of the city fell, and in the earthquake were slain of men seven thousand: and the remnant [remainder] were affrighted, and gave glory to the God of heaven." (Revelation 11:13)

The Lord concludes this most significant end times episode of martyrdom by sending an earthquake that destroys a tenth of the city of Jerusalem resulting in the deaths of seven thousand. The word translated *"remnant"* literally means rest or remainder indicating that those who were not killed *"were affrighted"*, or terrified being thrown into a state of great fear.

They obviously recognized exactly Who was the source of these supernatural events as they ascribe glory to God. In the plan and control of God, the deaths of these two are used to bring together His purposes, for even in their closing scene upon earth they will be extremely effective in bringing glory to God.

Additionally, the ministry of these two "People of the Apocalypse" takes on a much greater Biblical significance when these twelve parallels to the Lord Jesus Christ's earthly ministry are considered:
1. They will be anointed by the Holy Spirit.
   (Luke 4:18; Zechariah 4:14)
2. They will proclaim judgment to God's enemies.
   (Matthew 23; Revelation 11:5, 6)
3. They will minister on earth 3-1/2 years. (Length of the Lord's
   (4) Gospels ministry; Revelation 11:3)
4. They will complete their work on earth.
   (John 17:4; Revelation 11:7)

5. They will die at the hands of their enemies.
   (Matthew 27:19-53; Revelation 11:7)
6. They will die in Jerusalem. (Revelation 11:8)
7. They will remain dead for a similar time period.
   (Matthew 16:21; Revelation 11:11)
8. They will be miraculously resurrected.
   (Matthew 28:1-20; Revelation 11:11, 12)
9. Their resurrection will be accompanied by a great earthquake.
   (Matthew 28:2; Revelation 11:13)
10. Their resurrection/ascension will be witnessed by many
    (Acts 1:1-4, I Corinthians 15:6; Revelation 11:11-13)
11. They will ascend to heaven in a cloud.
    (Acts 1:8; Revelation 11:12)
12. They will bring glory to God.
    (John 17:1, 4, 5; Revelation 11:13)

The Woman of Revelation 12

The Lord Jesus Christ, addressing the faithful Israelites in the land of Judea at the mid-point of the 70th Week of Daniel said these words: *"When ye therefore shall see the ABOMINATION OF DESOLATION spoken of by Daniel the prophet, stand in the holy place, (whoso reads let him understand) Then let them which be in Judea flee into the mountains. Let him which is on the housetop not come down to take anything out of his house. Neither let him which is in the field return back to take his clothes. And woe unto them that are with child, and to them that give suck in those days! But pray ye that your flight be not on the sabbath day: For then shall be great tribulation, such as was not since the beginning of the world to this time, no nor ever shall be." (Matthew 24:15-21)*

This admonition from the Lord will apply to all the saints of that day, as the Antichrist's worldwide persecution will escalate at the mid-point of the 70th Week of Daniel for it is clearly described as: *"war with the saints" (Daniel 7:21; Revelation 13:7).*

His warning in this verse directly applies to the faithful of Judea. As the Lord Jesus indicated in Matthew 24:21, this spiritual and physical warfare will be the most intensive time of affliction for the saints in the history of the world. Satan's great wrath (Revelation 12:12), the Great Tribulation, will be focused upon the people of Israel as recorded in Revelation 12:1-17.

It is in this chapter where the symbolic title *"the woman"* is found referring to those faithful Israelites during the 70th Week of Daniel: *"And there appeared a great wonder in heaven, a woman clothed with the sun, and the moon under her feet, and upon her head a crown of twelve stars. And she being with child cried, travailing in birth, and pained to be delivered." (Revelation 12:1, 2)*

The *"woman"* is clothed in the most brilliant heavenly attire, standing upon the moon, with her crown of twelve stars symbolizing the twelve tribes, or twelve sons of Israel. She is about to give birth to the Son of God, the Lord Jesus Christ, and in the process fulfill the primary purpose for her existence:

"And there appeared another wonder in heaven; and behold a great red dragon, having seven heads and ten horns, and seven crowns upon his heads. And his tail drew the third part of the stars of heaven, and did cast them to the earth: and the dragon stood before the woman which was ready to be delivered, for to devour her Child as soon as it was born." (Revelation 12:3, 4)

Satan is the great red dragon. He casts one third of the stars to the earth displaying his furor followed by his confrontation of the woman in a vain attempt to destroy her Child, the Lord Jesus Christ, the Savior of mankind. In the next verse the Lord Jesus' history is given in a brief but significant synopsis:

"And she brought forth a Man Child, who was to rule all nations with a rod of iron: and her Child was caught up unto God and His throne." (Revelation 12:5)

The Lord's past incarnation through physical birth, His future role as the earthly King of kings, and His present exalted position at the right hand of God are clearly highlighted. Then, the focus turns upon the actions of those faithful of Israel in response to the Lord Jesus Christ's warning:

"And the woman fled into the wilderness, where she has a place prepared of God, that they should feed her there a thousand two hundred and three score days." (Revelation 12:6)

In that day, at the mid-point of the 70th Week of Daniel, when Satan's assault on the faithful intensifies, *"the woman"* will flee from population centers and take refuge in the protective environment prepared by God Himself.

In Revelation 12:7-12 open war breaks out in heaven and Michael and his angels are victorious over Satan and his angels, with the result being Satan and his angels are cast out of heaven unto the earth. The devil, now knowing he has only a short time, brings forth his *"great wrath"* upon the faithful:

And when the dragon saw that he was cast into the earth, he

persecuted the woman, which brought forth the Man Child. And to the woman were given two wings of [the] great eagle that she might fly into the wilderness into her place, where she is nourished for a time, and times, and half a time, from the face of the serpent."
(Revelation 12:13)

Satan's immediate response upon being cast out of heaven is the persecution of *"the woman"*, but she is supernaturally rescued being given flight from the place of affliction to a secret abode in the wilderness made ready by the Lord.

While some interpret *"the great eagle"* to be the United States coming to the aid of Israel, the Scripture reveals that God Himself has utilized *"eagles wings"* in the past to describe His own deliverance of His people Israel from Satan's assault:
"Ye have seen what I did unto the Egyptians, and how I bare you on eagles wings, and brought you unto Myself." (Exodus 19:4)

Revelation 12, which introduces and focuses upon *"the woman"*, closes by describing Satan's assault upon the faithful of Israel:
"And the serpent cast out of his mouth water as a flood after the woman, that he might cause her to be carried away of the flood. And the earth helped the woman, and the earth opened her mouth, and swallowed up the flood that the dragon cast out of his mouth. And the dragon was wroth with the woman and went to make was with the remnant of her seed, which keep the commandments of God, and have the testimony of Jesus Christ." (Revelation 12:15-17)

Although *"the woman"* is ultimately protected from Satan's wrath, the symbolic language here, paints a vivid word picture of a horrific attempt to drown *"the woman"*. The text brings to mind an all-consuming flood rushing in to devastate and destroy the faithful with only the earth itself being able to stave off this most intensive onslaught by *"the dragon"*.

She is given protection in her *"place prepared by God"* which parallels the Exodus account when the children of Israel were given a safe haven in the land of Goshen being protected from the plagues which God brought upon the Egyptians.

The Lord again provides shelter from the storm, not only protecting *"the woman"* from Satan's vicious persecution during Satan's great wrath, the great tribulation, but also gives her a safe haven during the seven trumpet judgments. They begin the Day of the Lord (Revelation 8, 9) when the Lord judges the planet and purifies His people Israel.

This specific series of plagues/judgments is also called *"the time of Jacob's trouble" (Jeremiah 30:7)*. The Lord will send these plagues to bring judgment to the world with the primary purpose of purifying His people (Isaiah 1:24-28, 6:10-13; Ezekiel 7:19, 20; Zechariah 13:8, 9; Malachi 3:1-3;). This prepares them for their Redeemer, the Lord Jesus Christ (Isaiah 59:20, Romans 11:26) Who will redeem them at the end of the 70th Week of Daniel.

The two secondary purposes of the Day of the Lord are:
1. Punishment of the People (Isaiah 2:10-17; Zephaniah 1:17; Revelation 9:20, 21, 19:20, 21)
2. Purging of the Planet (Psalm 102:26; II Peter 3:10-13)

The faithful woman will also be spared from this time of trouble as she is *"nourished for a time, and times, and half a time"*
(Revelation 12:14), which is the last 3-1/2 years of the 70th Week, in her Goshen-like place prepared of God, for the Great Tribulation and the seven trumpets make up the last half of the 70th Week of Daniel.

These faithful of Israel will join the 144 Thousand and those Israelites who will be saved eventually populating the promised land for the 1,000 year physical reign of Christ called the Millennium (Revelation 20:1-4) as described by the prophet Micah:
"Therefore will He [Messiah] give them up, until the time that she [Israel] which travails [The time of Jacob's trouble (Jeremiah 30:7)] has brought forth [all Israel saved]: then the remnant [rest/remainder] of His [Messiah's] brethren [The woman] shall return unto the children [sons] of Israel [the 144 Thousand]." (Micah 5:3)

Although the Authorized Version uses the word *"remnant"* here in this verse, this is not the word normally used to describe the *"remnant"* that God preserves referred to throughout the Old

Testament. This word simply means the remainder, the rest or ones leftover and may be larger or smaller than the former part.

Micah uses this word just once here in this verse but the word that refers to the preserved remnant of Israel he does use five other times: (Micah 2:12, 4:7, 5:7, 5:8, 7:18) highlighting the distinction he made here in this text.

He is referring to the remainder/rest of those other faithful Israelites who will be in *"a place prepared of God" (Revelation 12:6)* until the time the great gathering of the people of God takes place at the end of the 70th Week of Daniel.

Micah indicates that these three groups of Israelites will unite in that time which agrees with Jacob's prophecy:
"The scepter shall not depart from Judah, nor a lawgiver from between his feet, unto Shiloh [The Peaceful Ruler/ Lord Jesus Christ] come; and unto Him shall the gathering of the people [Israelites] be." (Genesis 49:10)

"The woman", will return from her place *"in the wilderness"* joining the 144 Thousand and those Israelites *"who will turn from transgression in Jacob" (Isaiah 59:20)* as they all will gather unto their Messiah, the Lord Jesus Christ Who will then sit upon:
"The throne of His father David, And He shall reign over the house of Jacob for ever; and of His kingdom there shall be no end." (Isaiah 9:7; Luke 1:32, 33)

20

The Remnant of Her Seed

In Revelation 12 *"the woman"* who represents the faithful nation of Israel is introduced with the main focus in this chapter upon Satan's attempts to eliminate the Jews as a people. God during this end of the age assault gives her supernatural protection, and His protection continues throughout the entire second half of Daniel's 70th Week.

The last verse of Revelation 12 introduces another group of Israelites who become Satan's target after *"the woman"* escapes:
"And the dragon was wroth with the woman, and went to make war with the remnant [rest] of her seed, which keep the commandments of God, and the testimony of Jesus Christ." (Revelation 12:17)

The word translated *"remnant"* means remainder or rest, and the phrase *"of her seed"* indicates the physical relationship this group has with the woman. They are Israelites and their spiritual qualifications, they *"keep the commandments of God and have the testimony of Jesus Christ",* are indicated in the remainder of the verse.

While some interpret this group to be *"the saints"* of Revelation 14:12, there is no Biblical precedent for *"the woman"* (the faithful nation of Israel) or any other group to be identified as the spiritual head of the saints as was Abraham:
"And if ye be Christ's, then are ye Abraham's seed, and heirs according to the promise." (Galatians 3:29)

The word translated *"seed"* in Revelation 12:17 and Galatians 3:29 is the same Greek word "sperma" which is used over forty times in the New Testament. Every time it occurs it refers to **physical** seed, as in Revelation 12:17, except for Galatians 3:29 which is the only time it is used to show Abraham as the spiritual fountainhead or father of the faithful. He as the physical father of the Israelites was also the first to have his faith recorded indicating the doctrine of justification by faith:

"And Abraham believed God and it was counted unto him for righteousness." (Genesis 15:16)

Now, all before him were also justified by faith *"by His [the Lord Jesus Christ's] blood" (Romans 5:9)*. But, it was Abraham, the father of the faithful, to whom it was first recorded in Scripture that *"it was imputed to him for righteousness" (Romans 4:22)*. Therefore he is the only one who can be defined as the spiritual fountainhead/father of the saints who are in Christ being justified by faith.

The purpose of this description in Revelation 12:17: *"the remnant [rest] of her [physical] seed, who keep the commandments of God and the testimony of Jesus Christ"* is to indicate exactly who Satan's focus will be after *"the woman"* flees to the wilderness. Three groups of Israelites will remain in the land as described in the book of Daniel 11, 12.

The vast majority of faithful Israelites are protected in a place prepared by God for the last half of the 70th Week, But, this select group of Israelites, the 144 Thousand, remains to serve the Lord becoming the primary focus of Satan's assault during the last 3-1/2 years of Daniel's 70th Week.

Their vital Redemption Ministry is necessary in the plan of God as it will be key to the conversion of many Israelites who will receive their Messiah, the Lord Jesus Christ:

"But the people that do know their God, shall be strong and do
exploits. And they that understand among the people shall instruct
many: yet they shall fall by the sword, and by flame, by captivity, and
by spoil many days. Now when they fall they shall be helped with a
little help: but many shall cleave to them by flatteries [hypocrisy].
And some of them understanding shall fall, to try them, and to purge,
and to make them white, even to the time of the end: because it is yet
for a time appointed." (Daniel 11:32-35)

These events occur during the days following the abomination of desolation at the mid-point of the 70th Week of Daniel that is recorded in the previous verse:

"And arms [forces] shall stand on his [the Antichrist] part, and they shall pollute the sanctuary of strength, and shall take away the daily sacrifice, and they shall place the abomination that makes desolate." *(Daniel 11:31)*

There will be those faithful Israelites who *"know their God"* and *"understand"* in the land after *"the woman...flees into the wilderness"* and, it will be their primary duty to minister to those who do not understand and are without Christ as the following verse affirms recording their success:

"And they that be wise shall shine as the brightness of the firmament; and they that turn many to righteousness as the stars for ever and ever." (Daniel 12:3)

The Lord's purpose of purifying those Israelites who remain in the land during *"the time of Jacob's trouble" (Jeremiah 30:7)* is also indicated in this chapter:

"Many will be purified and made white and tried; but the wicked shall do wickedly and none of the wicked shall understand; but the wise shall understand." (Daniel 12:10)

This prime group of soul winners will be performing their service to the Lord in the toughest and most crucial environment ever when Satan and his angels will be cast into the earth as he will be inflicting his *"great wrath" (Revelation 12:12)* upon the people of God.

This will be the most intense persecution upon the faithful ever:

"For then shall be great tribulation such as was not since the beginning of the world to this time, no nor ever shall be." (Matthew 24:21)

Martyrdom as described in the Daniel 11 passage above will be the norm rather than the exception as they *"will love not their lives unto the death" (Revelation 12:11)* demonstrating their willing self-sacrifice for the cause of the Lord Jesus Christ.

These words are spoken to the martyrs of that day after they inquired of God's judgment:

"And it was said unto them that they should rest yet for a little season, until their fellow servants also and their brethren, that should

be killed as they were, should be fulfilled." (Revelation 6:11)

As in all things concerning His children, God is in complete control. He has predetermined the exact number of martyrs during the Great Tribulation until the fulfillment of that segment of His plan is accomplished and the exact amount of His people remain to carry on His testimony during the Day of the Lord.

It is from this very group of faithful Jews, *"which keep the commandments of God and have the testimony of Jesus Christ"* that those *"servants of our God"* in Revelation 7:3-8, the 144 Thousand sons of Israel, will finally come forth to serve the Lord as His tried and purified army during the Day of the Lord.

Sixteen descriptive characteristics of *"the remnant of her seed"* are indicated in Daniel 11, 12 and Revelation 12:
1. They shall know their God (Daniel 11:32).
2. They shall be strong (Daniel 11:32).
3. They shall do exploits (Daniel 11:32).
4. They shall understand (Daniel 11:33).
5. They shall instruct many (Daniel 11:33).
6. They shall fall by the sword, and by flame, and by captivity, and by spoil many days (Daniel 11:33).
7. They shall be tried (Daniel 11:35).
8. They shall be purified through trials and made pure/white (Daniel 11:35, 12:10).
9. They shall be wise (Daniel 12:3).
10. They shall shine as the brightness of the firmament (Daniel 12:3)
11. They shall turn many to righteousness (Daniel 12:3).
12. They shall shine as the stars forever and ever (Daniel 12:3).
13. They shall overcome the Devil by the Blood of the Lamb and the word of their testimony (Revelation 12:11)
14. They shall love not their lives unto the death (Revelation 12:11)
15. They shall keep the commandments of God (Revelation 12:17b)
16. They shall have the testimony of Jesus Christ (Revelation 12:17b)

This group called *"the remnant of her seed"* will continue their Redemption Ministry to those who will be redeemed in the last half of the 70th Week (Matthew 24:15-28) and the Day of the Lord's seven trumpets (Revelation 8-11).

21

The Devil

While the amount of Bible text describing the Devil is brief in the book of the Revelation, it is clearly understood by the titles given him in the Revelation that he is at the root of all evil from the beginning of time itself. Here in this last book of the Bible he is called *"that old serpent"(Revelation 12:9)* identifying him as the one who tempted Eve bringing sin into the world in the Garden of Eden (Genesis 3:1).

He is introduced as *"another wonder in heaven; and behold, a great red dragon having seven heads and ten horns and seven crowns upon his heads"(Revelation 12:3).*

His description here clearly links him with the *"scarlet colored beast full of names of blasphemy, having seven heads and ten horns." (Revelation 17:3)* who is the coming Antichrist *"the eighth and is of the seven"(Revelation 17:11)* the final world ruler.

In the Revelation he is very busy about his ultimate goal of extinguishing Israel the people of God from which the Lord Jesus Christ, God in the flesh, would eventually come forth.

The faithful of Israel are introduced before the Devil as:
"a great wonder in heaven; a woman clothed with the sun, and moon under her feet, and upon her head a crown of twelve stars: And she being with child cried, travailing in birth, and pained to be delivered." (Revelation 12:1, 2)

The ages long conflict between God's people and the Devil is briefly described: *"the dragon stood before the woman which was ready to be delivered, for to devour her Child [the Christ] as soon as It was born." (Revelation 12:4)*

The culmination of the purpose of Israel is vividly pictured for the Messiah, the Lord Jesus Christ, entered the world through God's earthly people the Jews. Herein lies the central purpose for the people of God.

"And she brought forth a Man-Child, who was to rule all nations with a rod of iron: and her Child was caught up unto God, and to His throne." (Revelation 12:5)

Although the Devil expended his best effort to eliminate God's Son by devising an intricate plan of deception and betrayal including the ignorant defiance of the religious leaders in Israel who put the Lord Jesus Christ on the Cross, he, the Devil, unknowingly was playing right into the hand of God, for Christ's death, burial and resurrection formulate the very Gospel of God. (I Corinthians 15:3)

In (v.6) of Revelation 12 the text returns to action during the time of the end:

"And there was war in heaven: Michael and his angels fought against the dragon; and the dragon fought and his angels, And prevailed not; neither was their place found any more in heaven. And the great dragon was cast out, that old serpent, called the Devil, and Satan which deceives the whole world: he was cast out in to the earth, and his angels were cast out with him. And I heard a loud voice saying in heaven, Now is come salvation, and strength, and the kingdom of our God, and the power of His Christ: for the accuser of our brethren is cast down, which accused them before our God day and night." (Revelation 12:7-10)

The Devil is given a number of descriptive titles in this chapter:
1. *"the great red dragon" (v.3)*
2. *"the dragon" (v.4, 7, 13, 16, 17)*
3. *"the great dragon" (v.7, 9)*
4. *"that old serpent" (v.9)*
5. *"the Devil" (v.9, 12)*
6. *"Satan" (v.9)*
7. *"the accuser of our brethren" (v.10)*
8. *"the serpent" (v.14, 15)*

In the above text (12:9) four of his titles are given in succession unfolding the different tactics he utilizes in his assault upon men:
1. As *"the dragon"* his focus is upon destroying/devouring Israel
2. As the *"old serpent"* his focus is upon deceiving men

3. As *"the Devil"* his focus is upon falsely accusing believers
4. As *"Satan"* his focus is upon slandering believers

Although his titles are recorded in fifteen different places in this chapter, these four successive titles encompass his primary activities and cover all different people groups, the Jew, the Gentile, believer and unbeliever.

The believer's three-fold formula for overcoming the Devil is then clearly provided in (v.11):
"And they [the brethren] overcame him by the Blood of the Lamb and by the word of their testimony; and they loved not their lives unto the death."

His *"great wrath"*, which the Lord describes as *"great tribulation such as was not since the beginning of the world" (Matthew 24:21)*, is viciously poured out because *"he [the Devil] knows that he has but a short time." (Revelation 12:12)*

He is relentless in his pursuit and persecution of the faithful:
"And when the dragon saw that he was cast unto the earth, he persecuted the woman which brought forth the Man Child."
(Revelation 12:13)

The time frame for this intense persecution of the faithful of Israel is underlined here as it is already defined in (v.6) as ***"a thousand two hundred and three score days"***.
*"And to the woman were given two wings of a great eagle, that she might fly into the wilderness, into her place, where she is nourished for **a time, and times, and half a time** from the face of the serpent."*
(Revelation 12:14)

These are two of the Bible's descriptions of the last 3-12 years of the 70th Week of Daniel. This time period was first mentioned in Daniel's book where he utilized this same unit of time to describe this the most event-filled Satanic period during the end times.

The start of this 3-1/2 year period is pinpointed by this event: *"in the midst of the week he [Antichrist] shall cause the sacrifice and the oblation to cease, and for the overspreading of abominations he shall make it [holy place] desolate." (Daniel 9:27)*

The Lord refers to this same event in His most important discourse on the end times:
"When ye therefore shall see the abomination of desolation spoken of by Daniel the prophet stand in the holy place." (Matthew 24:15)

Daniel refers to this notable time period on two other occasions in his prophecy utilizing similar terms:
"And he [Antichrist] shall speak great words against the Most High and shall wear out the saints of the Most High, and think to change times and laws: and they [the saints] shall be given into his hand until ***a time and times and the dividing of time****." (Daniel 7:25)*

*"And sware by Him that lives for ever and ever that it [the great tribulation] shall be for **a time, times and a half**; and when he [Antichrist] shall have accomplished to scatter the power of the holy people all these things shall be finished." (Daniel 12:7)*

The Apostle John records this same period on five occasions using three different terms:
*"But the court which is without the temple leave out, and measure it not; for it is given unto the Gentiles; and the holy city shall they tread under foot **forty and two months**." (Revelation 11:2)*
*"And I will give power unto My two witnesses, and they shall prophesy **a thousand two hundred and threescore days**, clothed in sackcloth." (Revelation 11:3)*
*"And the woman fled into the wilderness where she hath a place prepared of God, that they should feed her there **a thousand two hundred and three score days**." (Revelation 12:6)*
*"And to the woman were given two wings of a great eagle, that she might fly into the wilderness, into here place, where she is nourished for **a time, and times, and half a time** from the face of the serpent." (Revelation 12:14)*
*"And there was given unto him [Antichrist] a mouth speaking great things and blasphemies; and power was given unto him [by Satan] to continue **forty and two months**." (Revelation 13:5)*

It is at the mid-point of the 70th Week of Daniel that the Devil's assault upon the faithful of Israel intensifies:

"And the serpent cast out of his mouth water as a flood after the woman, that he might cause her to be carried away of the flood. And the earth helped the woman, and the earth opened her mouth, and swallowed up the flood which the dragon cast out of his mouth. And the dragon was wroth with the woman and went to make war with the remnant [rest] of her seed, which keep the commandments of God and have the testimony of Jesus Christ." (Revelation 12:17)

He is shown to be the power source of the Antichrist as his evil career continues to be documented by the Apostle John:
"And the beast which I saw was like unto a leopard, and his feet were as the feet of a bear and his mouth as the mouth of a lion: and the dragon gave him his power, and his seat, and his great authority." (Revelation 13:2)

Satanic worship will be commonplace in that day even as it is rapidly escalating today in the world in which we live:
"And they worshipped the dragon which gave power [authority] unto the beast [Antichrist]." (Revelation 13:4)

Although it appears that the Devil finally has complete control of planet earth through his two henchmen, the Antichrist and the false prophet, the final chapter has already been written recording their end:
"And I saw an angel come down from heaven, having the key of the bottomless pit and a great chain in his hand. And he laid hold on the dragon, that old serpent, which is the Devil, and Satan, and bound him a thousand years. And cast him into the bottomless pit, and shut him up, and set a seal upon him, that he should deceive the nations no more, till the thousand years should be fulfilled: and after that he must be loosed a little season...And when the thousand years are expired, Satan shall be loosed out of his prison, And shall go out to deceive the nations which are in the four quarters of the earth God and Magog, to gather them together to battle: the number of whom is as the sand of the sea. And they went up on the breadth of the earth, and compassed the camp of the saints about, and the beloved city: and fire came down from God out of heaven, and devoured them. And the devil that deceived them was cast into the lake of fire and brimstone, where the beast [Antichrist] and the false prophet, and shall be tormented day and night for ever and ever."
(Revelation 20:1-3, 7-10)

This is the last word in Scripture concerning the unholy trinity, the Devil, the Antichrist, and the false prophet. They receive their just due as John recorded here outlining the final actions of the Devil's notorious career.

He will be bound for a thousand years (Revelation 20:1-3) during the earthly reign of the Lord Jesus Christ which is also called the Millennium. Even though the evil influence of the Devil is gone, there will be those who will continue to rebel against God *"the number of whom is as the sand of the sea" (Revelation 20:8).*

The Lord will allow him to be loosed and he formulates his last coalition against God and the saints. God will summarily crush him upon this final rebellion as clearly documented by the Apostle John.

Then he will join his two cohorts the Antichrist and false prophet to suffer eternal torment in the place which was originally *"prepared for the devil and his angels" (Matthew 25:41)!*

22

The Antichrist

The most mentioned end times character in the Word of God, besides the Lord Himself, is the Antichrist. The book of Daniel records the great majority of the information given about this wicked and notorious enemy of God beginning with king Nebuchadnezzar of Babylon who is a type of the Antichrist.

He, Nebuchadnezzar, had an image built and demanded the then known world to bow down and worship the image or be put to death: *"Then an herald cried aloud, To you it is commanded, O people, nations, and languages, That at what time ye hear the sound of the cornet, flute, harp, sackbut, psaltery, dulcimer, and all kinds of music, ye fall down and worship the golden image that Nebuchadnezzar the king hath set up: And whoso falls not down and worships shall the same hour be cast into the midst of a burning fiery furnace."* *(Daniel 3:4-6)*

This same tactic will be utilized by the Antichrist and implemented by his worship enforcer the false prophet: *"And he [the false prophet] had power to give life [spirit/breath] unto the image of the beast [the Antichrist], that the image of the beast should both speak, and cause that as many as would not worship the image of the beast should be killed."* *(Revelation 13:15)*

The Antichrist himself is also literally introduced in the book of Daniel: *"I considered the horns [ten horns of the fourth beast/Roman empire], and, behold, there came up among them another little horn, before whom there were three of the first horns plucked up by the roots: and, behold, in this horn were eyes like the eyes of man, and a mouth speaking great things."* *(Daniel 7:8)*

The *"little horn"* who comes up among the ten horns of the fourth beast is the Antichrist. His rise, rule and subsequent ruin are thoroughly detailed beginning here in chapter seven:

"I beheld then because of the voice of the great words which the horn spoke: I beheld even till the beast was slain, and his body destroyed, and given to the burning flame." (Daniel 7:11)

Daniel inquires of the meaning of what he saw in this vision, focusing upon the fourth beast, the ten horns and the little horn:

"Then I would know the truth of the fourth beast...And of the ten horns that were in his head, and of the other which came up, and before whom three fell; even of that horn that had eyes, and a mouth that spoke very great things, whose look was more stout than his fellows." (Daniel 7:19, 20)

Daniel continues to look:

"I beheld and the same horn made war with the saints, and prevailed against them; Until the Ancient of days came, *and judgment was given to the saints of the most High; and the time came that the saints possessed the kingdom." (Daniel 7:21, 22)*

He then receives a full, specific answer to his inquiry:

"The fourth beast shall be the fourth kingdom upon earth, which shall be diverse from all kingdoms, and shall devour the whole earth, and shall tread it down, and break it in pieces. And the ten horns out of this kingdom are ten kings that shall arise: and another [the little horn/Antichrist] shall rise after them; and he shall be diverse from the first, and he shall subdue three kings. And he shall speak great words against the most High, and shall wear out the saints of the most High, and think to change times and laws: and they [the saints] shall be given into his hand until a time and times and the dividing of time. But, the judgment shall sit, and they shall take away his dominion, to consume and destroy it unto the end. And the kingdom and dominion, and the greatness of the kingdom, under the whole heaven, shall be given to the people of the saints of the most High, whose kingdom is an everlasting kingdom, and all dominions shall serve and obey him. Hitherto is the end of the matter. As for me Daniel, my cogitations much troubled me, and my countenance changed in me: but I kept the matter in my heart." (Daniel 7:23-28)

Daniel's first vision provides specific information concerning:

I. <u>The Rise of the Antichrist</u> (Daniel 7:7, 8, 11)

1. He rises from the fourth beast/Roman Empire.
2. He rises after the ten horns/kings.
3. He is called the "*little horn*" and "*the beast*".
4. He has eyes like a man and mouth speaking great things.
5. He comes up among the ten horns/kings.

II. The Rule of the Antichrist (Daniel 7:8b, 21, 24, 25)
1. He subdues three of these ten kings.
2. He speaks great [boastful] words against the most High.
3. He makes war [global] with the saints.
4. He prevails against them and they are given into his hand for a time, times and dividing of time [3-1/2 years).
5. He is diverse/different than the ten kings.
6. He is more stout/opposing than the ten kings.
7. He shall think to change times and laws.

III. The Ruin of the Antichrist (Daniel 7:11, 26, 27)
1. He shall have his dominion taken away, to consume and destroy it unto the end.
2. He is ultimately slain, his body destroyed and given to the burning flame.
3. He is destroyed just before the kingdom and dominion is given to the people of the saints of the most High.

Chapter seven, Daniel's introductory vision, is global in scope, applying to both Jew and Gentile and provides the necessary framework for the end times and the remainder of the book of Daniel, with the Antichrist and his actions being the primary focal point.

Most of the first chapters of Daniel's prophecy are written in Aramaic/Chaldee (Daniel 2:4-7:28) and are mainly historical except for chapter seven, which applies to the saints worldwide who are rescued by the rapture when the great tribulation is shortened (Matthew 24:21-31).

The second of Daniel's visions in chapter eight is written in Hebrew as are the remaining two visions in chapters nine and ten through twelve. These three visions specifically focus upon Israel and her people. The vision in chapter eight begins by describing a ram and a he goat symbolizing two kingdoms. The ram is the kingdom of the Medes and Persians, being overcome by the he goat, the kingdom of Greece. The he goat having a *"notable horn"* refers to Alexander the great (Daniel 8:2-7).

When he [Alexander] dies: *"The great horn was broken" (Daniel 8:8a)* and his kingdom is divided into four parts *"toward the four winds of heaven" (Daniel 8:8b). "And out of one of them came forth a little horn [the Antichrist] which waxed exceeding great, toward the south, and toward the east, and toward the pleasant land [Israel]." (Daniel 8:9)*

"The little horn" comes *"out of one of them"* indicating one of the four divisions which are part of the previous ten horns and the Roman Empire. The detail of Daniel 8:1-9 is given in order to accurately pinpoint the country from which the Antichrist will rise with the choice coming from one of the *"four notable ones toward the four winds of heaven"*.

The Antichrist will come from one of these *"four kingdoms...in the latter time [end of days] of their kingdoms" (Daniel 8:22, 23)* being clearly interpreted by the angel. These four countries are from the kingdom of Alexander the Great when upon his death it was divided into Syria (North), Egypt (South), Turkey/Armenia (East), Greece (West). Their locations are in respect to the land of Israel.

In chapter eleven the Antichrist is identified as *"the [last] king of the north" (Daniel 11:21-45)* indicating he will rise from the present-day country of Syria which should be no surprise as Assyria of old was one of Israel's major adversaries just as it continues to be today.

Isaiah prophesied indicating this truth:
"Therefore, thus saith the Lord God of hosts, O My people that dwell in Zion, be not afraid of the Assyrian [Antichrist]: he shall smite thee with a rod, and shall lift up his staff against thee, after the manner of Egypt. For yet a very little while, and the indignation shall cease, and My anger in their destruction. And the LORD of hosts shall stir up a scourge for him [Antichrist] according to the slaughter of Midian at the rock of Oreb: and as His rod was upon the sea, so shall He lift it up after the manner of Egypt. And it shall come to pass in that day [Day of the Lord], that his [Antichrist] burden shall be taken away from off thy shoulder, and his yoke from off thy neck, and the yoke shall be destroyed because of the anointing." (Isaiah 10:24-27)

"The LORD of hosts hath sworn, saying, Surely as I have thought, so shall it come to pass, and as I have purposed, so shall it stand. That I will break the Assyrian [Antichrist] in My land, and upon My mountains tread him under foot: then shall his yoke depart from off them [Israel], and his burden depart from off their shoulders. This is the purpose that is purposed upon the whole earth: and this is the hand that is stretched out upon all the nations. For the LORD of hosts hath purposed, and who shall disannul it? And His hand is stretched out, and who shall turn it back?" (Isaiah 14:24-26)

"For in that day [Day of the Lord] every man shall cast away his idols of silver, and his idols of gold, which your own hands have made unto you for a sin. Then shall the Assyrian [Antichrist] fall with the sword, not of a mighty man; and the sword, not of a mean man, shall devour him: but he shall flee from the sword, and his young men shall be discomfited. And he shall pass over to his strong hold for fear, and his princes shall be afraid of the ensign, saith the LORD, Whose fire is in Zion, and His furnace in Jerusalem." (Isaiah 31:7-9)

Micah the prophet, a contemporary of Isaiah, also prophesied concerning the future demise of the Antichrist:
"And this Man [Messiah] shall be the peace, when the Assyrian [Antichrist] shall come into our land: and when he shall tread within our palaces, then shall we raise against him seven shepherds and eight principal men. And they shall waste the land of Assyria with the sword, and the land of Nimrod in the entrances thereof: thus shall He [Messiah] deliver us from the Assyrian, when he comes into our land, and when he treads within our borders." (Micah 5:5, 6)

But first of all, here in Daniel chapter eight, the Antichrist's actions are more specifically defined as they apply to Israel:
"And it waxed great, even to the host of heaven; and it cast down some of the host and of the stars to the ground, and stamped upon them. Yea, he magnified himself even to the Prince of the host, and by [from] Him the daily sacrifice was taken away, and the place of His sanctuary was cast down. And an host was given him against the daily sacrifice by reason of transgression, and it cast down the truth to the ground; and it practiced, and prospered." (Daniel 8:10-12)

The extent of the Satanically empowered Antichrist's greatness is

described as *"even to the host of heaven"* when he will, as Satan's instrument *"cast down some of the host and of the stars to the ground"* which is also recorded in Revelation:
"And he [dragon/Satan] drew the third part of the stars of heaven, and did cast them to the earth." (Revelation 12:4)

His self-magnification reaches *"even to the Prince [the Lord Jesus Christ] of the host"* as the Antichrist will stop the daily sacrifice and set up his image in *"the place [the holy place] of His [the Lord's] sanctuary"*. He is given *"An host...by reason of transgression"* which evidently indicates some of the angelic host of heaven being given over to the Antichrist for a time. The first reference to the renown *"abomination of desolation"* occurs here in Daniel's vision of chapter eight, with the purpose of this vision focusing upon the Antichrist, his Actions and the Actual Time his actions will have effect.

In (v.1-8) unfolds The Ascertaining of His Country, (v.9) The Ascendancy of the Antichrist, and (v.10-14) indicates The Actual Time/Actions of the Antichrist. Although the introduction of this vision includes the rise and fall of certain kingdoms from a long past era, the timeframe and emphasis of this revelation is *"The time of the end...the last end [Ack-ah-reeth'] of the indignation" (Daniel 8:17, 19)* indicating exactly when all of these events will take place.

The Hebrew word pronounced Ack-ah-reeth' is found in the Old Testament over sixty times. It is used numerous times to indicate the last days/latter days/time of the end/end of days, beginning with this proclamation given by the patriarch Jacob:
*"And Jacob called unto his sons, and said, Gather yourselves together, that I may tell you that which shall befall you in the **last days.**" (Genesis 49:1)*

Moses also utilized this same word:
*"When thou art in tribulation, and all these things are come upon thee, even in the **latter days** , if thou turn to the LORD thy God, and shall be obedient unto His voice; (For the LORD thy God is a merciful God) He will not forsake thee, neither destroy thee, nor forget the covenant of thy fathers which He sware unto them." (Deuteronomy 4:30, 31)*

The prophet Isaiah describes the future time of the Millennium using this same term:
*"And it shall come to pass in the **last days** , that the mountain of the LORD'S house shall be established in the top of the mountains, and shall be exalted above the hills, and all nations shall flow unto it."* *(Isaiah 2:2)*

Ezekiel's end times prophecy also records this word twice:
*"After many days thou [Gog] shall be visited: in the **latter years** thou shall come into the land that is brought back from the sword, and is gathered out of many people, against the mountains of Israel, which have always been waste: but it is brought forth out of the nations, and they shall dwell safely all of them...And thou [Gog] shall come up against My people of Israel, as a cloud to cover the land; it shall be in the **latter days**, and I will bring thee against My land, that the heathen may know Me, when I shall be sancified in thee, O Gog, before their eyes."* *(Ezekiel 38:8, 16)*

Two of the most significant instances of this Hebrew word are found in the prophecy of Daniel when this word is used to indicate exactly when the information Daniel was given in two of his visions will come to pass:
*"And he [Gabriel] said, Behold, I will make thee know what shall be in the **last end** of the indignation: for at the time appointed the end shall be."* *(Daniel 8:19)*

This vision in Daniel chapter eight applies to the future *"time of the end"* as Gabriel also indicated earlier:
"So he [Gabriel] came near where I stood: and when he came, I was afraid, and fell upon my face: but he said unto me, Understand, O son of man: for at the time of the end shall be the vision." *(Daniel 8:17)*

In Daniel's last vision he once again is told:
*"Now I [the angel] am come to make thee understand what shall befall thy people in the **latter days**: for yet the vision is for many days."* *(Daniel 10:14)*

It is clear from the text that the information given to Daniel in these two visions applies to those future days at the time of the end. While some interpret much of these two important end times visions as completed history, Daniel was explicitly told without exception that these visions would come to pass:

"At the time of the end...at the last end of the indignation...in the latter days." (Daniel 8:17, 18, 10:14)

The information given in Daniel 8:9-14, 23-26 and 11:21-45 pertains to future events which will occur during the latter days/time of the end. This is the literal and therefore the most accurate interpretation of these two visions for the following reasons:

1. The text explicitly indicates *"the time of the end"* as the specific time these two visions will be fulfilled which is the **only** evidence required in order to apply these visions to that future time.

2. The Word of God **alone** is all that is necessary to know God's plan for *"the time of the end"* (knowledge of ancient history is not a primary prerequisite for understanding God's truth)

3. There is no reason to record centuries of ancient history not clearly interpreted by the angel in order to illuminate the focus of the text which is *"the time of the end"*.

4. The same feature in the text divides past history from the future *"time of the end"* in both visions:

   a. *"Therefore the he goat waxed very great: and when he was strong, the great horn was broken; and for it came up four notable ones **toward the four winds of heaven**." (Daniel 8:8)*

   b. *"And when he shall stand up, his kingdom shall be broken, and shall be divided **toward the four winds of heaven**." (Daniel 11:4)*

5. Both visions then unfold information pertaining to the time of the end and the Antichrist:

   a. Chapter eight immediately details specifics concerning the Antichrist (Daniel 8:9-12, 23-26).

   b. Chapter eleven includes two *"king[s] of the north"* (Daniel 11:5-20) just prior to the Antichrist's description(Daniel 11:21-45).

6. The interpretation of the visions given to Daniel by the angel providing the actual names of the pertinent countries is the only ancient history necessary to understand these two visions:

"The ram which thou saw having two horns are the kings of Media and Persia. And the rough goat is the king of Greece: and the great horn that is between his eyes is the first king. Now that being broken, whereas four stood up for it, four kingdoms shall stand up out of the

nation, but not in his power." (Daniel 8:20-22)

"And now I will show thee the truth. Behold, there shall stand up yet three kings in Persia; and the fourth shall be far richer than they all: and by his strength through his riches he shall stir up all against the realm of Greece. And a mighty king shall stand up, that shall rule with great dominion, and do according to his will. And when he shall stand up, his kingdom shall be broken, and shall be divided toward the four winds of heaven; and not to his posterity, nor according to his dominion which he ruled: for his kingdom shall be plucked up, even for others beside those." (Daniel 11:2-4)

7. Both of these visions begin with and refer to this same initial historical sequence. Their primary purpose is to clearly indicate the Antichrist's country of origin:

*"And **out of one of them** [four notable ones toward the four winds of heaven] came forth a little horn [Antichrist] which waxed exceeding great, toward the south, and toward the east, and toward the pleasant land." (Daniel 8:9)*

8. *"The abomination of desol*ation" referred to by the Lord Jesus Christ (Matthew 24:15) is recorded only once in the Daniel chapter eight vision indicating the end times actions of the Antichrist at the mid-point of the 70th Week (Daniel 9:27):

"Yea, he magnified himself even to the prince of the host, and by him the daily sacrifice was taken away, and the place of his sanctuary was cast down." (Daniel 8:11)

9. This same "a*bomination of desolation"* is only indicated once in the Daniel 11:5-45 sequence:

"And arms [forces] shall stand on his part, and they shall pollute the sanctuary of strength, and shall take away the daily sacrifice, and shall place the abomination that makes desolate." (Daniel 11:31)

   a. There is only one personage recorded in Daniel chapter eight after the introductory history. There is no break in the narrative given in Daniel 11:5-45 in order for the theree "*kings of the north"* to be separted by an interval of time.
   b. The country which the three "*king(s) of the north"* (Daniel 11 5-45) rule over, north of Israel, is present-day Syria, which is one of those four kingdoms *"divided toward the four winds of heaven"*.
   c. Daniel 11:5-45, which chronicles the activities of the three "*king[s] of the north*", is referring to three rulers of Syria.

10. The last *"king of the north"* is responsible for the only mention of the *"abomination of desolation"* in chapter eleven revealing that he, the last king of the north, is the renown time of the end Antichrist.

The Antichrist's involvement with the *"daily sacrifice"* begins after he confirms a covenant with the Jews, at the beginning of the 70th Week (Daniel 9:27), and continues 2300 days or *"evenings and mornings" (Daniel 8:14)*.

Just exactly what his involvement will include is not clearly specified. However, he may preside over it, possibly taking a position of authority regarding the Jews temple worship after 220 days, or a little over seven months, after confirming the existing covenant at the beginning of the 70th Week of Daniel.

After this time, the host and regular sacrifice will be given over to the Antichrist lasting for the next 1040 days with the culmination of his evil influence coming at the mid-point of the 70th Week. Then his forces stop the regular sacrifice and pollute the sanctuary by setting up his image in the holy place for the remaining 1260 days of the 70th Week which is the *"abomination of desolation"* indicated by the Lord Jesus Christ (Matthew 24:15).

Some apply the vision in chapter eight to the history of Antiochus Epiphanes, an historic type of the Antichrist, who desecrated the temple during his assault upon the Jews and their worship during the second century B.C. But, Gabriel, who interpreted the vision for Daniel, clearly states exactly when this vision will come to pass:
*"O son of man: for at **the time of the end shall be the vision**...Behold I will make thee know what shall be in **the last end of the indignation**: for at the time appointed **the end** shall be."*
(Daniel 8:17, 19)

In addition, there are three events mentioned in this vision that were not fulfilled in the second century B.C. by Antiochus Epiphanes:
1. He did not "*cast down some of the host and of the stars to the ground, and stamped upon them.*" *(Daniel 8:10)*
2. He did not "*magnify himself even to Prince of the host/stand up against Prince of princes*" *(Daniel 8:11, 25)*

272

3. He was not *"broken without hand [Human agency: NASB]."*
   (Daniel 8:25)

These three events are prophesied and will occur during the end times:

1. *"And his [Great red dragon/Satan] tail drew the third part of the stars of heaven, and did cast them to the earth."*
   (Revelation 12:4)
2. The Antichrist will open *"his mouth in blasphemy against God, to blaspheme His name, and His tabernacle, and them that dwell in heaven"* *(Revelation 13:6)* fulfilling the second event.
3. The Antichrist will *"be broken without hand."*
   (Daniel 2:34, 35; Revelation 19:20)

This passage recording the 2300 days the Antichrist is involved with the *"daily sacrifice"* indicates he may, early on during the 70th Week of Daniel, have an integral position of authority regarding the Jews worship and possibly preside over the *"evening and morning"* or *"regular sacrifice"*.

Daniel 8:12 gives the reason the Antichrist is given this opportunity:
"And on account of transgression the host will be given over to the horn along with the regular sacrifice; and it will fling truth to the ground and perform its will and prosper." NASB

This verse not only gives the cause for the Antichrist's intrusive ability to invade these sacred areas, but it also underlines the two events that will occur during those 1040 days prior to the *"abomination of desolation"* which occurs at the mid-point of the 70th Week:

1. The host will be given over to the horn [During the 1040 days]
2. The regular sacrifice will also be given over to the horn [During the 1040 days]

These two actions occur because of sin, transgression in particular, a word that emphasizes the settled attitude of open and full rebellion against God. This is the same word used in Daniel 9:24, *"Seventy weeks are determined upon thy people and thy holy city, to finish the* **transgression**", describing the first reason the Lord has decreed these

70 weeks or 490 years.

The Lord Jesus Christ spoke of this last and most blatant rejection of the Messiah and reception of the Antichrist by the Jews:
"I am come in My Fathers name, and ye receive Me not: if another shall come in his own name, him ye will receive." (John 5:43)

The majority of Jews will in fact continue to reject the Lord Jesus Christ and embrace the Antichrist, just as their Caesar of old (John 19:15). The final rejection of the Messiah, will be this transgression as the Jews: *"have intelligence with" (Daniel 11:30)* the Antichrist in open rebellion against God.

This transgression or rebellion by those who *"forsake the holy covenant" (Daniel 11:30)* will likely provide the Antichrist with the ability to intervene. The host will be given over to him, along with the regular sacrifice, eventually resulting in the stopping of the regular or daily sacrifice and his image being set up in the holy place at the mid-point of the 70th Week (Daniel 9:27).

One saint [holy one/angel] questions the length of time::
"How long shall be the vision concerning the daily sacrifice, and the transgression of desolation, to give both the sanctuary and the host to be trodden under foot? And he said unto me, Unto two thousand and three hundred days; then shall the sanctuary be cleansed."
(Daniel 8:13, 14)

Daniel then receives the interpretation of the vision beginning with the time it will occur:
"Understand O son of man: for at the time of the end shall be the vision...And he said, Behold, I will make thee know what shall be in the last end of the indignation: for at the time appointed the end shall be." (Daniel 8:17, 19)

He is told exactly who the ram and the he goat represent
(Daniel 8:20-22), but, in the closing verses the emphasis again focuses upon the Antichrist:
"And in the latter time of their kingdom [Persia: Iran/Iraq and Greece], when the transgressors are come to the full [Have run their course], a king of fierce countenance [The Antichrist], and

understanding dark sentences, shall stand up. And his power shall be mighty, but not by his own power: and he shall destroy wonderfully, and shall prosper, and practice, and shall destroy the mighty and the holy people [Jews]. And through his policy also he shall cause craft to prosper in his hand; and he shall magnify himself in his heart, and by peace shall destroy many: he shall also stand up against the Prince of princes [Lord Jesus Christ]; but he shall be broken without hand. And the vision of the evening and the morning which was told is true; wherefore shut thou up the vision, for it shall be for many days." (Daniel 8:23-26)

This second vision of Daniel uncovers additional detailed information concerning the Antichrist:

I. The Rise of the Antichrist (Daniel 8:9, 10)
 1. He *"the little horn"* will come *"Out of one of them"* [The Four divisions of Alexander's kingdom]
 2. He will wax exceeding great toward the south [Egypt], the east [Turkey/Armenia] and toward the pleasant land [Israel]
 3. He will even grow up to the host of heaven and cast some of the host and of the stars down to the ground

II. The Rule of the Antichrist (Daniel 8:11, 12, 23-25)
 1. He magnifies himself even to the Prince/Commander of the host
 2. He takes away His [Prince/Commander] daily sacrifice
 3. He casts down the place of His [Prince/Commander] sanctuary
 4. He is given an host by reason of transgression
 5. He casts down truth to the ground and practices and prospers
 6. He causes the daily sacrifice to be stopped and implements the transgression [abomination] of desolation
 7. He treads under foot the sanctuary and the host for 2300 days
 8. He is a king of fierce countenance and understanding dark sentences
 9. He shall be powerful but not of his own power [Satanic]
 10. He shall destroy the mighty and the holy people [Israel]
 11. He shall cause craft to prosper through his policy
 12. He shall magnify himself in his heart
 13. He shall destroy many by peace

III. The Ruin of the Antichrist (Daniel 8:25)
 1. He shall stand up against the Prince of princes

[Lord Jesus Christ]
2. He shall be broken without hand [Human agency]

In chapter nine, after telling Daniel the truth concerning this coming one who will oppose God and end the regular sacrifice, the *"little horn"* of chapters seven and eight, also called the *"king of fierce countenance" (Daniel 8:23)*, this same Antichrist *"confirms the covenant for one week" (Daniel 9:27)*. He causes the daily sacrifice to cease at the mid-point of this week, which is the last week or seven years also known as the 70th Week of Daniel (Daniel 9:27).

The information supplied by these verses (Daniel 9:26b, 27) concerning the Antichrist appears to be minimal on the surface but in reality these few brief facts provide the information which supplies the bond of unity of Daniel's visions and unfolds the crucial timing of the Antichrist's actions and their key relationship to the nation of Israel at the time of the end.

I. The Rise of the Antichrist (Daniel 9:26b, 27a)
   1. He is out of the Roman Empire.
   2. He is *"the prince that shall come"*.
   3. He shall *"confirm the covenant with [the] many [of Israel] for one week [70th Week of Daniel]"*.

II. The Rule of the Antichrist (Daniel 9:27b,c,d)
   1. He shall *"cause the sacrifice and oblation to cease in the midst of the week [70th Week of Daniel]"*.
   2. He shall *"make it [Holy place] desolate [because of] the overspreading of abominations"*.
   3. He shall *"cause the sacrifice and oblation to cease...make it [Holy place] desolate even until the consummation"*.

III. The Ruin of the Antichrist (Daniel 9:27e)
   1. He shall come to his end.
   2. When *"that determined is poured out upon the desolate"*.

After Daniel is told by the angel Gabriel of the *"seventy weeks"* that God *"determined upon thy people [Israel] and upon thy holy city [Jerusalem]" (Daniel 9:24)* he was given both the purpose and the unfolding of this time period. The following three verses indicate how it would all come to God's predetermined conclusion.

These four verses are some of the most quoted verses in Scripture dealing with eschatology, the doctrine of last things. They unfold the entire history of the nation of Israel from the day *"the commandment"* was given in 445 B.C. (Nehemiah 2:4-8) *"to restore and to build Jerusalem unto the Messiah the Prince [The Lord Jesus Christ]"* until His triumphant entry (Matthew 21:1-9) into Jerusalem.

Then the Messiah *"shall be cut off"* referring to His death on the Cross. *"The people [Romans] of the prince that shall come [Antichrist] shall destroy the city [Jerusalem] and the sanctuary [temple]; and the end shall be with a flood, and unto the end of the war [A.D.70] desolations are determined."* (Daniel 9:26)

The last verse (Daniel 9:27) supplies the bulk of the information which applies to the Antichrist. Daniel 9:26 also underlines two important facts concerning the Antichrist: He is called the *"prince that shall come"* and is considered to be a representative of the Roman Empire [The fourth beast (Daniel 7)]. This same Roman Empire did in fact conquer all of the nations that made up Alexander the great's empire that was divided into four parts, from which the Antichrist eventually will rise.

The last, longest and most informative vision of Daniel is found in the last three chapters (Daniel 10-12) of the book. This vision was given to literally fill in the blanks for Daniel concerning the vision of chapter eight that he did not fully understand at the time it was given (Daniel 8:27).

Chapter ten is introductory and does not advance the vision's timeline, but it is precious in content as it contains a majestic view of the Lord Jesus Christ and the effect it had upon the aged prophet (Daniel 10:5-9) for he is estimated to be in his late eighties at the time this last vision was given to him by God,

He speaks with the Lord during the remainder of the verses in this section (Daniel 10:10-17) and is strengthened by an angel at the close of this most informative chapter. It unveils the communication and warfare by the demonic princes of Persia and Greece against the angel and his only angelic ally *"Michael your [Israel's] prince"* (Daniel 10:21).

This vision, like the two before it (Chapter 8 & 9), focuses upon Israel during the end times. The introductory information found in Daniel 10:1-11:1 is given to harmonize and couple with what had already been given in the previous visions and the prophetic truth Daniel would be given in the remainder of this great vision.

Beginning with (Daniel 11:2) the angel gives Daniel future information starting with the day the vision was given to him:
"And now will I show thee the truth. Behold, there shall stand up yet three kings in Persia; and the fourth shall be far richer than they all; and by his strength through his riches he shall stir up all against the realm of Greece And a mighty king [Alexander] shall stand up, that shall rule with great dominion, and do according to his will. And when he shall stand up, his kingdom shall be broken, and shall be divided toward the four winds of heaven; and not to his posterity, nor according to his dominion that he ruled: for his kingdom shall be plucked up, even for others beside those." (Daniel 11:2-4)

There would be three more Persian kings to come then the last would be conquered by Alexander and his kingdom would be divided into four parts, which is what Daniel was told in his second vision (Daniel 8:8).

In chapter eight, immediately after these four divisions are recorded, the account moves to the end times, and the [Antichrist] *"little horn"* is introduced as coming out of one of these four divisions or countries.

In this last vision Alexander's kingdom is *"broken, and shall be divided toward the four winds of heaven" (Daniel 11:4)*. This repeats the same pattern of Daniel 8:8 and immediately the vision is fast-forwarded to the *"time of the end"*. Starting with Daniel 11:5 through the end of the chapter, this section chronicles the generations and conflicts of *"the king of the south [Egypt]"* with *"the king of the north [Syria]"*.

The last of these kings of the north (Daniel 11:21-45) is the same *"little horn"*, *"king of fierce countenance"* who is the Antichrist of the previous visions. This conclusion is based upon a comparison of the information given concerning the Antichrist in Daniel's visions of chapters seven and eight compared with chapter eleven listed below:

(7:25) "He shall speak great words against the most High"

(11:36) "He shall speak marvelous things against the God of gods"

(7:25) "He shall think to change times and laws"

(11:37) "Neither shall he regard the gods of his fathers" etc.

(7:21, 22) "The same horn prevailed until the time came that the saints possessed the kingdom."

(11:36) "He shall prosper till the indignation be accomplished"

(8:9) He waxed great "Towards the pleasant land"

(11:41) "He shall enter also into the glorious land"

(8:17) "At the time of the end shall be the vision"

(11:40) "At the time of the end" etc.

(8:19) "In the last end of the indignation"

(11:36) "He shall prosper till the indignation be accomplished"

This brief comparison was taken from the commentary: "Tregelles on Daniel" pp.83 written by Dr. Samuel P. Tregelles LL.D. nearly a century and a half ago.

He also records the repeated pattern in chapters eight and eleven of the four divisions of Alexander's kingdom being immediately followed by time of the end prophecies concerning the Antichrist.

He rightly contends that the subject matter in all of these visions is repeatedly said to be focused upon the time of the end as indicated by the text, and not merely centuries of history that have no bearing whatsoever upon the end times.

The brief historic content of Daniel's visions interpreted by the angel was given only to illuminate, magnify and verify the future events concerning the nation of Israel and the actions of the Antichrist during the end times:

I. The Rise of the Antichrist (Daniel 11:20, 21)
   1. He shall be a vile person
   2. He shall not be given the honor of the kingdom

3. He shall come in peaceably
4. He shall obtain the kingdom by flatteries [intrigue]
5. He shall have the arms [forces] overflow from before him and they shall be broken including the prince of the covenant
6. He shall work deceitfully after the league [covenant] is made with him
7. He shall come up and become strong with a small people [force]
8. He shall enter peaceably even upon the fattest [richest] places of the province [realm]
9. He shall do that which his fathers/ancestors have not done: scatter the prey, and spoil and riches
10. He shall forecast his devices against the strongholds

II. The Rule of the Antichrist (Daniel 11:24-45)
1. He shall stir up his power and his courage against the king of the south with a great army, the king of the south shall be stirred up to battle with a very great and mighty army, but the [King of the south] shall not stand for they shall forecast devices against him. Yea, they that feed of the portion of his meat shall destroy him, his army shall overflow: and many shall fall down slain.
2. And both these kings' [King of the north & king of the south] hearts shall be to do mischief, and they shall speak lies at one table; but it shall not prosper: for yet the end shall be at the time appointed.
3. He [king of the north] shall return into his land with great riches; and his heart shall be set against the holy covenant
4. He shall do exploits, and return to his own land [Syria]
5. He shall return, and come toward the south; but it shall not be as the former, or as the latter
6. He shall be grieved for the ships of Chittim [Cyprus] shall come against him
7. He shall return, and have indignation against the holy covenant; so shall he do
8. He shall even return, and have intelligence with them that forsake the [Jews] holy covenant
9. And arms [forces] shall stand on his part, and they shall pollute the sanctuary of strength, and shall take away the daily sacrifice, and they shall place the abomination that makes desolate

10. He shall corrupt by flatteries [smooth words] such as do wickedly against the [holy] covenant
11. He shall do according to his will
12. He shall exalt himself, and magnify himself above every god
13. He shall speak marvelous [monstrous] things against the God of Gods
14. He shall prosper till the indignation be accomplished: for that is determined to be done
15. He shall not regard the god of his fathers
16. He shall not regard the desire of women
17. He shall not regard any god
18. He shall magnify himself above all
19. He shall honor the god of forces
20. He shall honor with gold and silver and precious stones, and pleasant things a god whom his fathers knew not
21. He shall honor this strange god in the most strong holds
22. He shall acknowledge and increase with glory this strange god
23. He shall cause them to rule over the many
24. He shall divide the land for gain
25. At the time of the end shall the king of the south push at him and the king of the north shall come against him [king of the south] like a whirlwind, with chariots, and with horsemen, and with many ships
26. He shall enter into the countries, and shall overflow and pass over
27. He shall enter also into the glorious land [Israel] and many countries shall be overthrown: but these shall escape out of his hand, even Edom, and Moab, and the chief of the children of Ammon
28. He shall stretch forth his hand also upon the countries: and the land of Egypt shall not escape
29. He shall have power over the treasures of gold and of silver, And over all the precious things of Egypt; and the Libyans And Ethiopians shall be at his step [follow at his heels]
30. He shall be troubled by tidings out of the East, out of the North
31. He shall go forth with great fury to destroy and utterly make many away
32. He shall plant the tabernacles of his palace between the seas [Dead Sea & Mediterranean Sea] in the glorious holy

mountain [Mt. Zion/Jerusalem]
III. The Ruin of the Antichrist (Daniel 11:45b)
1. He shall come to his end
2. And no one shall help him

This vision unfolds the most detailed information concerning The Rise, Rule and Ruin of the Antichrist as Daniel 11:21-45 is wholly focused upon this notorious end times character.

He does not receive the kingdom honorably as those before him. Instead this despicable despot through intrigue in a time of peace seizes the throne. He practices deception; he devises schemes; he speaks lies; he turns on the Jews and the holy covenant; he utilizes smooth words to gain his way; he does as he pleases, magnifying himself, speaking blasphemous things against God; he shows no regard for the god of his fathers but instead magnifies himself above all gods; he is constantly in the midst of warfare, destroying and annihilating many. He is a formidable foe indeed, but, thank God, he will come to his end, and no one will help him.

While the book of Daniel definitely supplies the most detail concerning the Antichrist, the book of the Revelation also provides many parallels to Daniel's prophecy and much new information:

I. The Rise of the Antichrist (Revelation 13:1, 2a)
1. He shall rise up out of the sea.
2. He shall have seven heads. [Seven previous beast kingdoms]
3. He shall have ten horns [kings] and upon his horns ten crowns.
4. He shall have upon his heads the name of blasphemy.
5. He shall be called the beast.
6. He shall be like unto a leopard, and his feet were as the feet of a bear, and his mouth as the mouth of a lion.
II. The Rule of the Antichrist (Revelation 13:2b-8, 16:13. 14. 17:3-13)
1. He shall receive his power, seat [throne] and great authority [right to rule] from the dragon [Satan].
2. He shall have one of his heads wounded to death; and his deadly wound [miraculously] healed.
3. He shall be wondered after by all the world
4. He shall be worshipped by all the world just as the dragon

[Satan].

5. He shall be worshipped because of his warfare invincibility.
6. He shall have a mouth speaking great things and blasphemies.
7. He shall have power [authority] given to him [by Satan] to continue forty and two months [3-1/2 years].
8. He shall blaspheme the name of God, and His tabernacle, and them that dwell in heaven.
9. He shall make war with the saints.
10. He shall overcome them.
11. He shall have [worldwide] authority given him [by Satan] over all kindreds, and tongues, and nations.
12. He shall be worshipped by all that dwell upon the earth, whose names are not written in the book of life of the Lamb slain from the foundation of the world.
13. He shall be one of the sources of unclean spirits as they proceed out of his mouth during 6th vial judgment for they are the spirits of devils, working miracles which go forth unto the kings of the earth of the whole world to gather them to the battle of that great day of God Almighty. [Armageddon]
14. He is the scarlet colored beast upon whom the woman, Mystery Babylon [false religion/Romanism] sits.
15. He was and is not and yet is.
16. He shall ascend out of the bottomless pit, and go into perdition.
17. He shall be wondered at by them that dwell upon the earth, whose names were not written in the book of life from the foundation of the world.
18. He shall be the 8th in the series of kings of which five are fallen, and one is [John's day: Nero, the 6th], and the other [Hitler, the 7th] is not yet come; and when he comes he must continue a short space [approximately 7 years].
19. He [Antichrist] shall be given the power and strength of the ten kings for one hour [brief period].

23

<u>The False Prophet</u>

I. <u>The Rise of the False Prophet</u> (Revelation 13:11)
   1. He shall come up out of the earth
   2. He shall have two horns like a lamb
   3. He shall speak as a dragon

II. <u>The Rule of the False Prophet</u> (Revelation 13:12 18, 16.13, 14)
   1. He shall exercise all the power [authority] of the first beast
   2. He shall cause the earth and them that dwell therein to worship the first beast whose deadly wound was healed.
   3. He shall do great wonders making fire to come down from heaven on the earth in the sight of men.
   4. He shall deceive them that dwell on the earth by those miracles which he had power to do in the sight of the beast.
   5. He shall have an image of the beast made by them that dwell on the earth.
   6. He shall have the power to give life [spirit/breath] unto the image of the beast that the image should both speak, and cause that as many as would not worship the image of the beast should be killed.
   7. He shall cause all both small and great, rich and poor, free and receive a mark in their right hand or in their foreheads: that no man might buy or sell, save he that had the mark, or the name of the beast, or the number of his name
   8. The number of the beast is the number of man, which is 666
   9. He shall also be one of the sources of unclean spirits as they proceed out of his mouth during the 6th vial judgment for they are the spirits of devils, working miracles which go forth unto The kings of the earth and of the whole world to gather them to the battle of that great day of God Almighty [Armageddon]

III. <u>The Ruin of the False Prophet & Antichrist</u> (Revelation 19:19, 20)
   1. The beast [Antichrist] was taken and with him the false prophet that wrought miracles before him, with which he deceived them that worshipped his image.

2. These both were cast alive into a lake of fire burning with fire and brimstone.

The information God supplies in His Word concerning His two time of the end archenemies, the Antichrist and the false prophet, is unfolded in a certain pattern for our understanding. Although they will have supernatural authority and power given them by Satan, they are merely men whom Satan possesses having turned themselves over to him in order to perform his wicked purposes against God and all of humanity.

However, the bottom line concerning these two wicked characters is pronounced upon them repeatedly in the infallible Word of God:

"And in the days of these kings shall the God of heaven set up a kingdom, which shall never be destroyed: and the kingdom shall not be left to other people, but it shall break in pieces and consume all these kingdoms, and it shall stand for ever." (Daniel 2:44)

"I beheld then because of the voice of the great words which the horn spoke: I beheld even till the beast was slain, and his body destroyed, and given to the burning flame." (Daniel 7:11)

"But the judgment shall sit, and they shall take away his dominion, to consume and to destroy it unto the end." (Daniel 7:26)

"He shall also stand up against the Prince of princes; but he shall be broken without hand." (Daniel 8:25)

"And he shall confirm the covenant with many for one week: and in the midst of the week he shall cause the sacrifice and the oblation to cease, and for the overspreading of abominations he shall make it desolate, even until the consummation, and that determined shall be poured upon the desolate [desolator/Antichrist]." (Daniel 9:27)

"And he shall plant the tabernacles of his palace between the seas in the glorious holy mountain; yet he shall come to his end, and none shall help him." (Daniel 11:45)

"And the beast was taken and with him the false prophet that wrought miracles before him...These both were cast alive into a lake of fire burning with brimstone." (Revelation 19:20)

Their end has been clearly prophesied in the inspired Word of God seven times over…they shall not escape their deserved judgment.

24

<u>The Israelites Saved</u>

Paul's record of this coming end times event is clear:
"For I would not, brethren, that ye should be ignorant of this mystery, lest ye should be wise in you own conceit; that blindness in part is happened to Israel until the fullness of the Gentiles be come in. And so all Israel shall be saved: as it is written, There shall come out of Zion the Deliverer, and shall turn away ungodliness from Jacob: For this is My covenant unto them, when I shall take away their sins."
(Romans 11:25-27)

He explains that the Jews are presently blinded to the gospel of Jesus Christ, having initially rejected Him and His message when they cried out for His crucifixion almost 2,000 years ago. This rejection and open condemnation of their Messiah has brought the judgment of God upon the Jews as a people just as they requested in that day:
"His blood be on us and on our children," (Matthew 27:25)

This national blindness will end when they recognize the Lord Jesus Christ as their Lord and Redeemer. Then He will come to redeem Israel at the end of the 70th Week of Daniel. At that time the Lord will bring to completion exactly what He has decreed:
"Seventy weeks are determined upon thy people [Israel] and upon thy holy city [Jerusalem], to finish the transgression, and to make an end of sins, and to make reconciliation for iniquity, and to bring everlasting righteousness, and to seal up the vision and prophecy, and to anoint the most holy." (Daniel 9:24)

Their Deliverer and Redeemer, the Lord Jesus Christ, will come *"bringing in everlasting righteousness"* at the end of the 70th Week in order to redeem Israel as the prophet Isaiah's record of this event indicates:
"And the Redeemer shall come to Zion, and unto them that turn from transgression in Jacob, said the LORD." (Isaiah 59:20)

Notice, the Lord Jesus Christ will redeem those who *"turn from transgression in Jacob"* indicating that His salvation will be dependent upon those who turn to Him by faith, repenting of their sin, being saved in the same way salvation has been realized throughout the ages.

Before this event can take place, in the plan of God, the Jews will suffer through the *"time of Jacobs trouble"* *(Jeremiah 30:7.)* They will be purged and purified coming forth as gold (Daniel 11:35, 12:10; Zechariah 13:9) when they receive their Redeemer at the end of the 70th Week of Daniel.

These end times Jews are spoken of in Daniel 9:27 where *"the many"* in the land of Israel confirm a covenant with the Antichrist for seven years or one week which is the last week of Daniel's seventy weeks.

They will align themselves with the Antichrist, with some eventually forsaking the *"holy covenant"* *(Daniel 11:28, 30, 32)* actually having *"intelligence"* with the Antichrist supporting his wicked actions.

But many Israelites will turn the opposite direction being instructed by those *"who know their God"* and *"shall be strong, doing exploits"* *(Daniel 11:32)*. These will be among those at the end of the 70th Week of Daniel who are redeemed by the Lord Jesus Christ:
"And they that understand among the people shall instruct many: yet they shall fall by the sword, and by flame, by captivity, and by spoil, many days." (Daniel 11:35)

Also, some of those Israelites who *"forsake the holy covenant"* *(Daniel 11:30)* could be part of this same group who turn from transgression and receive their Messiah, unless they join themselves to the Antichrist and take his mark during the great tribulation.

Tragically, many Jews will take the mark of the beast and suffer the consequences:
"And it shall come to pass, that in all the land, saith the LORD, two parts therein shall be cut off and die; but the third part shall be left therein. And I will bring the third part through the fire, and will refine

287

them as silver is refined, and will try them as gold is tried: they shall call on My name, and I will hear them: I will say, It is My people: and they shall say, the LORD is my God." (Zechariah 13:8, 9)

Notice, Zechariah tells us these Jews will *"call on My name"* indicating another prerequisite for salvation:
"For whosoever shall call upon the name of the Lord shall be saved." (Romans 10:13)
Also, *"They shall say, the LORD is my God"* confessing the name of the Lord:
"If thou shall confess with thy mouth the Lord Jesus and believe in thine heart God has raised Him from the dead thou shall be saved." (Romans 10:9)

The purifying process which causes them *"to turn from transgression" (Isaiah 59:20)* and call upon the Lord, confessing His name (Zechariah 13:8, 9), will take place during the Day of the Lord judgments of Revelation 8-11. Then over 1/3 of the earth's inhabitants will die during the seven trumpet judgments with the seventh trumpet sounding at the end of Daniel's 70th Week (Revelation 11:15) bringing an end to Israel's refining process also called *"the time of Jacob's trouble" (Jeremiah 30:7).*

The Lord has spoken through His prophets concerning this future time of purifying:
"Therefore saith the Lord, the LORD of hosts, the mighty One of Israel, Ah I will ease Me of Mine adversaries, and avenge Me of Mine enemies. And I will turn My hand upon thee, and purely purge away thy dross, and take away all thy sin." (Isaiah 1:24)

"For thus says the LORD: We have heard a voice of trembling, of fear, and not of peace. Ask ye now, and see whether a man doth travail with child? Wherefore do I see every man with his hands on his loins, as a woman in travail, and all faces are turned into paleness? Alas for that day [Day of the Lord] is great, so that none is like it: it is even the time of Jacob's trouble; but he shall be saved out of it. For it shall come to pass in that day, says the LORD of hosts, that I will break his [Antichrist] yoke from off thy neck, and will burst thy bonds, and strangers shall no more serve themselves of him." (Jeremiah 30:5-8)

288

"Behold, I will send My messenger, and he shall prepare the way before Me: and the Lord, whom ye seek, shall suddenly come to His temple, even the Messenger of the covenant, whom ye delight in: behold, He shall come, says the LORD of hosts. But, who may abide the day of His coming? And who shall stand when He appears? For He is like a refiner's fire, and like fullers' soap: And He shall sit as a refiner and purifier of silver: and He shall purify the sons of Levi, and purge them as gold and silver, that they may offer unto the LORD an offering of righteousness." (Malachi 3:1-3)

This purification and eventual deliverance of Israel by their Redeemer, the Lord Jesus Christ, is one of the major events in God's plan. The Lord Jesus will come to earth for The Grand Redemption, which is the second of His three appearances that make up His Second Coming:

1. The Glorious Reception [The Rescue/Rapture/Resurrection of the Saints] (Matthew 24:29-31; John 14:3; I Thessalonians 4:13-18; Revelation 7:9-17)
2. The Grand Redemption [The Salvation of Israel] (Isaiah 59:20; Romans11:25-27; Revelation 14:1)
3. The Great Retribution [The Battle of Armageddon] (Revelation 16:16, 19:11-21)

He appears on Mt. Zion in His role as Redeemer, the Lamb slain, with the 144 Thousand at the end of the 70th Week of Daniel. Heaven and earth rejoice together (Revelation 14:1) for *"the time of Jacob's trouble"* is over upon the completion of the 70 Weeks of Daniel when Israel's transgression is finished, their sin is ended and reconciliation for their iniquity has been made, and *"all Israel shall be saved" (Romans 11:26).*

25

The Gentiles Saved

Although not specifically designated as Gentiles, the Lord does give a warning to a group of His people just prior to the destruction of *"Babylon the great"*:

"And I heard another voice from heaven, saying, Come out of her, My people, that ye be not partakers of her sins, and that ye receive not of her plagues. For her sins have reached unto heaven, and God hath remembered her iniquities." (Revelation 18:4, 5)

The Lord in this passage uses the term *"My people"* which often refers to His earthly people, the Jews. However, He does call Egypt *"My people" (Isaiah 19:25)* when they come to Him at the end of the age. It also indicates His present-day title for the saints, Jew and Gentile alike, as recorded by the Apostle Peter:

*"But ye are a chosen generation, a royal priesthood, an holy nation, a peculiar people; that ye should show forth the praises of Him who has called you out of darkness into His marvelous light. Which in time past were not a people, but are now **the people of God**: which had not obtained mercy, but now have obtained mercy." (I Peter 2:10, 11)*

At this point, the 70th Week of Daniel has ended with the sounding of the seventh trumpet (Revelation 11:15). *"The kingdoms of this world are become the kingdoms of our Lord and of His Christ"* and the national conversion of Israel takes place completing God's 70 Week program for the Jews as described in Daniel 9:24.

This is followed by 75 days (Daniel 12:10, 11) during which the seven vial judgments (Revelation 16), the judgment of Babylon (Revelation 17, 18) and the battle of Armageddon (Revelation 19:11-21), the closing event of the Day of the Lord take place, in that order.

When the Lord gives the command to *"come out"* to those in Babylon, the seven vial judgments have just ended (Revelation 16:1-21). These judgments focus primarily upon the Antichrist and his kingdom, and are followed by *"one of the seven angels which had the seven vials" (Revelation 17:1)* talking with the apostle John.

The angel explains to him the circumstances of the coming judgment of Mystery Babylon in great detail, unfolding the specific description of certain kings and kingdoms which have crossed the stage of history and also those who will eventually come, including the Antichrist and the ten horns/kings (Revelation 17:1-17).

It is in this explanation that the identity of *"MYSTERY, BABYLON THE GREAT, THE MOTHER OF HARLOTS AND ABOMINATIONS OF THE EARTH" (Revelation 17:5)* is given.

The detailed description given to John indicates that at the end of the age, Romanism/Roman Catholicism may well be *"the whore"*. She is the embodiment of false religion and has been responsible for shedding *"the blood of the saints and...the martyrs of Jesus." (Revelation 17:6)*

The city of Rome is alluded to which has seven hills: *"The seven heads are seven mountains [hills], on which the woman sits," (Revelation 17:9.* She is in fact the time of the end representative of all organized false religion that has held sway over mankind throughout the past sixteen centuries of world history.

The earliest records of false religion begin with the humanistic bent of Adam and Eve which was devised and offered to Eve by Satan, then to Cain who practiced his own brand of neo-orthodoxy, and to Nimrod who is the first to be connected with Babylon/Babel (Genesis 10:8, 9).

It became the birthplace of the Satanic Babylonian cult which merged with a false form of Christianity during the early centuries after the Lord's ascension as false religion continued its monstrous growth throughout the Church Age and will continue to mushroom into this "MOTHER OF HARLOTS" one-world organization.

Recently the head of the United Nations stated that the future of the world is in the hands of those women who gathered from all so-called religions of the planet to unite in an effort to bring world peace.

Under the support and auspices of the U.N., this gathering took place providing the Bible believer with indications of the nearness of the end of this age.

The Lord Jesus Christ told us that many false Christs will appear as a sign of His Coming and the end of the age (Matthew 24:5, 24). We are living within the realization of this prophecy as many of the major cults with their false Christ's have risen during the past few centuries.

The Mormons, the Seventh Day Adventists, the Jehovah's (false) Witnesses, and Christian Science and others have all surfaced and grown during this time period. But the most notorious cult to date is Roman Catholicism, even though Islam is now competing for this title. It could well be that Islam, the fastest growing false religion of our day, will become the source of the martyrdom among God's people during the end times.

Revelation 20:4 tells of the beheading of *"the witnesses of Jesus"* which is the preferred method of execution used by the radical Islamists even at this present hour. Therefore, it is likely that Islam will replace Romanism/Roman Catholicism after she, the great whore, is destroyed by the ten kings (Revelation 17:16, 17).

With these facts in mind, the 19th and 20th centuries could be designated the period of time which the Lord referred to when He spoke the prophetic warnings concerning false Christ's and false prophets during His most informative discourse on the end of the age, Matthew 24:3-31.

Here in Revelation 17 and 18 and the beginning of chapter 19, the Lord deals with the judgment of this, the greatest force for evil in the history of the world. It is this system of false religion that receives the most descriptive and complete judgment in the book of the Revelation during God's Day the Day of the Lord.

Two full chapters and part of a third are dedicated to the past, present and future of Mystery Babylon, including the cataclysmic judgment of this great enemy of God. This mighty judgment brings forth the most powerful occurrence of praise to God in all of Scripture.

The famous Hallelujah Chorus where heaven sounds forth *"Alleluia"* on three occasions in chapter 19, is heaven's response to God's full and complete judgment upon this notoriously wicked and false religious system which has been the corrupter of the earth from the beginning.

The prophet Isaiah refers to this judgment of Babylon on a number of occasions beginning in chapter Isaiah 13:1-22 showing its occurrence at the end of the age during the Day of the Lord. Again it appears in Isaiah 21:9 where the fall of Babylon is proclaimed and repeated by the prophet Jeremiah in Jeremiah 51:8 about 150 years later with the Revelation documenting this same refrain on two occasions (Revelation 14:8, 18:2).

Revelation 17:1-17 sets the stage describing *"Babylon...the whore"* and the succession of kings past, present and future including the ten kings who will eventually be used of God to destroy her. But, just before God physically destroys her, He calls to His people who are in the path of His coming judgment to physically get out. That these are Gentile believers is likely because Gentiles make up the majority of present-day Romanism.

We know that some of these people who remain within this wicked false religious system are definitely saved because of the command made by the Lord. The Lord's command to those believers within Roman Catholicism reveals certain end of the age Gentiles who will be saved during the Day of the Lord after the rapture has occurred.

This direct command by the Lord is similar to the one the Apostle Paul gave to the Corinthians:
"Wherefore come out from among them and be ye separate saith the Lord, and touch not the unclean thing; and I will receive you, And will be a Father unto you, and ye shall be My sons and daughters, saith the Lord Almighty." (II Corinthians 6:17, 18)

The Lord speaks to all believers through this pointed ultimatum requiring separation from unbelievers and any form of idolatry (I Corinthians 6:14-16) which is exactly what Roman Catholicism emphasizes.

It teaches and practices the idolatrous worship of saints with the Lord's mother Mary being the worship/focus of this un-Biblical idolatry. However, this command to God's people was not new with the Apostle Paul:

"Depart ye, depart ye, go ye out from hence, touch no unclean thing: get ye out of the midst of her; be ye clean, that bear the vessels of the LORD." (Isaiah 52:11)

Isaiah's plain injunction given to the Old Testament priests of God is paraphrased by Paul and applied to the New Testament priests of God, that is, all the born-again Bible believers who name the name of the Lord Jesus Christ. This clear command applies to every single child of God. The prophet Isaiah also records the conversion of other Gentiles during the Day of the Lord:

"In that day [Day of the Lord] shall Egypt be like unto a woman: and it shall be afraid and fear because of the shaking of the hand of the LORD of hosts, which He shakes over it...In that day there shall be an altar to the LORD in the midst of the land of Egypt...and He shall send them a Savior, and a Great One, and He shall deliver them. And the LORD shall be known to Egypt, and the Egyptians shall know the LORD in that day, and shall do sacrifice and oblation; yea, they shall vow a vow unto the LORD, and perform it, And the LORD shall smite Egypt: He shall smite and heal it: and they shall return even to the LORD, and He shall be entreated of them, and shall heal them. In that day shall there be a highway out of Egypt to Assyria, and the Assyrian shall come into Egypt, and Egyptian into Assyria, and the Egyptians shall serve with the Assyrians. In that day shall Israel be the third with Egypt and with Assyria, even a blessing in the midst of the land: Whom the LORD of hosts shall bless saying, Blessed be Egypt My people, and Assyria the work of My hands, and Israel My inheritance." (Isaiah 19:16-25)

Although this end times passage has Millennial applications, the phrase *"In that day"*, referring to the Day of the Lord, is found repeatedly along with definite acts of Gods judgment: *"The shaking of the hand of the Lord, which He shakes over it...the LORD shall smite Egypt...He shall smite"*. This is followed by the healing and conversion of the most unlikely of peoples, the notorious age-old enemies of Israel, the Arabs of Egypt and Assyria.

Additional Gentiles will also come to the Lord when they see the many miraculous supernatural plagues/judgments from God during the Day of the Lord as the prophet Micah indicates:

"As in the days when you [Israel] came out from the land of Egypt,
I will show you miracles [miraculous plagues of judgment].
Nations will see and be ashamed of all their might.
They will put their hand on their mouth,
Their ears will be deaf.
They will lick the dust like a serpent
Like reptiles of the earth.
They will come trembling out of their fortresses;
To the LORD our God they will come in dread,
And they will be afraid before Thee." (Micah 7:15-17) NASB

All praise to the Lord God of heaven, for there will definitely be Gentiles saved during the Day of the Lord, as these passages indicate. Unfortunately, the vast majority of the earth's inhabitants will take the mark of the beast and worship his image remaining openly rebellious and unrepentant toward God:

*"And the rest of the men which were not killed by these plagues [seven trumpet judgments] yet **repented not** of the works of their hands, that they should not worship devils, and idols of gold, and silver, and brass, and stone, and of wood: which neither can see, nor hear, nor walk: **Neither repented** they of their murders, nor of their sorceries, nor of their fornication, nor of their thefts."*
(Revelation 9:20, 21)

Similar words describe the actions of these same people during and after the seven vial judgments:

*"And men were scorched with great heat, and blasphemed the name of God, which hath power over these plagues: and they **repented not** to give Him glory...And blasphemed the God of heaven because of their pains and their sores, and **repented not** of their deeds...and men blasphemed God because of the plague of hail; for the plague thereof was exceeding great." (Revelation 16:9, 11, 21)*

Notice in the verses above it is stated four times that these men would not repent indicating that they had the opportunity to repent, but they instead refused. However the Lord will save some, in that day, for He is not a God of judgment but of mercy, for judgment is

295

"His strange work" (Isaiah 28:21), but His mercy is abundantly given, and *"endures forever" (Psalm 136:1-26)*.

Although He does extend His mercy to all men, deadly judgment will come upon those who refuse to repent in that day, for the Day of the Lord will be an almost indescribable time of devastating fiery destruction upon planet earth and its inhabitants:

"Howl ye, for the day of the Lord is at hand; it shall come as a destruction from the Almighty. Therefore, shall all hands be faint, and every man's heart shall melt: And they shall be afraid: pangs and sorrows shall take hold of them; they shall be in pain as a woman that travails: they shall be amazed one at another; their faces shall be as flames. Behold, the day of the Lord comes, cruel both with wrath and fierce anger, to lay the land desolate: and he shall destroy the sinners thereof out of it. For the stars of heaven and the constellations thereof shall not give their light: the sun shall be darkened in his going forth, and the moon shall not cause her light to shine. And I will punish the world for their evil, and the wicked for their iniquity; and cause the arrogance of the proud to cease, and will lay low the haughtiness of the terrible." (Isaiah 13:6-11)

"The great day of the LORD is near, it is near, and hastes greatly, even the voice of the day of the LORD: the mighty man shall cry there bitterly. That day is a day of wrath, a day of trouble and distress, a day of wasteness and desolation, a day of darkness and gloominess, a day of clouds and thick darkness. A day of the trumpet and alarm against the fenced cities, and against the high towers. And I will bring distress upon men, that they shall walk like blind men, because they have sinned against the LORD: and their blood shall be poured out like dust, and their flesh as dung." (Zephaniah 1:14-17)

Upon some, these judgments from God will bring hardening, causing their hearts to grow even harder, as they remain blatantly rebellious and unrepentant. Upon others, these same judgments, through the merciful grace of God, will soften their hearts causing them to turn to the Lord and be saved.

The Lord's mercy will continue to operate during His Day of the Lord judgment bringing salvation to both Jew and Gentile. The Lamb will be exalted throughout eternity for His sacrifice on the Cross as it provides the power to save every soul that ever enters this world (I John 2:2).

After the Day of the Lord is over, during the following 1000 year earthly reign of Christ called the Millennium (Revelation 20:1-4), multitudes will come to God's sacrificial Lamb, slain from the foundation of the world, the Lord Jesus Christ. They will put their faith in His Blood (Ephesians 1:7), repenting of their sins being saved just like all saints have been saved during the previous ages.

It should not be surprising, that the Lord will continue to redeem many Gentiles during the time He judges the earth for He will freely offer His great gift, salvation by grace through faith (Ephesians 2:8, 9) to any and all who will believe and turn to Him.

26

<u>The Ten Kings</u>

These Ten Kings are first indicated in Scripture as part of the *"great image"* in Nebuchadnezzar's vision:
"Thou, O king, saw, and behold a great image. This great image, whose brightness was excellent, stood before thee; and the form thereof was terrible. This image's head was of fine gold, his breast and his arms silver, his belly and his thighs brass, His legs of iron, his feet part of iron and part of clay." (Daniel 2:31-33)

Daniel gave Nebuchadnezzar a detailed interpretation telling him that he [king of Babylon] was *"this head of gold" (Daniel 2:38)*. Then Daniel revealed the next three kingdoms:
"And after thee shall arise another kingdom inferior to thee [Medes and Persians/Silver Breast and Arms], and another third kingdom of brass [Grecian/Brass Belly and Thighs] which shall bear rule over all the earth [Alexander the Great]. And the fourth kingdom [Roman/legs of iron and feet of iron and clay] shall be strong as iron: forasmuch as iron breaks in pieces and subdues all things: and as iron that breaks all these, shall it break in pieces and bruise."
(Daniel 2:39, 40)

The Roman kingdom becomes the primary focus and is explicitly detailed down to the [ten] toes of the feet, which parallels the ten kings of the revived Roman empire that will rise during the end times as attested to by Daniel at the beginning of his interpretation:
*"But there is a God in heaven that reveals secrets, and makes known to the king Nebuchadnezzar what shall be **<u>in the latter days</u>**."*
(Daniel 2:28)

Daniel also indicated this same truth at the conclusion of his interpretation:
"And in the days of these kings shall the God of heaven set up a Kingdom (Revelation 11:15), which shall never be destroyed: and the Kingdom shall not be left to other people, but it shall break in pieces

and consume all these kingdoms (Revelation 19:11-21), and it shall stand forever." (Daniel 2:44)

1. The purpose of this vision is to provide information concerning *"the latter days"*. (Daniel 2:28, 44)
2. These four kingdoms will be active during *"the latter days"*. (Daniel 2:44).
3. The Kingdom of God will be set up on earth *"in the days of these kings"* [the latter days]. (Daniel 2:44a; Revelation 11:15).
4. The Kingdom of God will *"never be destroyed nor left to other people"*. (Daniel 2:44b).
5. The Kingdom of God will *"break in pieces and consume all these kingdoms"*. (Daniel 2:44c, Revelation 19:11-21).
6. The Kingdom of God will be eternal. *"It shall stand forever."* (Daniel 2:44d).

The ten kings are later introduced as *"ten horns"* in Daniel's first vision:

*"After this I saw in the night visions, and behold a fourth beast, dreadful and terrible, and strong exceedingly; and it had great iron teeth: it devoured and brake in pieces, and stamped the residue with the feet of it: and it was diverse from all the beasts that were before it; and it had **ten horns**. I considered the horns, and, behold, there came up among them another little horn, before whom there were three of the first [ten] horns plucked up by the roots: and, behold, in this [little] horn were eyes like the eyes of a man, and a mouth speaking great things." (Daniel 7:7, 8)*

When the ten kings [ten horns] are mentioned, immediately *"there came up among them another little horn"* who is the Antichrist as the remaining visions of Daniel clearly affirm. He [*the little horn*] conquers three of the ten horns during his rise to power.

Daniel is told during the interpretation of this vision just exactly what these *"ten horns"* are:

"And the ten horns out of this kingdom [4th Beast/Revived Roman Empire] are ten kings that shall arise: and another [little horn/Antichrist] shall rise after them; and he shall be diverse from the first [ten], and he shall subdue three kings." (Daniel 7:24)

These ten kings of the revived Roman Empire are not mentioned

299

again in the book of Daniel but they are clearly indicated in the book of the Revelation of Jesus Christ:

"And I stood upon the sand of the sea, and saw a beast rise up out of the sea, having seven heads and ten horns, and upon his horns ten crowns, and upon his heads the name of blasphemy."
(Revelation 13:1)

In this reference the Antichrist is described as having seven heads that represent the seven beast kingdoms of history with the eighth beast kingdom yet future:

<u>The Eight Beast Empires of the Ages:</u>

1. Egypt: (Exodus 1:15-22; Acts 7:19, 20)
   1800-1445 B.C. [Ancestor of Ham]

2. Assyria: (II Kings 17:6)
   722 B.C. [Ancestor of Shem]

3. Babylonia: (Daniel 1:4)
   586 B.C. [Ancestor of Shem]

4. Medo-Persia: (Daniel 2:39; Esther 3:10)
   445 B.C. [Ancestor of Japheth]-----------<u>Beginning of 70 Weeks
   of Daniel</u>

5. Greece: (Daniel 2:39)
   330-175 B.C. [Ancestor of Japheth]

6. Rome: (Daniel 2:40)
   63 B.C.-70 A.D. [Ancestor of Japheth]

7. Germany/The Third Reich: (Revelation 17:10)
   1938-1945 A.D. [Ancestor of Japheth]

8. World Ruler/Antichrist/Ten Kings (Revelation17: 3, 11-13)
   [Ancestor of Shem]-------------------------<u>End of 70 Weeks
   of Daniel</u>

This list unfolds in world history and the pages of Scripture and is encapsulated in Revelation 17:3-5

"And here is the mind which hath wisdom. The seven heads are seven mountains, on which the woman sits. And there are seven kings: five are fallen, and one is [Nero-John's day] and the other is not yet come; and when he comes he [Hitler] must continue a short space. And the beast [Antichrist] that was and is not, even he is the eighth and is of the seven and goes into perdition." (Revelation 17:9-11)

The Antichrist, who is the head of the revived Roman Empire, will be heavily allied with false religion during his meteoric rise to power. The political and religious authorities of that day will unite during the initial days of the 70th Week of Daniel. As this chapter reveals, this unity will not last throughout the Antichrist's rule:

"And the ten horns which thou saw are ten kings, which have received no kingdom as yet; but receive [from Satan] power [authority] as kings one hour with the beast. These have one mind, and shall give their power and strength [authority] unto the beast. These shall make war with the Lamb, and the Lamb shall over come them: for He is Lord of lords and King of kings: and they that are with Him [the 144 Thousand] are called, and chosen, and faithful."
(Revelation 17:12-14)

Satan gives the ten kings authority which they in turn give to the Antichrist when they go to war against the Lord Jesus Christ at Armageddon. However, before that event comes to pass, these ten kings will be used to destroy Babylon bringing upon her the devastating judgment of Almighty God:

"And the ten horns which thou saw upon the beast, these shall hate the whore, and shall make her desolate and naked, and shall eat her flesh, and burn her with fire. For God has put in their hearts to fulfill His will, and to agree, and give their kingdom unto the beast, until the words of God shall be fulfilled." (Revelation 17:17)

When the judgment of Babylon and its aftermath are surveyed, three different groups will lament her destruction:
1. The kings of the earth (Revelation 18:9, 10)
2. The merchants of the earth (Revelation 18:11-17a)
3. The merchants of the sea (Revelation 18:17b-19)

Within their laments each of these groups of men emphasize the brief period of time it took for Babylon to be destroyed:

"For in __one hour__ is thy judgment come…For in __one hour__ so great riches is come to nought…For in __one hour__ is she made desolate." (Revelation 18:10, 17, 19)

This brief time reference corresponds to the short period of time that the ten kings give their full allegiance to the Antichrist:
"[The ten kings] receive [from Satan] power [authority] as kings __one hour__ with the beast." (Revelation 17:12)

The ten kings will also make war with the Lamb as recorded above, which occurs at Armageddon, ending the Day of the Lord (Revelation 19:11-21). It appears that the judgment of Babylon (Revelation 17, 18), which is accomplished by the ten kings, will occur just before Armageddon, and immediately after the seven vial judgments have ended (Revelation 15, 16).

27

The Purpose of God

The record in Scripture is clear, God has never left, nor will He ever leave His planet earth without a human witness to His great and glorious grace demonstrated by His redemption of men through the finished work of the Lord Jesus Christ on the Cross.

Based upon this one single unwritten principle which is taught by example and precept throughout the written Word of God, including the 2,000 year history of the Church, it can be said that there will continue to be people of faith upon the earth, throughout the time of the end, the 70th Week of Daniel and the Day of the Lord.

As the previous messages have set forth, the 70th Week of Daniel, which God has determined upon His earthly people the Jews (Daniel 9:24), will also be utilized to purify the saints before they, *"the elect"*, are gathered by the angels (Matthew 24:31) and gloriously received into heaven (Revelation 7:9-17).

Before that magnificent event occurs, the Lord will call, prepare and seal 144 Thousand *"sons of Israel" (Revelation 7:1-8)* in order to provide the continuing testimony of His redemptive grace through the agency of redeemed men as He has chosen to do from the beginning of time itself.

While the Lord will call and utilize many different people to accomplish His end times purposes, these *"servants of our God" (Revelation 7:3)* are the focal point of "The People of the Apocalypse". For, when the Scripture is examined, it reveals that they are unlike any other group of believers ever to be set forth in the Word of God.

Their Redemption Ministry has been thoroughly planned and prophesied by the Lord as they will be His literal end times disciples *"following Him wherever He goes"' (Revelation 14:4.)*

They become the ultimate *"fishers of men"* according to Jesus own promise*:*
"Come ye after Me and I will make you to become fishers of men."
(Mark 1:17)

Their task will be enormous as their great number indicates. For, at the beginning of this age the Lord chose, trained and sent out twelve disciples and they *"Turned the world upside down"* (Acts 17:6). But then, during the end times, in order for His continuing purpose of redemption to be fulfilled, He has deemed it necessary to once again follow this same pattern of utilizing personal disciples.

He will not call and train a mere twelve disciples like at His first Coming. He will need ***twelve thousand sets of twelve disciples*** to accomplish His great end times purpose of redemption. Their sheer number reveals the overwhelming magnitude of the ministry these young men will undertake.

It is imperative that the present-day Church of Jesus Christ recognizes its part in raising up these young men in order for the Lord to bring to pass His marvelous and miraculous plan. The end of this age is closing rapidly when He will most certainly come again just as He has promised in His Word (John 14:3; Matthew 24:30, 31) *"Even so come Lord Jesus" (Revelation 22:20).*

However, it is **after** He comes to resurrect, rescue, rapture, and receive the saints that these 144 Thousand disciples of Christ will embark upon their most intensive Redemption Ministry. Then they will carry the message of the Gospel of Jesus Christ (Daniel 11:32-35, 12:3) to those who also have been written in the Lamb's book of life (Revelation 13:8, 17:8).

There will be many that will *"**Turn** from transgression in Jacob" (Isaiah 59:20)* and *"shall **call** on My name, and I will hear them: I will say, It is My people: and they shall say, **The Lord is my God**" (Zechariah 13:9).*

The unfolding of the lives and ministry of the 144 Thousand is indicated in Scripture as has been documented in previous chapters. In order to conclude these messages and clearly emphasize their great significance in God's plan for the time of the end, the following outline summarizes their future:

I. They are part of *"the remnant of her [the woman's] seed" (Revelation 12:17b)*
    *Time: The Beginning of the Great Tribulation
   1. They are from the twelve tribes of Israel (Revelation 7:3-8)
   2. They are young men (Psalm 110:3; Revelation 14:4a)
   3. They are persecuted by Satan (Revelation 12:17b)
   4. They keep the commandments of God (Revelation 12:17b)
   5. They have the testimony of Jesus Christ (Revelation 12:17b)

II. They will *"know their God" (Daniel 11:32, 35)*
    *Time: During the Great Tribulation [Redemption Ministry]
   1. They shall be strong
   2. They shall do exploits
   3. They will have understanding
   4. They will instruct many
   5. They [some] shall fall, to try them, and to purge, and to make them white, even to the time of the end

III. They are *"the servants of our God" (Revelation 7:3)*
    *Time: During the Day of the Lord [Redemption Ministry]
   1. They are sealed <u>before</u> the Day of the Lord judgments (Revelation 7:1-3)
   2. They are protected <u>during</u> the Day of the Lord judgments (Revelation 9:4)

IV. They *"shall be willing in the day of Thy [Lord Jesus] power" (Psalm 110:3)*
    *Time: During the Day of the Lord [Redemption Ministry]
   1. They are the time of the end priests unto God (Exodus 19:5, 6; Psalm 110:3; I Peter 2:5; Revelation 14:4, 5)
   2. They are the holy nation/time of the end Israel of God (Exodus 19:5, 6; Psalm 110:3; Revelation 14:4)

V. They will *"shine as the brightness of the firmament" (Daniel 12:3)*
    *Time: During the Day of the Lord [Redemption Ministry]
   1. They are wise
   2. They turn many to righteousness
   3. They shine as the stars forever and ever

VI. They are *"with the Lamb" (Revelation 14:1, 17:14)*
    *Time: During the Day of the Lord

1. At the end of the 70th Week of Daniel
   (Revelation 14:1)
2. At the battle of Armageddon (Revelation 17:14)

VII. They gather unto the King of kings populating the Promised Land
   (Genesis 49:10; Micah 5:3)

   *Time: During the Millennium

   1. Along with the Israelites who will be saved at the end of the
      70th Week of Daniel (Isaiah 59:20; Micah 5:3)
   2. And faithful Israel, "the Woman" of Revelation 12
      (Micah 5:3)

As God continues to unfold His end times plan, He will raise up this mighty army of soldiers of Christ from the twelve tribes of Israel many of whom will likely come out of the families of the faithful in the Church (Revelation 7:1-8, 14:4).

The Gospel emphasis of the Lord Jesus Christ and the Apostle Paul: *"to the Jew **first** and also to the Greek [Gentile]" (Romans 1:16)* must now be the clear priority and compelling emphasis of evangelism in the present-day Church of Jesus Christ throughout the world.

For, in order for the Lord to return and bring this age to a close, these end times disciples of Christ must be called and prepared so that they might also *"turn the world upside down"*, fulfilling the plan of God for their lives and thereby exalt and glorify the Lord Jesus Christ.

But, the question arises: "Just where will this great number of faithful Jews physically come from?" The answer is: From across the earth, as alluded to in the following passages:

*"And after these things I saw four angels standing on the four corners of the **earth**, holding the four winds of the **earth**, that the wind should not blow on the **earth**, nor on the sea, nor on any tree. And I saw another angel ascending from the east, having the seal of the living God: and he cried with a loud voice to the four angels, to whom it was given to hurt the earth and the sea, Saying, Hurt not the **earth**, neither the sea, nor the trees **till we have sealed the servants of our God** in their foreheads. And I heard the number of them which were sealed: and there were sealed an hundred and forty and four thousand of all the tribes of the children [sons] of Israel."*

306

(Revelation 7:1-4)

*"And they sung as it were a new song before the throne, and before the four beasts, and the elders: and no man could learn that song but the hundred and forty and four thousand, which were redeemed from the **earth**." (Revelation 14:3)*

These verses give credence to the conclusion that the 144 Thousand will come from throughout the earth. The four angels to *"whom it was given to hurt the [entire] earth and the sea"* were delayed from accomplishing their global mission of judgment until these young men were sealed, providing them with God's protection (Revelation 9:4) in the midst of His Day of the Lord judgment.

Notice, all four angels were delayed, not just the one angel who would bring judgment to the land of Israel where most of the world's present-day Jews reside. This great number of *"servants of our God"* will likely be called from across the planet being *"redeemed from the [entire] earth."*

As mentioned above, world evangelization of the Jews must be the clear priority of the church today as it definitely was the focus of the Lord and the early church, including the Apostle Peter and the Apostle Paul. Even though Paul was unmercifully persecuted and soundly rejected by the great majority of the Jews during his ministry, he continued to go to their synagogues in each city attempting to win them to Christ (Acts 9:20, 13:5, 14:1, 17:1, 10, 17, 18:4, 19).

He was simply following his heart (Romans 1:15, 16, 10:1) and the emphasis that his Lord utilized during His earthly ministry. For, at the end of the Lord Jesus Christ's first coming, He gave this brief but vividly descriptive portrait of His public ministry:

"I spoke openly to the world; I ever taught in the synagogue, and in the temple, whither the Jews always resort; and in secret have I said nothing." (John 18:20)

In God's purpose there is coming a day, at the end of the 70th Week of Daniel, when *"the veil shall be taken away" (II Corinthians 3:16b)* from the spiritual eyes of His earthly people the Jews. Then, their *"Redeemer shall come to Zion, and unto them that turn from transgression in Jacob, saith the Lord." (Isaiah 59:20)*

"And so all Israel shall be saved: as it is written, There shall come out of Zion the Deliverer, and shall turn away ungodliness from Jacob." (Romans 11:26)

But at the present hour *"the veil is upon their heart"* *(II Corinthians 3:15)* and the age-old methods used by the Lord Jesus Christ and the Apostle Paul continue to be the best ways to reach the Jews. They utilized Old Testament Messianic preaching: (Luke 4:15-21; Acts 13:16-39, 17:1-3, 18:28) and confrontational one-on-one evangelism: (John 3:1-21, 4:1-26; Acts 16:31, 18:4, 19:8).

In the purpose of God, it is the clear duty of the Church of Jesus Christ to pray for the Lord to send forth laborers into His harvest. They must focus their Holy Spirit filled soul-winning compassion upon the earthly people of God, the Jews, wherever they may be found as we close in on the Second Coming of the Lord Jesus Christ.

The time is drawing near when these young men, the 144 Thousand, will be called, prepared and later sealed for their Day of the Lord service to God. This great conversion of the earthly people of God may well take place during the powerful restoration/revival ministry of Elijah whom God will send (Malachi 4:5, 6) to His people.

He will of necessity follow the pattern of his two predecessors, Elijah and John the Baptist, preaching repentance and revival, *"Turning hearts... and restoring all things" (Malachi 4:5, 6; Matthew17: 11; Mark 9:12)* in the process.

It is likely that the Lord will use this mighty prophet to also bring revival to the Church of Jesus Christ and spearhead the mass evangelization of His earthly people, including the 144 Thousand, during the first half of the 70th Week of Daniel. The 144 Thousand are given a unique title that points to this very likely possibility:
*"These were redeemed from among men, being **the firstfruits unto God and to the Lamb**." (Revelation 14:4c)*

These young men appear to be the first Jews to be redeemed during the 70th Week of Daniel, which is the last week of the *"seventy weeks are determined upon thy people and thy holy city." (Daniel 9:24)* There will be many Jews saved later at the end of this restored *"holy* covenant" *(Daniel 11:28-32)* Jewish dispensation when the Lord intervenes as the completion of His first three purposes (Daniel 9:24) come to pass at which point in history:

"The Redeemer shall come to Zion...And all Israel shall be saved."
(Isaiah 59:20; Romans 11:25, 26)

Before that day takes place the saints will experience the rise and rule of the Antichrist during Satan's *"great wrath" (Revelation 12:12)* *"the great tribulation" (Revelation 7:14)* which is the time just prior to their sealing. The Lord describes this period of intense persecution:

"When ye therefore shall see the abomination of desolation spoken of by Daniel the prophet, stand in the holy place; (whoso reads let him understand) then let them which be in Judea flee into the mountains...For then shall be great tribulation, such as was not since the beginning of the world to this time, no, nor ever shall be. And except those days should be shortened, there should no flesh be saved: but for the elect's sake those days will be shortened."
(Matthew 24:15, 21, 22)

The Antichrist will make *"war with the saints" (Daniel 7:21; Revelation 13:7)* pointing to the wholesale martyrdom of God's people which is also described in other passages:

"And they that understand among the people shall instruct many: yet they shall fall by the sword, and by flame, by captivity and by spoil many days...And some of them understanding shall fall."
(Daniel 11:33, 35)

"And when He had opened the fifth seal, I saw under the altar the souls of them that were slain for the word of God, and for the testimony which they held: And they cried with a loud voice, saying, How long, O Lord, holy and true, dost Thou not judge and avenge our blood on them that dwell on the earth? And white robes were given unto them; and it was said unto them, that they should rest yet for a little season, until their fellowservants also and their brethren, that should be killed as they were, should be fulfilled." (Revelation 6:9-11)
"And when they [two witnesses] shall have finished their testimony, the beast that ascends out of the bottomless pit shall make war against them, and shall overcome them, and kill them."
(Revelation 11:7)

"And they [the brethren] overcame him [Satan] by the blood of the Lamb and the word of their testimony; and they loved not their lives unto the death." (Revelation 12:11) And I heard a voice from heaven saying unto me, Write, Blessed are the dead which die in the Lord from henceforth: Yea, saith the Spirit, that they may rest from their labors; and their works do follow them."
(Revelation 14:13)

"And I saw thrones, and they sat upon them, and judgment was given unto them: and I saw the souls of them that were beheaded for the witness of Jesus, and for the word of God, and which had not worshipped the beast, neither his image, neither had received his mark upon their foreheads, or in their hands; and they lived and reigned with Christ a thousand years." (Revelation 20:4)

This heinous slaughter of God's people will be cut off by the intervention of the Lord when He 'amputates' this period called *"the great tribulation" (Matthew 24:21; Revelation 7:14)* which is authored by the Satanically energized Antichrist and his false prophet.

At that time the Lord will rescue *"the elect" (Mathew 24:22, 31)* when He comes in the clouds to rapture His church which is the closing event of this present age. But, before He comes, many Jews and Gentiles will die a martyr's death during this last and most severe holocaust of the people of God as is told to some of the martyrs of this same era:
"Rest for a little season, until their fellowservants also and their brethren, that should be killed as they were, should be fulfilled."
(Revelation 6:11)

When God's purpose is fulfilled for the *"great tribulation"*
(Matthew 24:21, 22), He will bring it to an end in His timing. He will send His Son, the Lord Jesus Christ, to rescue and gather *"His elect"* *(Matthew 24:31)* by rapture cutting off this vicious martyrdom of His people.

There will be three groups of believing Jews who will remain on earth to carry on the Lord's purposes during the Day of the Lord which immediately follows the resurrection, rapture, rescue, reception of the saints (I Thessalonians 4:13-18; Revelation 7:9-17).

1. The two witnesses prophesy during the entire last half of Daniel's 70th Week (Revelation 11:3-13)
2. The woman [faithful Israel] is preserved during the entire last half of Daniel's 70th Week (Revelation 12:6, 13-16)
3. The 144 Thousand also serve during the entire last half of Daniel's 70th Week (Daniel 11:32-35, 12:3, 10; Revelation 7:1-8, 9:4, 12:17, 14:1-5, 17:14)

God's priority for His 144 Thousand disciples is the one-on-one evangelization of His people. They will witness of their Messiah and His glorious grace to their brethren, the twelve tribes of Israel, preparing them for that day when *"all Israel shall be saved" (Romans 11:26)* at the end of the 70th Week of Daniel. Herein, is the primary purpose of God…The Grand Redemption of His earthly people.

This event has long been foretold:
"The scepter shall not depart from Judah, nor a lawgiver from
between his feet, until Shiloh [The Lord Jesus Christ] come; and unto
Him shall the gathering of the people be." (Genesis 49:10)

"And the Lord thy God will bring thee into the land which thy fathers
possessed, and thou shall possess it; and He will do thee good, and
multiply thee above thy fathers. And the Lord thy God will circumcise
thine heart, and the heart of thy seed, to love the Lord thy God with
all thine heart, and with all thy soul, that thou may live."
(Deuteronomy 30:5, 6)

"And the Redeemer shall come to Zion, and unto them that turn from
transgression in Jacob, saith the Lord. As for Me this is My covenant
with them, saith the Lord; My Spirit that is upon thee, and My words
which I have put in thy mouth, shall not depart out of thy mouth, not
out of the mouth of thy seed, nor out of the mouth of thy seed's seed,
saith the Lord, from henceforth and for ever." (Isaiah 59:20, 21)

"Behold the days come, saith the Lord, that I will make a new
covenant with the house of Israel, and with the house of Judah: Not
according to the covenant that I made with their fathers in the day
that I took them by the hand to bring them out of the land of Egypt;
which My covenant they brake, although I was an husband unto them,
saith the Lord: But this shall be the covenant that I will make with the

house of Israel; After those days, saith the Lord, I will put My law in their hearts; and will be their God, and they shall be My people." (Jeremiah 31:31-33)

"Behold, I will gather them out of all countries, whither I have driven them in My anger, and in My fury, and in great wrath; and I will bring them again unto this place, and I will cause them to dwell safely: And they shall be My people, and I will be their God: And I will give them one heart, and one way, that they may fear Me for ever, for the good of them, and of their children after them: And I will make and everlasting covenant with them, that I will not turn away from them, to do them good; but I will put My fear in their hearts, that they shall not depart from Me. Yea, I will rejoice over them to do them good, and I will plant them in this land assuredly with My whole heart and with My whole soul." (Jeremiah 32:37-41)

"For I will take you from among the heathen, and gather you out of all countries, and will bring you into your own land. Then will I sprinkle clean water upon you, and ye shall be clean: from all your filthiness, and from all your idols, will I cleanse you. A new heart also will I give you, and a new spirit will I put within you: and I will take away the stony heart out of your flesh, and I will give you and heart of flesh. And I will put My Spirit within you, and cause you to walk in My statutes, and ye shall keep My judgments, and do them. And ye shall dwell in the land that I gave to your fathers; and ye shall be My people, and I will be your God." (Ezekiel 36:24-28)

In the sure purpose of God, He will surely bring forth this great company of His servants, the 144 Thousand during this last "Jewish" dispensation, the 70th Week of Daniel. They will prepare the hearts of His people in order to accomplish His continuing plan of redemption when the Lord Jesus Christ the:
"Redeemer comes to Zion, and unto them that turn from transgression in Jacob." (Isaiah 59:20)

As the outline [shown above] underlines the 144 Thousand's Day of the Lord Redemption Ministry, it is clear that they will undergo vital preparation during the Great Tribulation when they will *"instruct...many"* who do not understand (Daniel 11:33).

They will be the Lord's life-line to His chosen people, the Jews, during the end of this age and the ensuing Day of the Lord for He will thoroughly prepare His servants for their time of the end Redemption Ministry when:

1. The Jews will be a *"people" (Daniel 9:24)*
2. The Jews will be in their *"own [promised] land"* (Deuteronomy 30:1-18; Ezekiel 36: 24-26, 37:21ff; Daniel 9:24)
3. The Jews will occupy/control their *"holy city"* Jerusalem (Daniel 9:24)
4. The *"prophet Elijah"* will be sent "first" to revive/restore (Malachi 4:5, 6: Matthew 17:11; Mark 9:12)
5. The *"holy covenant"* will be restored (Daniel 11:28-32)
6. The *"temple of God"* will be rebuilt (II Thessalonians 2:1-4: Revelation 11:1, 2)
7. The *"holy place"* included (Matthew 24:15)
8. The *"regular sacrifices"* will be offered (Daniel 8:11, 12, 9:27, 11:31, 12:11)
9. The Jews will worship in *"the temple of God"* (Revelation 11:1, 2)
10. *"The Sabbath"* will be honored (Matthew 24:28)
11. The sending of *"prophets"* to the Jews will occur (Malachi 4:5, 6: Revelation 11:3-17)
12. The tribal system will be restored as the twelve tribes of *"the sons of Israel" (Revelation 7:1-8)* will eventually be sealed

It appears evident that the Lord will bring to pass the same conditions that prevailed during the first 69 weeks of this prophesied time period during the remaining week or seven years, which is the 70th Week of Daniel.

At the present time [2007] He has already put the first three conditions into place. The Jews have become a people/nation, they have been in the land for well over a half-century and they have occupied their holy city Jerusalem for four decades.

The next event on God's prophetic timetable appears to be the sending of Elijah the prophet for he *"truly shall **first** come, and restore all things" (Matthew 17:11)* referring to those necessary *"holy covenant" (Daniel 11:28-32)* conditions listed above.

That Elijah will be sent *"**first**"* before the Second Coming of Jesus Christ is underlined by this statement in the Apostle Peter's second sermon:

*"And He shall send Jesus Christ, which before was preached unto you: Whom the heaven must receive **until the times of restitution [restoration] of all things** which God hath spoken by the mouth of all his holy prophets since the world began." (Acts 3:20, 21)*

Just as certain orthodox Jews await God's sending of Elijah the prophet to this very day, so also should the Church of Jesus Christ look for the Lord to send this mighty Hebrew prophet who will revive hearts and *"restore all things"(Matthew 17:11) "**before** the coming of the great and dreadful day of the Lord" (Malachi 4:5).*

This future sending of Elijah follows a previous pattern when the temple and Jerusalem were destroyed in 586 B.C. Later the Jews returned to the land, rebuilt the temple, and eventually God sent the first Elijah-like prophet, John the Baptist, to His people before the Lord came to earth the first time.

This pattern is in the process of being repeated today for the temple and Jerusalem were destroyed in A.D. 70, the Jews have returned to the land and will eventually rebuild the temple. Then God will send the last Elijah-like prophet who will *"restore all things"* (Mark 9:12) which will be followed by the Lord's return.

In addition to the certain fulfillment of the above Bible prophecies, there will also be other major events taking place on the world stage in order for the end times to continue to unfold:

1. The rise of the Antichrist/*"king of the north"* (Daniel 11:21ff)
2. The economic/political growth of Romanism (Revelation 17, 18)
3. The *"safety"* [peace] in the land of Israel (Ezekiel 38:8, 11)

As the Lord continues to prepare the earth for His Second Coming and Day of the Lord judgment all these things will definitely come to pass and thereby drastically alter the present-day [2007] complexion of planet earth.

These events will most certainly take place in God's perfect timing in order that His primary purpose is realized which is the loving redemption of those who have been written in *"the Lamb's book of life...from the foundation of the world"!*

Therefore, this question must be asked: "If you were to die today, are you ***sure*** you would go to heaven?" The Lord Jesus Christ made the requirements perfectly clear:
*"**Except** a man be born again, he cannot see the kingdom of God...**Except** a man be born of water [physical birth] and of the Spirit [spiritual birth], he cannot enter into the kingdom of God...Marvel not that I said unto you, Ye **must** be born again."*
(John 3:3, 5, 7)

The Apostle Paul explained:
"For by grace are ye saved through faith and that not of yourselves it is the gift of God not of works lest any man should boast."
(Ephesians 2:8,9)
*"Testifying both to the Jews, and also to the Greeks, **repentance** toward God and **faith** toward our Lord Jesus Christ. (Acts 20:21)*

It is through faith that you are saved, faith in what the Lord Jesus Christ did for you on the Cross for He lovingly shed His Blood to pay the penalty for your sin. When you believe this truth [faith] and turn from your sin [repent] and pray to **receive** the Lord Jesus Christ as your Savior, **then** you will be born from above by the Holy Spirit!

*"But as many as **received** Him, to them gave He power [authority] to become the sons of God, even to them that **believe** on His name."*
(John 1:12)

If you have prayed to receive the Lord Jesus Christ as your Savior, please contact us at http://www.btmi.org/ and we will send you Bible study information to help you grow in grace and in the knowledge of the Lord Jesus Christ.

28

THE AUTHOR'S BACKGROUND INFORMATION

-PERSONAL INFORMATION-

-Gloriously Saved March 7, 1980: Age 35
-Graduate of Bob Jones University (1986):
   Bachelor of Arts Degree: Bible Major / Greek Minor
-Ordained: Independent Baptist / Bible Preacher (1987)

-MINISTRY EXPERIENCE-

-Local Church Revival & Evangelistic Meetings
-Prophecy Preaching / Teaching - www.prewrath.com
-Interim Pastor
-Adult Sunday School Teacher
-Tent Evangelism Ministry
-Rescue Mission Preaching & Discipleship Ministry
-Family Nursing Home Ministry
-Street Preaching Ministry
-Prison Preaching & Discipleship Ministry
-Internet Evangelism Ministry-www.btmi.org
-Author: Booklet, Tri-folds, Discipleship Series Gospel Tracts,
   Scripture Memory Plan & Bible Reading Plan
-Testimony Tract Ministry
-Author: "The People of the Apocalypse" Book

-DOCTRINAL BELIEFS-

-The Verbal, Plenary Inspiration & Inerrancy of Scripture
-The Deity & Virgin Birth of the Lord Jesus Christ
-His Vicarious Atonement by the Shedding of His Blood on the Cross
-His Bodily Resurrection, Ascension, & Literal Pre-Millennial Return
-Literal, Eternal Heaven for Saints & Literal, Eternal Hell for the Lost
-Salvation by Grace through Faith in the Shed Blood of Christ
-The Eternal Life [Security] of the Saints
-The Autonomy of the Local Church
-Biblical Separation from the World, Compromise & Apostasy